Called to Preach, Condemned to Survive

Called to Preach, Condemned to Survive

The Education of Clayton Sullivan

Clayton Sullivan

MERCER

ISBN 0-86554-173-6

All books published by Mercer University Press are produced
on acid-free paper that exceeds the minimum standards set by
the National Historical Publications and Records Commission.

Library of Congress Cataloging in Publication Data
Sullivan, Clayton, 1930–
    Called to preach, condemned to survive.

    1. Sullivan, Clayton, 1930–   .   2. Baptists—
United States—Clergy—Biography.   3. Southern Baptist
Convention—Clergy—Biography.   I. Title.
BX6495.S7988A32   1985   286'.132'0924 [B]   85-13654

Contents

Foreword

EDITORS, AS A RULE, should neither be seen nor heard. If we do our work well, no one should be able to see us doing it; if we do not perform well, everyone will know. This book is an exception to the rule. It is a remarkable document, a story of one human life. It is not "inspirational" or "uplifting"; it is not intended to be. It is not a scholarly "contribution to knowledge" in the usual sense of those words.

What then is it? It is a story of one human life: a story that both attracts and repels; a story about quickening, living, and dying in the American South; a story about Christian preaching and ministry; a story about theological education; a story about critical study of the New Testament; a story about racial conflict and human rights; a story about teaching religion and philosophy; a story about higher education and the academic life; a story about human feelings and human dignity. This story touches almost every issue that matters to us as makers of books. For that reason, and no other, we publish this story, and we commend it to every reader for whom these issues are vital.

Clayton Sullivan is an enigma, even to himself. Blessed with an extraordinary memory and a novelist's eye for detail, he has become a trenchant observer of human folly. Yet he can also be singularly obtuse; the angle of his forward vision is incredibly confined. The record of his "education," as he has written it here, is at once unsparing and self-serving. Some readers will commend his candor; others will find it frightening; still others will note telling omissions. Few of us would wish to be remembered in the way that Clayton Sullivan presents himself. A number of people have read this book in

manuscript; none of them could put it down. That is not to say that
they came away caring very much about Clayton Sullivan.

Clayton Sullivan is a white Mississippi Baptist preacher. He is also
a Doctor of Theology and a professor of religion and philosophy in
a state university. He is, he likes to think, a "redneck." He is, indeed,
the son and grandson of rednecks, but while he is of that world he
is no longer in it. He is a white Mississippian by birth and by choice.
He is a Baptist preacher because he was "called." As he frequently
observes, it is not easy to be a white Mississippian. It has never been
easy to be a Baptist preacher. Clayton Sullivan's story calls for sym-
pathy, but it is not easy to sympathize.

Clayton Sullivan was born in Mississippi at the depth of the Great
Depression to parents who had obtained just enough education to
teach in country schools. With both parents working the Sullivans
could subsist in a more genteel poverty than many white Mississippians could manage in that desperate time. They had food on the
table and a roof over their heads, trips to town on Saturday and to
the State Fair once a year, and respectability in the community. Yet
Clayton Sullivan bears in body and soul the scars of inadequate nu-
trition, indifferent sanitation, intense longings, and inevitable dis-
appointments. Poverty of opportunity is far more insidious than
simple starvation. Clayton Sullivan did not starve, although others
did; he and his family survived the Depression. At the onset of World
War II his father found the secure job he had sought all his life, in
the venereal disease section of the Mississippi Health Department.
The Sullivans moved to a boarding house in Jackson and young
Clayton, before and after school, went to work—selling newspapers, serving sodas and sandwiches, unpacking shoes, scrubbing
floors and slicing oranges in a hotel kitchen, "struggling to become
somebody who mattered."

In the kitchen of the Heidelberg Hotel, slicing oranges and
squeezing them for the "somebodies" of Mississippi, Clayton Sullivan yielded to "an imposed, unsought compulsion" that had besieged
him for months. His heroes were the entrepreneurs of Jackson; he
craved wealth and the things that money would buy. But a voice
within him, rising from sources he did not understand, called him to
quite another kind of life. The Sullivans were Baptists, of course; yet
young Clayton "had no abundance of religion." He could not explain

the "call," and he could not resist it. It was a "call," he writes, "quite specific and limited: *a 'call' to be a Southern Baptist preacher,* a 'call' so real to me that I began to dread the consequences of not capitulating to it." The consequences of capitulating he could not foresee.

Clayton Sullivan's prayer in the kitchen of the Heidelberg—"Dear God, if you want me to be a preacher, I'll be one"—led him "down the slippery slope into religious fanaticism." At Mississippi College he became a sweating, shouting, pulpit-pounding boy preacher, haranguing country churches on Sundays and leading a team of student revivalists on missions all over Mississippi. He constructed, so he tells us, "an artificial world—based on fragile assumptions—within which I was to live for years." His preaching condemned sin, but the "artificial world" he had created knew nothing of the problem of evil. He would be, he decided, "completely dedicated to Jesus," but the Christianity he espoused, "devoid of intellectual difficulties," was a religion indistinguishable from Southern culture. "Indeed," he writes now, "I believed that the states of the Old Confederacy constituted the geographical center of Christendom, and I believed that the Southern Baptist Convention embodied quintessential Christianity."

So believing, Clayton Sullivan came to Southern Baptist Theological Seminary. Straying for the first time beyond the borders of Mississippi, he experienced an intellectual awakening. With the energy he had once devoted to pleasing his employers, he now devoured every book his professors mentioned in passing. With the zeal that had assailed the sinners and backsliders of Mississippi, he now engaged the critical study of the New Testament, mastering its language and its forms but not quite comprehending its message. For eight years he became a "married monk," immersed in the minutia of his studies in "an isolated, warm, secure world of scholarship." Near the end of that time, as he was preparing to write his doctoral dissertation, the warmth, security, and isolation of his world exploded in the so-called "Battle of Lexington Road." The "married monk" fled to Harvard and its libraries to continue the tranquil composition of his scholarly masterpiece in peace.

But there was to be no peace for Clayton Sullivan. He returned to Louisville, dissertation in hand, to find his professors in exile and a new regime with a new agenda in place. Whatever the mixture of motives, attitudes, and ideals that had led to the confrontation between faculty and administration at Southern, some of the new faculty members had definite ideas about their predecessors and definite remedies in mind for their students. Clayton Sullivan was told, by the dominant member of his new committee of advisors, that he would have to rewrite his dissertation to conform to "conservative" expectations. Not only was his work "too liberal," he was told, but its author had "no moral right to be a Southern Baptist preacher." Shattered by this verdict, fearful that all his work would be wasted and his degree denied, certain that all of his dreams were about to be dashed on the rocks of ideology, Clayton Sullivan "decided to crawl." He rewrote and revised his dissertation, working round the clock, and "loaded it with references to 'conservative' scholars." He "groveled" before the members of his dissertation committee. He became a Doctor of Theology. He survived.

From his experience at Southern Seminary, Dr. Sullivan learned "that religion is the only field of human inquiry where a premium is placed on intellectual dishonesty." From his professors and his reading he had absorbed ideals of "critical scholarship" and "intellectual honesty." He did not know, he says now, that he was not supposed to believe what he heard and read or practice what he was taught. "I did not understand the chemistry of religious conservatism," he writes. "No law required me to say everything I believed. I should have kept my mouth shut. At times duplicity and compromise are in order. As the Bulgarian proverb teaches, 'My child, one is allowed to walk with the devil until one has crossed over the bridge and is out of danger.' "

That axiom continued to guide Clayton Sullivan as he became the preacher of the First Baptist Church in "the cream pitcher," a "two-traffic-light town" in South Mississippi. His theological education and his advanced study of the New Testament had failed to penetrate the "artificial world" of his religious illusions; it had, therefore, ill prepared him to contend with the undeserved suffering of some members of his church or to confront the community's "caste system" that excluded him from any real participation in its affairs. Almost from the moment of his arrival in Tylertown, Clayton Sullivan decided that he should "be cautious about what I said" about the one issue that overshadowed all others—"the niggers." The demand of black Mississippians for civil rights stirred white Mississippians to paroxysms of fury. Clayton Sullivan's racial views had, he tells us, undergone a profound change in his years at Southern Seminary. There he had come in contact with blacks who did not fit the stereotypes ingrained in his youth. Yet whatever the depth of his change of attitude, he did not speak out against racism in Tylertown. Indeed, as the civil rights struggle reached its climax in 1965, he wrote a still controversial essay for the *Saturday Evening Post* in order to present the views of white Mississippians to the rest of the nation. The editors of the *Post* retitled the piece so that, Clayton Sullivan writes now, "I came across not as an observer trying to explain *why* segregation existed but as a racist *defending* segregation." For more readers than one, the distinction will seem rather fine.

Later in that year the Tylertown Baptist Church voted "to adopt an open-door policy toward Negroes" during a tumultuous open business meeting. Not one of the church's "liberals"—who privately disapproved of segregation and whispered to one another of racial "moderation"—was present for the meeting or the vote. No blacks applied for membership or even attempted to attend services, but the decision, as Clayton Sullivan recalls it now, engendered "a firestorm of criticism."

It was a fearful thing for a white Mississippian, in those terrible years, to appear to support the black demand for freedom and respect. As Clayton Sullivan tells us, it was an especially traumatic time to be a Christian minister in Mississippi's white churches. A healing word would be greeted with scorn, a prophetic word with fire. White Mississippians found themselves—isolated, angry, and bewildered—on a collision course with history. They told story after obscene story in which their hero, Governor Ross Barnett, made John F. Kennedy and Martin Luther King seem foolish and contemptible. To most of the rest of the nation it was Ross Barnett and his loyal followers who seemed foolish and contemptible, even criminal. In their pathetic attempts to ridicule their enemies white Mississippians continued to delude themselves. Even then it was clear that they would not win; things would never again be the way they had been for a hundred years. But white Mississippians wanted to believe they would win. Their rage and contempt would issue first in filthy stories and then in the shedding of blood. But their enemies kept coming— the black students and the Northern white preachers and the federal marshals and the civil rights lawyers—and they could not kill them all. And in the end, as Clayton Sullivan rightly says, "the Negro's liberation from raw racism has delivered Southern whites from raw racism also." Which is not to say that either blacks or whites are yet delivered from racism. It is to say that the terror is over. Clayton Sullivan is an important witness to the evolution of white racial attitudes in Mississippi. However one may fault him for where he has been or where he is now, for what he did or did not do, he has articulated a point of view rarely seen in print.

Despite his uncharacteristically forthright and successful support of the symbolic "open door" to blacks, his inability to cope with the fallen sparrows among his flock, and his discomfort with his position in the community, Clayton Sullivan survived in Tylertown until the opportunity arose—he does not tell us exactly how—to become a professor of religion and philosophy at the University of Southern Mississippi in Hattiesburg. Preparing courses in philosophy and comparative religions led him to yet another intellectual awakening that forced him "to rearrange the furniture in my mind." For the first time he studied non-Christian religions, grappling with ideas he had not encountered at Southern Seminary. But he came to the university in the last years of the reign of a despotic president who ruled the institution through brutal "commanders." Denied tenure and dismissed from his post after several years of service, Clayton Sullivan elected to confront "the General" himself. "Dressed in my very best suit and with my shoes freshly polished," he groveled before his tormentors once again, and once again he survived.

Today, after two more firings and a change of administration, Clayton Sullivan is still at the University of Southern Mississippi, a tenured professor of religion and philosophy. "I have *survived!*" he tells us, with perhaps more resignation than exultation. "I have done whatever I had to do, and I have outrun the hounds. I have outlasted Louisville liberalism, Texas fundamentalism, cream pitcherism, and bureaucratic brutality. I have survived, and survival is the essence of a Mississippi redneck."

Some readers may find Clayton Sullivan's survival heroic; others will not. Some readers will not forgive him for surviving. Some readers will blame him because he did not become a martyr, a now forgotten witness for the truth—whether that truth be intellectual

freedom or doctrinal purity, human rights or white supremacy, re-
sistance to oppression or submission to authority. Most martyrs do
not survive in memory. But truly Clayton Sullivan is "condemned to
survive," and perhaps that survival is his most eloquent testimony.

Clayton Sullivan's story, as it is told here, is not quite a seamless
garment; there are, in fact, some unseemly gaps. We never learn even
the name of Mrs. Sullivan, who must be a remarkable woman. We
may be sure that her resources accounted for their survival on more
than one occasion, but she is, in this account, little more than a piece
of furniture or a useful appliance. It is never quite clear in this narrative just how or why Dr. Sullivan's transition from preacher to professor was arranged. We never learn exactly how he survived three
dismissals at the University of Southern Mississippi. Yet what we are
told rings true to any reader who has traversed any of the territory.

We are not called to judge Clayton Sullivan—God will do that,
in his own good time—but we can learn from his story. Clayton Sullivan is not where he started out to be. But at last he seems to feel
that he is "over the bridge and out of danger." So he seems to believe, and so we may hope. This is his story, told as he wants to tell
it. Others could tell other stories, but Clayton Sullivan is at last secure enough to tell this one. That grace may make it worth the telling. Certainly it is worth the reading.

14 February 1985
Mercer University Press
Don Haymes, *Editor-in-Chief*

PART I

Getting Started
in Mississippi

1

In the Beginning

I WAS BORN IN MISSISSIPPI at the beginning of the Great Depression. My father, Henry Clay Sullivan, was from Smith County in South Central Mississippi and was from an area in Smith County known locally as Sullivan's Hollow. Until two or three decades ago Sullivan's Hollow, about which books have been written, constituted a subculture where frontier conditions lingered. People lived in log houses of dog-trot design, used corn cobs for toilet paper, raised watermelons and cotton, distrusted outsiders, had fist fights on Saturday night, and sang hymns in church on Sunday morning.

My father, one of twelve children, was born into this subculture on a cotton farm between Magee and Mize, close to the line dividing Smith and Simpson counties. The profit from this farm went to sending sons (not daughters) to college. My daddy received a partial college education that enabled him (while in his early twenties) to secure a teaching job at a crossroads community in Lincoln County named Enterprise.

At Enterprise my father lived in the home of Mr. Bill McGraw, a county supervisor whose wife maintained a boarding house for the local teachers. At McGraw's boarding house Daddy met the woman who was to be his wife and my mother. She was Mildred Paxton, also a school teacher who had been reared on a Mississippi cotton farm. Mother, a beautiful woman, was impressed with Daddy's Model A Ford. They courted, fell in love, and became husband and wife.

Soon after their marriage my father and mother lost their teaching jobs, a common occurrence for teachers during the Great Depression. They moved from Enterprise to Jackson, the state's capital, then a country town that centered around Capitol Street. My father got a job pumping gas at a Standard Oil service station. By then Mother was pregnant, and early on the morning of 6 July 1930 I was born. I was born at a time when Herbert Hoover was our country's president and when Theodore G. Bilbo, later a race-baiting United States senator, was serving a second term as Mississippi's governor.

From what others have told me, my daddy—before his marriage—was a happy-go-lucky dandy of the Roaring Twenties. He wore white shoes and a circular straw hat and drove his Model A Ford on sidewalks across the campus of Mississippi College in Clinton. His collapse from a dandy to a jobless school teacher working at a service station was traumatic for him. Years later, when I was grown, he told me that on the morning I was born at the Jackson Infirmary, he contemplated hopping a freight train and disappearing. He toyed with this possibility as a means of escaping both discouragement and the financial pressure of having become a father.

But time passed, and my parents' fortunes improved. They secured teaching jobs in Lemon, a farming community in Smith County. They moved into a three-room shack a farmer had used for storing his feed and fertilizer. Mother and Daddy scrubbed this house down with boiling water and Octagon soap to get rid of the fertilizer odor. For me this structure is significant because it is the place marking my emergence from infancy's unawareness into personal awareness. One day a chicken snake crawled into this shack. I was in diapers and watched with fascination as the snake crawled across the floor toward me. My mother came into the room, screamed, grabbed the snake, and threw it out the door. This chicken snake episode is my mind's anchor, my earliest memory.

For years Mother and Daddy made their living as school teachers. We moved across Mississippi from one rural community to another and from one town to another. From these years of my youth I've brought into adulthood a mixture of impressions. The strongest impression concerns *poverty*. For in my Mississippi youth I experienced the rural South as portrayed in the writings of William Faulkner, Eudora Welty, and Erskine Caldwell. Practically everyone I knew when I was a youngster was poor. This poverty we Mississippians didn't comprehend because we didn't know there was any other way to live. If we had reflected on the issue, I'm certain we would have surmised that people everywhere wore overalls, lived in unpainted houses, washed clothes out in the yard in iron pots, and ate sweet potatoes, turnips, and cornbread. That places like Boston or Paris or Zürich existed was beyond our conceptual horizon.

One of my pastimes as a boy was eating what we called a "molasses hole." I made a molasses hole by sticking my finger into a cold biscuit—thereby creating a hole—and then filling the hole with molasses. I've reflected on the happenstance that while I sat in the shade of cotton sheds munching on molasses holes, youngsters in other places were being exposed to museums, to art galleries, to libraries, to concerts and lectures, to Broadway plays, and to transatlantic crossings. Of such I knew nothing. I didn't have time for art galleries or museums; I was too busy pole fishing and squirrel hunting with my father. With the exception of a Bible, the only book I recall seeing around our home was *Gone with the Wind*. Mother had a copy of this Margaret Mitchell novel and read it aloud to neighbors.

Yet people were content in this Mississippi world of red hills, cotton fields, and one-street towns. We didn't feel sorry for ourselves. People lived entire lives within miles of their birthplaces, never imagining there were other visions and life-styles to experience.

A second impression from my youth concerns *Negroes*. Sinclair Lewis, the Minnesota novelist, wrote that he never saw a Negro until he traveled east to attend Yale. By contrast, I can't recall a time in my life void of blacks. They were a part of the landscape, like broomsage, creeks, and corn cribs. As a youngster I didn't perceive the caste system within which they lived. I took for granted that Negroes wore ragged clothes, spoke in a different dialect, went to the back door, walked instead of rode, and said "Yassah" when speaking to white men. I recall blacks being called "hands"—"hands" for the chopping and picking of cotton—and having names like Hiccups, Possum, Broom Stick, and Hip Pocket. And I remember discussions in which white farmers (while chewing tobacco) argued about whether Negroes had souls. A view commonly expressed was that they didn't but were animals like cows or mules.

Thus from my birth I lived with race prejudice in the James K. Vardaman[1] tradition. Prejudice was in the air I breathed, and we Mississippi youngsters absorbed the racial attitudes of the white majority. A rural proverb frequently repeated was, "A nigger ought to stay in his place." I remember the doggerel we repeated when playing childhood games.

> Enee, Menee, Minee, Mo!
> Catch a nigger by his toe,
> If he hollers make him pay
> Fifty dollars every day!

We used Enee, Menee, Minee, Mo when choosing who was going to be "It" in a game. As a boy I yelled this doggerel hundreds of times, never sensing a racial insult. That maybe Negroes didn't like going to the back door or being called Hip Pocket were possibilities I didn't entertain. A major adjustment for Southern whites has been a rethinking of the Negro's identity in American society. For me this rethinking didn't come until I was grown.

A third impression from my Mississippi youth concerns *religion*. Mother had been reared a Methodist, Daddy a Baptist. Consequently, we attended Methodist and Baptist worship services in the communities where Mother and Daddy taught school. When Sundays and Wednesday nights rolled around, our family went to church. But so did other families. In the rural South during the 1930s the church mattered. It was a focal institution, serving multiple roles. For couples the church was a place to go courting; for farmers, a place to discuss crops; for kids, a place to play hide and seek; for politicians, a place to run for sheriff; for housewives, a place to visit; for some of everyone, a place for worship and prayer.

Church services played an entertainment role in our lives, breaking the monotony of rural life. The best-liked preachers were those who spiced sermons with stories and humor. To have the preacher visit and eat a meal in your home was an honor. Housewives slaved

---

[1]James K. Vardaman was governor of Mississippi from 1904 to 1908 and United States Senator from 1913 to 1918. Ever hostile to blacks, he earned the title "Great White Father" for his advocacy of white supremacy.

for hours over wood stoves "cooking for the preacher"—preparing vegetables, meats, breads, and pies. Clergymen (unaware of the vice of gluttony) cultivated reputations for ravenous appetites.

In my youth Methodist camp meetings were a vital part of rural life, and for years I attended Shiloh Camp Meeting Ground out from Brandon in Rankin County. This meeting ground was dominated by an open frame pavilion with a tin roof. The pavilion was surrounded by rows of simple, wooden cabins. In the fall of the year farm families temporarily lived in these cabins and attended revival services conducted in the pavilion. The pavilion had no floor. Instead, its rows of wooden benches sat on the sawdust-covered ground. Toward the front was a platform with pulpit and piano. Before this platform, farmers and wives—their dresses made of flowered fertilizer sacks— gathered morning, afternoon, and night to listen to sermons and to sing hymns like "The Old Rugged Cross," "When the Roll Is Called Up Yonder," "Brighten the Corner Where You Are," and "Onward, Christian Soldiers."

Visiting clergymen who preached at these Methodist camp meeting services were viewed by us as celebrities. One year at Shiloh the visiting evangelist was from Texas. I had never seen a person from Texas, and I recall gaping at the visiting minister's boots, cowboy hat, and white suit. His manner was theatrical, and his sermons bore Western titles like "The Final Roundup" and "The Meanest Man in Texas."

This rural religion to which I was exposed in Baptist and Methodist churches was neither mystical nor reflective. Southern rural religion wasn't a matter for intellectual analysis. Rather, this "Old Time Religion" consisted of a core of unquestioned beliefs taught authoritatively by preachers—beliefs "straight out of the Bible" and laden with emotion and passed on from one generation to the next through hymns. We rural Southerners didn't *think* our religion; rather, we sang and we clapped and we *felt* our religion.

Moreover, this Old Time Religion seems to me now to have been without an appeal to the aesthetic. Church buildings of imposing architecture and religious music in the tradition of a Bach or a Handel were unknown. At a later stage in life I would witness services like mass in St. Peter's in Rome or a midnight Christmas celebration in Grace Cathedral on Nob Hill in San Francisco. Such services with their overpowering music and pageantry were unknown to us who lived in Mississippi's rural areas in the 1930s. To us, attending church meant going to a square frame building (with no screens over the windows) where we sat on hard pews, listened to exegetical sermons, and cooled ourselves with hand-held, cardboard fans that advertised Jesus on one side and Baldwin's or Hartman's funeral homes on the other.

2

Gulde

MY PARENTS—earning their livelihood as teachers—wandered across South and Central Mississippi from one community to another. The rural community where my parents taught that I remember most vividly is Gulde (rhymes with "fool-bee"), a settlement in Rankin County half-way between Brandon and Pelahatchie. Gulde is about a mile off Highway 80, down a road that leaves the highway near the Illinois Central overpass.

My parents moved to Gulde before I was old enough to attend school, and they taught there until I'd finished the third grade. So for five years my world was this Rankin County community of farmers and dirt roads. Back in the mid-1930s the most imposing structure in Gulde was the two-story, white frame schoolhouse, where Mother and Daddy taught. This building has since disappeared; students now ride yellow buses to the consolidated school in Brandon. We lived across the road from this school building in a house that everyone called "the teacher's home," a structure that was one of Rankin County's earliest WPA projects.

Next to this "teacher's home" was the Gulde Methodist Church—a wooden building painted gray—where we attended services two Sundays each month. On alternate Sundays my parents drove into Brandon, the county seat, to attend services at the Baptist Church.

Right beyond the Methodist Church—around a curve in the road—were the Illinois Central railroad tracks with a rail siding for pulpwood cars. And just beyond the railroad tracks—down a slight incline and past a pond—was the farm belonging to Mr. and Mrs. Henry Robbins. In Gulde titles of family relationships were used indiscriminately (with reference to both whites and blacks). That's why everyone referred to Mr. Robbins as "Uncle Henry" and to his wife as "Aunt Cora." Their grandson, Billy Bert Robbins, lived with them. Billy Bert was my age, and he and I were constant companions— going fishing together, chasing rabbits, and whittling on wood with our pocket knives.

Adjacent to Uncle Henry's farm was a shotgun shack where Aunt Mandy, a black woman, lived. Aunt Mandy was the wealthiest black person in the Gulde community. She received a monthly government check because a son had been killed in World War I. But Aunt Mandy could neither read nor write nor add. She couldn't tell a dime from a dollar.

When Aunt Mandy discovered that her relatives were fleecing her out of money, she turned to my father (whom she called "the 'fessor") for assistance. Month by month she gave her government check (endorsed with an "X") to Daddy and entrusted to him the dispensing of her funds. Daddy made certain that Aunt Mandy always had a supply of groceries and Levi Garrett snuff.

Daddy and Aunt Mandy became the best of friends. When peanut butter first came out, it created a sensation and was viewed by us in rural Mississippi as a delicacy. My father spread peanut butter on soda crackers (making what we called "peanut-cracker sandwiches"). Time and again my father would fix for Aunt Mandy a plate of "peanut-cracker sandwiches" and I'd carry them down the road to the shotgun shack where Aunt Mandy lived.

The Methodist Church, the Illinois Central railroad tracks, Uncle Henry's farm (where Billy Bert lived), and Aunt Mandy's house were all east of the teacher's home. Our immediate neighbor to the west was Alex, a black farmer. Alex's wife was named Melissa, and his son was named Booker T. Booker T. was my age and—like Billy Bert—was another of my boyhood companions.

I never knew Alex's last name. Blacks didn't have last names. They were known only by first names. In the Gulde community Alex was referred to as a "good nigger." A "good nigger" was a black person who worked hard and minded his business and "stayed in his place." Particularly did Melissa, Alex's wife, mind her business. She was a recluse, always staying inside her house.

Alex and Melissa insulated their home against cold weather by covering the walls and ceilings with layers of newspapers. With the passing of time this newspaper insulation became brittle and flammable as gasoline. One January morning a spark from Alex's fireplace ignited these insulating newspapers, and in minutes Alex's house was engulfed in fire with black smoke billowing into the air. Seeing the smoke, people came from all over the Gulde community to help, but there was nothing anyone could do. To this day I carry in my mind a mental picture of Alex's house going up in fire and smoke like a Vesuvian eruption. After the fire the neighbors, both black and white, pitched in for a "house building," and in a matter of days Alex, Melissa, and Booker T. were living in a new house, the walls of which were never insulated with newspapers.

Just beyond Alex's farm was where Mr. Tom Rogers lived. His wife was Miss Laura. Mr. Tom was the dominant farmer and citizen in the Gulde community. If you needed to borrow money, Mr. Tom was the man you went to see. No person ran for sheriff or supervisor without first consulting Mr. Tom and asking for his support.

Mr. Tom's children (Thomas, Anna, and Laura Jean) were grown when we moved to Gulde, and in their absence Mr. Tom let me follow him around like a shadow, watching while he plowed mules (yelling "gee" and "haw" to the mules to indicate desired direction), pitched hay into his barn loft, and banged away on the anvil in his blacksmith's shop.

Mr. Tom, a man my father described as the best friend he ever had, was a reservoir of witticisms. I remember his remarking one day to my father, "Sullivan, all my neighbors must be mad at me. It's nine o'clock in the morning and not a single one of 'em has come by to borrow something from me."

Mr. Tom was a Methodist. On Sundays when services were conducted at the Gulde Methodist Church he always attended and sat on the front pew. He invariably had a pocket full of change (nickels, dimes, quarters). During the prayers Mr. Tom stuck his fingers in his pockets and rattled his change, providing an unsought background for the minister's petitions to the Almighty.

On a cold day in January or February Mr. Tom killed hogs. Mr. Tom and the blacks who lived on his place would tie the hogs' hind legs together and suspend the hogs with ropes and chains from tree limbs. The hogs' throats were cut and—with the hogs squealing madly—the blood came gushing out in red streams that flowed across the ground in many-fingered patterns. Mr. Tom and his black helpers then butchered the hogs, preparing the meat for salting and storage in the smoke house.

The night after hog killing was when Mr. Tom and Miss Laura had a chitterling (a word we pronounced "chitlins") supper for the community. "Chitlins" (a hog's small intestines) were to depression-ridden Mississippians what oysters are to people in Southern New Jersey—a culinary pleasure to be eaten in banquet fashion. Miss Laura, Aunt Cora, and my mother spent hours in the kitchen frying "chitlins" and baking crackling bread. As many as twenty people turned up for one of Mr. Tom's and Miss Laura's "chitlin" suppers, which were replete with creamed potatoes, butter beans, potato salad, and pecan pie. For hours neighbors sat around Mr. Tom's table, eating fried "chitlins" while talking and visiting.

More entertainment in Gulde came at syrup-making time in the fall of the year. All the farmers around Gulde raised sugar cane, but only a few had mastered the art of transforming raw sugar cane into molasses. A farmer who had perfected this art was Mr. Ed Rhodes, who lived a stone's throw down the road from Mr. Tom's. Farmers for miles around brought their sugar cane to Mr. Rhodes's syrup mill, and for several weeks in the fall of the year the syrup mill became Gulde's social center, with people standing around smelling and watching the syrup-making activity.

The juice of the sugar cane was extracted by feeding the cane stalks into revolving counter-rollers (called grinders) that were turned by a pair of mules walking around and around in a circular path. The cane juice flowed into open cooking vats that were heated under an open shed over a wood fire. The secret was to know when the cane juice had cooked enough. Undercooked syrup was thin and would turn sour; overcooked syrup would turn to sugar. As the cane juice cooked, a brown, bubbly foam formed on the top, a foam which Mr. Rhodes scraped off with wooden paddles. Gradually the juice thickened into syrup which was then drained off into gleaming tin cans for storage.

As days of syrup making passed, the pile of squeezed sugar cane stalks behind Mr. Rhodes's syrup mill got higher and higher, forming a spongy, pliable hill. Pushing an empty barrel before us, Billy Bert, Booker T., and I would climb to the top of this hill of sugar cane stalks (called "mash"). On reaching the top, we'd all three get into the barrel and—yelling as the barrel turned over—we'd roll down to the bottom of the sugar cane pile, a feat we performed hundreds of times. Rolling down Mr. Rhodes's "mash" hill in a barrel was almost as exciting to us as rides at the Mississippi State Fair.

Nine months of the year were spent going to school. Only whites attended the Gulde school where my father and mother taught. Booker T. went to a separate school called the "nigger school." The Gulde school knew nothing of what is now referred to in educational jargon as "open classrooms" and "learning centers." Instead we sat in straight rows in desks that were attached to the floor. To speak in class, unless the teacher was calling on you to recite, was an unpardonable sin.

Before school and during recess, unless it was raining or was too cold, we played marbles. Every boy brought marbles to school, and the best way to bring marbles was to carry them in our back pockets in red Prince Albert tobacco cans or in Country Gentleman tobacco bags, white in color with a yellow draw string. To play marbles we dug a series of holes in the ground with a pocket knife, each hole three or four inches deep and approximately three inches in diameter. The point of the game was "to shoot" a marble—propelling it with a snap of thumb against forefinger—from hole to hole without missing. At least two persons, taking turns, played at the same time. We would keep shooting until we missed a hole. Then it would be someone else's turn. The person who "shot" all the holes first won. Experience taught us that the closer we got to the ground (stretching out on our stomachs so we could aim with precision) the better we could play. That's why by the end of the day we'd be covered with dust from head to toe. If the teacher wasn't looking, we played "for keeps." Playing "for keeps" meant we got to keep marbles belonging to someone we beat in a game. By the end of the day (if I were lucky) my Country Gentleman tobacco bag could be bulging with marbles I had won from classmates.

During recesses we also played hide-and-go-seek and pop-the-whip. To pop the whip we formed a straight line and joined hands. Holding tightly to one another we ran as fast as we could across the

schoolyard. Then the "pivot"—a person on one end of the line—
"popped the whip" by stopping suddenly and allowing the running
line of handholding children to continue in an arc. Centrifugal force
caused the children on the other end of the line to run faster and
faster, eventually hurtling them to the ground. As we "popped" off
the end of the whip we yelled with mock fright, tumbling over the
earth like autumn leaves tossed by the wind.

We had morning recess and afternoon recess, and in the middle
of the day we ate lunch. Everybody brought lunches to school (in
paper bags, syrup cans, or lard buckets) until they put in the WPA
lunch room. Everyone then had a hot plate lunch at noon. Aunt Cora
was in charge of the WPA lunch room, and she and her helpers
cooked meals using government commodities—hams, eggs, crowder peas, cheese (tons of it!), macaroni, rice. At Christmas they'd fix
everybody a Santa Claus. Each Santa Claus was made out of an apple, with raisins for eyes and with toothpicks and marshmallows for
arms and legs.

I could tell those for whom the WPA lunch was a primary source
of food. They'd clean their plates and then ask for seconds—a request Aunt Cora never denied.

When we finished our meals we could leave the lunch room and
go out in the school yard and play until the school bell rang and
classes resumed. Leaving the lunch room involved a set procedure.
We put our forks and spoons across our plates, stood up and slid our
chairs under the table, and while walking to the door we said, "Enjoyed my lunch, Aunt Cora." Day after day this phrase was spoken
dozens of times as one by one the pupils headed for the lunch room
door saying, "Enjoyed my lunch, Aunt Cora."

Once a year the Coca-Cola man came to Gulde. He'd drive on
the school yard in a red truck that had Coca-Cola painted on the
sides. When the Coca-Cola man arrived all classes were dismissed
and everyone got in a line. One by one we'd pass by the red truck
to receive Coca-Cola advertisements—a red pencil, a red tablet, and
a ruler on which was imprinted the Golden Rule: "Do unto others as
you would have them do unto you."

And once a year a representative from the State Health Department came. Usually this representative was Miss Eyrick. Miss Eyrick
was a spinster. We lined up for her as we had lined up for the Coca-

Cola man. Miss Eyrick inspected our teeth, looking for cavities. She exhorted us to brush our teeth and to eat an apple every day. Each time Miss Eyrick came we'd have a school assembly in the auditorium so Miss Eyrick could tell us a story. One year she told a story about a king who rode in a carriage shaped like an apple. While Miss Eyrick told the story she held an apple in her hand. Somehow a star was a part of the story's plot, and at one point in her narrative Miss Eyrick took a knife and sliced the apple she was holding in a way I'd never seen an apple sliced before. She cut it at its widest circumference (horizontally across the core instead of vertically through the core) and held the sliced apple before us revealing—miracle of miracles—a star in the middle of the apple! I couldn't believe my eyes. A star on the inside of an apple! For months thereafter I insisted on slicing apples as Miss Eyrick had done and invariably the apple's core appeared star-shaped, a phenomenon that eventually lost its novelty.

One year the representative from the State Health Department was a man instead of Miss Eyrick. And instead of coming with an apple he came with portable metal cabinets shaped like suitcases that had trays. On each tray were rows of metal cans, each can in diameter about the size of a quarter and approximately a half-inch high—cans suggesting the ones Aunt Mandy's Levi Garrett snuff came in. That something mysterious was involved in his coming was obvious because all the boys were called to the auditorium with no girls present. This mass separation by sex was unprecedented at the Gulde school. The man from the Health Department stood up and informed us that we were to be tested for hookworms. He held up one of the shiny metal cans and told us we were to take a can home with us and bring it back the next day with a bowel specimen, saying, "Take a small amount of fecal matter and enclose it in the can. Insert the can into the brown envelope, making certain you have printed your name on the label."

As the instructions sank in, a stunned silence descended on the male student body of the Gulde school. When we cut through the fancy language, what the man from the Health Department was saying—so it dawned on our boyish minds in categories we understood—was that every person was to carry a can home and bring it back the next day with some shit in it. Silence was followed by whispering followed by giggles. Everyone started talking, some making cracks. "Hey, Paul, do you think you'll have any trouble sittin' on your can and takin' a crap?" My father, who as school principal knew how to read the riot act, made everyone quiet down. Orders were orders, and the next day every person brought back to school a stool specimen in a little metal can. Life had its absurdities.

The climax of the school year at Gulde came when the graduating class presented "the senior play." Everybody in Gulde came to see these dramatic productions. The school auditorium was always jammed with mothers and fathers, brothers and sisters, aunts and uncles who came to witness the thespian skills of the graduating seniors. One year the play's plot involved a shooting. A person was "murdered" with a pistol right there on the stage. My daddy added a note of realism to the play by having his double-barrel shotgun backstage. At the precise moment when the play's "murder" took place, Daddy fired his shotgun out a backstage window, firing it into the air. The blast was deafening! Women in the audience screamed. One lady jumped up out of her seat—much to the delight of those who knew ahead of time what was going to happen.

In connection with one of those senior plays at Gulde, I had my first remembered encounter with guilt. Between acts of the senior play girls of the 4-H Club sold homemade candy to raise money for their club treasury. On the day of the senior play 4-H members brought to school platters of candy (fudge, divinity, peanut brittle) that they stored for the day in Miss Hopson's room. They left the candy there until evening when they sold it between acts to people in the audience. Late in the afternoon, after school was out and when everyone had temporarily left the school building (before returning that evening for the senior play), I slipped into Miss Hopson's room and surreptitiously ate several pieces of homemade fudge and divinity. I sensed at once that what I had done was wrong. Later I would "confess" this transgression to a preacher.

Summer in Gulde was a busy time. It was a season for labor in which everyone worked. The women, using steam pressure cookers, canned vegetables, putting up butter beans, string beans, crowder peas, and tomatoes in glass jars with the words "Ball" or "Knox" on them. By summer's end Miss Laura and Mother had rows of canned vegetables stored in their pantries—enough food to carry us through the winter.

Summer was when farmers "chopped" cotton. Chopping cotton meant thinning out stalks and getting rid of grass growing around the stalks so the cotton could grow tall. You thinned out cotton with a hoe. Everyone pitched in—sons and daughters, aunts and grand-mothers. That's why we didn't have school in the summer—so everybody could work in the cotton fields. White women who worked in the fields wore bonnets and gloves so the sun wouldn't hit them. No white woman wanted tanned skin. In the rural South un-tanned skin was seen as evidence of delicacy and femininity.

So they'd have labor to chop cotton (and pick it in the fall) was the reason Mr. Tom and other farmers had Negroes living on their farms. Early in the morning, at sunrise, you'd see the "hands" headed for the fields, hoes over their shoulders, hoes carried like soldiers carry rifles when marching. While Mr. Tom and his "hands" were out in the field working the cotton, Miss Laura was home cooking a noonday meal. In the middle of the day, when Miss Laura had din-ner ready, she'd go out on the back porch and ring the dinner bell, a signal for Mr. Tom and his "hands" to come to the house and eat. Mr. Tom ate inside the house. The blacks ate outside, sitting on the back steps or sitting under trees.

After dinner while the sun was at its hottest, everybody took a noonday nap. The blacks stretched out on the ground where there was shade. Mr. Tom took his nap in his "back porch bedroom," a room lined with windows to catch the breeze and a room that fas-cinated me because on a nail in a corner hung Mr. Tom's pistol—a revolver that he kept always loaded. Time and again Miss Laura and Mr. Tom warned me, "Clayton, don't you go near that pistol." This warning I took seriously.

I wasn't old enough to chop cotton, but Mr. Tom let me help out (and earn money) by being his water boy. I'd pump water out of Mr. Tom's cistern and carry it in buckets to the field. Mr. Tom and his "hands" would always be wet with perspiration. When I came up with a bucket of water, they'd stop hoeing and take a drink of water with the dipper.

In late summer and early fall the cotton was picked and carried to the gin. You haven't really lived unless you've ridden to the Pelahatchie gin on a truck load of Mr. Tom's cotton. While going to the gin Billy Bert, Booker T., and I stretched out on the cotton as if it were a bed, looking up at the sky and feeling the breeze against our faces as Mr. Tom drove his truck down the road from Gulde to Pelahatchie where the gin was.

The cotton and corn fields were worked Monday through Friday. Saturday was the day everybody, blacks and whites alike, went to town. The blacks went in wagons pulled by mules. Some rode horses. Others walked. The whites drove to town in cars and trucks. Some folks went to Pelahatchie, others to Brandon. By Saturday afternoon people were so thick on Main Street in Pelahatchie and Brandon you couldn't stir them with a stick. People went to town to buy on credit what they needed for the coming week and to visit. Going to town was a way of escaping the isolation of farms and the boredom of manual labor. To that end blacks and whites ambled up and down the street. Walking back and forth, going in and out of stores, constantly milling, going everywhere and going nowhere. In Brandon white farmers hunkered in front of the courthouse. By hunkering, I mean they squatted close to the ground. They hunkered in groups where they'd roll cigarettes—using Prince Albert tobacco—and where they'd gossip about politics and talk about the crops. The blacks horsed around, slapping one another on the back, speaking loudly to each other, breaking out in guffaws that could be heard blocks away. This conduct was referred to by whites as "acting like a nigger." Although Mother and Daddy were not farmers, we went to town on Saturday like everyone else did. When we went to Brandon, Daddy always bought me a vanilla ice cream cone at Overby's Drug Store. I'd take my ice cream cone out on the sidewalk and stand in the shade, licking the ice cream and watching the folks go by. When we went to Pelahatchie on Saturday, we did our shopping at Mr. Andrew Glaze's store where Daddy bought me Cracker Jacks, which I opened always hoping that the toy inside was a "cricket."

In the summer I found delight in going barefooted. When I was barefooted I could scratch my dog with my toes and feel the dew on the morning grass and go wading in Uncle Henry's pond below the railroad tracks. Yet going barefooted had its perils. I got stickers in my feet, and stumped my toes on tree roots, and accidentally stepped in chicken shit and felt it oozing up between my toes.

In summer I also ran the risk of getting risins. "Risins"—pronounced RYE-zins—was the name we gave to skin infections. Why these boils came I don't know. Maybe they came upon us because of diet deficiency, or because the soaps we used were chemically inadequate. Whatever the reason, they came, as many as a half-dozen risins at the same time. They'd appear on our arms, legs, stomachs, backs—even on our butts, making it painful to sit down. I could tell a risin was on its way when a spot on my arm or leg or back would start getting red. I could feel the boil developing beneath my skin, getting hard and sore. Days passed and the risin got bigger and bigger—some as big as silver dollars. Then they'd start "getting ripe." By "getting ripe," I mean a head of pus started developing. A ripening risin was cause for family conferences. We had to wait for the right moment to "mash" a risin, squeezing out the pus. If we mashed a risin too soon, before it was ripe, it came back with a vengeance, more inflamed and painful. But if we played it right and waited and mashed a risin after it was ripe, we'd get rid of it. My father and I made a daily reconnaissance of my risins, studying them as soldiers study the enemy on fields of battle. When we mutually decided a risin was ripe—when it was all a mass of soft, yellow pus—we'd mash it. Mashing a risin was a process of several steps. Daddy sterilized a needle with a match and then wiped the carbon off by rubbing the needle on his pants. With the needle he'd prick the risin's head and the pus started flowing out. Daddy and I took turns mashing the risin, causing a stream of pus to gush forth. You'd know you'd won the battle when the core, a hardened mass of infection, appeared. And you'd know all the pus was out when the risin started bleeding, leaving a raw, red place where it had been—a place we called the risin's "socket." Then came the part that really hurt. Daddy took cotton soaked in rubbing alcohol and cleaned the socket, causing the socket to burn like it was on fire. I'd start crying and yelling, but Daddy would keep on wiping the socket despite my protests. He'd yell, "Son, we've got to get the socket sterilized," but this explanation did not lessen the pain. Risins were, it seemed then, a penalty we rural Southerners paid for being who we were and living where we lived.

Summer was also the season when we youngsters had ample time to watch the trains pass by. Several times during the day and night trains, spewing steam and smoke, sped through Gulde on the Illinois Central railroad tracks. For Billy Bert, Booker T., and me, watching these trains hurtling by was high drama, an encounter with the awesome! We'd walk down to the tracks and wait for a train to come. Far down the tracks you'd see the train coming. Sometimes coming from the direction of Brandon. Sometimes coming from the direction of Pelahatchie. Billy Bert, Booker T., and I would stand in the middle of the tracks to watch the train's approach. What a spectacle! The engine's headlight rotating, even in daylight! Smoke billowing out of the engine! The whistle blowing, penetrating the air with its shrill sound! The bell ringing! The engine chugging! Closer and closer the train came while Billy Bert, Booker T., and I stood on the tracks, visually absorbing the grandeur of the approaching iron monster. As the train came still closer we'd get off the tracks and stand a few feet away from the railway bed, enthusiastically waving our hands and arms at the engineer. Without fail the engineer, leaning out of the cab with goggles on and a cap on his head and a red handkerchief around his neck, his hand on the throttle, waved back at us. What an honor! What a thrill! To have our waving returned by an Illinois Central engineer! Somehow the engineer's handwave at Billy Bert, Booker T., and me gave us significance and suggested we too had a place in the cosmos.

Most of the trains that came through Gulde were freights. Some of them were long, taking an eternity to pass by. Some freights stopped at Gulde and attached rail cars loaded with pulpwood. Passenger trains never stopped; they never even slowed down. Maybe that's why they suggested mystery to my boyish mind. Through their windows I saw people speeding by, some reading newspapers and smoking cigars, some sitting at tables in diners. What surpassing luxury! To sit at a table in a diner and to eat food brought to you on trays by black waiters wearing white coats! Who were these people, dressed in suits, the ladies wearing hats, who sped through Gulde in mechanized elegance? Whence did they come? Where were they going? These questions puzzled my youthful Mississippi mind.

The event of events, surpassing all others in power to exhilarate, was the annual trip in October to the Mississippi State Fair. In the

1930s there were no "Disney Worlds" or amusement parks like "Six Flags over Texas." Thus the wonderland of wonderlands, the ultimate in excitement and stimulation, the last word in the exotic was the Mississippi State Fair in Jackson. Potent searchlights, sending beams into the night sky, proclaimed the fair's presence. Gulde was twenty miles east of Jackson, and at night I'd sit on the back steps where I could see in the distance those beams of light moving back and forth across the sky like illuminated fingers, beckoning people to come to the fair. The fair lasted a week and Friday of fair week was always a school holiday. On this holiday people from all over Mississippi converged en masse on the fairgrounds in downtown Jackson. The fairgrounds extended eastward from the base of the hill on which Mississippi's Old Capitol building is located. My Daddy would put me on his shoulders and carry me to a vantage point behind the Old Capitol where I'd look down on the fair in all its color, pomp, and pageantry. What a miracle to behold at night! An illuminated, iridescent wonderland! Multicolored lights as far as the eye could see! The Royal American Midway in all its glory!

We'd spend all day Friday and part of Friday night at the fair, where the attractions were endless. There were exhibition barns where farmers displayed ribbon-winning chickens, cows, bulls, horses, and sheep. There were buildings with displays of canned vegetables, flowers, quilts, and wood crafts. And out in the open were displays of farm equipment—tractors and wagons and combines.

Then there was the Midway where the rides, vendors, and sideshows were. Some vendors sold candied apples. Others sold cotton candy or popcorn or taffy. There were hamburger stands operated by organizations like the Lion's Club and the Shriners. There were rides like the Moon Rocket and the Chinese Dragon. There was the Hall of Mirrors where I'd get lost and couldn't tell whether I was coming or going. And the Crazy House with trap doors, sliding floors, and secret tunnels. The marvel of marvels was a sideshow—shaped like a huge barrel—where a man rode a motorcycle around and around inside the circular enclosure with a live lion beside him in a sidecar—a spectacle I found unbelievable! There were booths where men guessed your age or your weight; if they didn't guess close enough you'd win a prize—like a statue of Jesus made out of plaster of Paris. The freak shows featured the fattest woman in the world and a two-headed calf from Kansas. And at night there was the grandstand performance replete with a band, dancers, clowns, and bears riding bicycles.

Tucked at the end of the Midway, before you got to the Ferris wheels, were girlie shows. Daddy never stopped at the girlie shows. When we got to them he'd say, "Son, don't look at them. They're dirty." But I'd look long enough to see ladies without many clothes on, standing before the crowd, winking and smiling while the barkers exhorted, "Come on in, Folks! The show starts in ten minutes! Take a look at the most beautiful girls between New Orleans and St. Louis!" I noticed the girlie shows drew more customers than any other attraction on the Midway. But I took Daddy's evaluation of them seriously and conjectured that these girlie shows were contemporary versions of the wicked cities of Sodom and Gomorrah that Miss Willie Bea told us about in Sunday School at the Gulde Methodist Church.

3

Memories

OUR WAY OF LIFE in Gulde during the 1930s was as innocent as buttermilk in the winter and as harmless as a butterfly in the springtime. For me life was a Mississippi version of a Tom Sawyer and Huckleberry Finn existence, and memories of that guileless life linger to this day in my mind.

Memories of Aunt Mandy sitting on her front porch in the shade of a chinaberry tree, dipping her Levi Garrett snuff and snoozing the afternoon away.

Memories of Daddy getting up early in the morning, putting on a pot of coffee, and then sitting on the back steps in his underwear while drinking a cup of coffee. All Sullivans are coffee drinkers. Indeed, at our house drinking coffee was a family ritual. My daddy brewed coffee morning, noon, afternoon, and night. When company came his inevitable reaction was, "Let's put on a pot of coffee!" At the end of his life my father made a statement about a coffee pot that will haunt me the rest of my days.

Memories of watching Mother churn butter, and then watching her dip the butter out of the churn with a spoon and put it into a wooden butter mold—a mold that left the impression of a star on the top of the circular mound of butter.

Memories:

Of eating watermelons and then seeing how far I could spit the seeds.

Of going squirrel hunting with Daddy in the Pelahatchie swamp.

Of stretching out on hay in Mr. Tom's barn during a summer thunderstorm and watching the rain coming down in sheets while listening to the rain hitting on the barn's tin roof.

Memories:

Of rolling a tire, its tread gone, up and down the dusty road in front of the WPA teacher's home where we lived, while pretending I was a truck roaring down U.S. 80 toward Pelahatchie.

Of eating cornbread crumbled in "pot likker" (our name for the broth of turnip greens).

Of watching Daddy wring a chicken's neck and then watching the headless chicken stand up and run around and around in the backyard—a paradigm of futility.

Memories:

Of making daily visits to the outhouse and on January days feeling the wind chilling my bare behind.

Of stretching out on the ground at night while looking for shooting stars.

Of gathering blackberries in the Pelahatchie swamp . . . blackberries that Mother cooked into jam that I ate with hot biscuits for supper.

Of watching Aunt Mandy sweep her front yard with a broom made of dogwood branches.

Memories:

Of watching Mr. Tom slop his hogs and feed his mules.

Of standing beside the road and watching a black funeral pass by, the funeral procession consisting of three or four mule-pulled wagons with the coffin homemade of pine boards.

Of going to Mr. Mills's house at night for a communitywide peanut boil; there we'd boil peanuts in an iron washpot over a wood fire, with everybody laughing and singing "Old McDonald Had a Farm" and "She'll Be Coming 'Round the Mountain When She Comes" while Mr. Gilmore played his harmonica.

And memories:

Of listening at night on the radio to Amos 'n Andy.

Of reading the *Farmer's Almanac* to see if it was going to snow in January.

Of going to basketball tournaments in Brandon and yelling while teams from Brandon, Pisgah, Johns, and Puckett battled to see who'd be the county champions in basketball.

Of shooting firecrackers and eating "niggertoes" (our name for Brazil nuts) at Christmas.

Of going home with Miss Willie Bea Rhodes after church on Sunday. (Miss Willie Bea, my Sunday School teacher, would make delicious homemade vanilla ice cream. Her husband, Mr. Rufus, farmed and drove the school bus.)

Yet evidence suggested that all was not well with the world. For homeless tramps got off the freight trains that stopped at Gulde to attach rail cars loaded with pulpwood. These tramps were the flotsam and jetsam of the Great Depression. They dressed in ragged and dirty clothes. They had heavy beards, wore caps pulled over their faces, and carried their belongings on their backs. These beggars we called "hoboes." No one was afraid of these men who looked down at the ground as they walked and who spoke in low voices.

I'd hear my dogs barking and I'd look down the road toward the Illinois Central railroad tracks and I'd see a hobo coming. I'd call off my dogs, and the hobo would come on down the road and make his way to the back door and in a quiet manner ask Mother if she had food he could eat. My Mother and Miss Laura and Aunt Cora never turned away a hobo. A hobo always got something to eat—like a plate loaded with vegetables and a pork chop and corn bread. That's why Mr. Tom and Miss Laura had two gardens, so they'd have food to give away. I remember Miss Laura saying, "Not feeding a hobo would go against the parable of the Good Samaritan." After the hobo had eaten, he'd put his pack on his back and head for the railroad tracks where he'd disappear as silently as he'd appeared, fading away like dew in the morning sun.

Somewhere, exactly where I didn't know, was an all-wise leader. His name was President Roosevelt, Franklin Delano Roosevelt (a name that we pronounced ROW-se-velt). What a name! His name we spoke with reverence, like the names George Washington, Abraham Lincoln, and Robert E. Lee.

In rural Mississippi during the 1930s all good things came either from God or from Franklin Delano Roosevelt. From God came rain, sunshine, sugar cane for molasses, cotton, and corn. From Franklin

Delano Roosevelt and the Democrats came WPA projects, commodities, CCC camps, and the REA.

Before REA we saw at night by means of a candle or a kerosene lamp. But after REA came through, we had electricity. Men wearing boots and driving trucks came down the road erecting poles and stringing lines. They strung wire to Aunt Mandy's shack and to Mr. Tom's house and to the WPA teacher's home where we lived. In the middle of each room an electric cord was dropped from the ceiling. On the end of the cord was a socket where we screwed in a light bulb. There were no light fixtures or lamp shades. Just bare bulbs, hanging exposed like glass onions, which we turned on and looked at and rejoiced over. A burning light bulb, suspended by a cord four feet from the ceiling: the ultimate in convenience!

Before REA Daddy bought ice from the ice man who came by in a truck three times a week. We kept ice in a wooden ice box. In summer Daddy bought extra blocks of ice and wrapped them in a blanket or covered them with sawdust and stored them in the fireplace. But after REA we had refrigerators that made ice cubes in trays.

Lights at night and ice all the time—boons made possible by Franklin Delano Roosevelt who lived far away, whom no one ever saw, but whose voice Mother and Daddy listened to at night on the radio and whose picture hung on the wall of the Gulde school beside a picture of George Washington, our country's founder.

Whereas everyone spoke well of President Roosevelt, holding him in awe, no one spoke well of his wife. Her name was Eleanor. People made fun of Mrs. Roosevelt's buck teeth and cracked jokes about her appearance.

> QUESTION: "Why does President Roosevelt take his wife with
>   him everywhere he goes?"
> ANSWER: "So he won't have to kiss her goodbye!"

Mrs. Roosevelt had "outlandish ideas," ideas having to do with blacks and Jews. They said she sang to President Roosevelt the doggerel:

> I'll kiss the niggers
> And you kiss the Jews.
> And we'll stay in office
> As long as we choose.

In the distance was rumbling of thunder. Sometimes at night Mr. Tom, Uncle Henry, Doc (Mr. Tom's bachelor brother who drove a dump truck), and my Daddy sat for hours on Mr. Tom's front porch. They'd roll cigarettes from Prince Albert tobacco and smoke and talk in low, concerned voices, while Billy Bert and I sat on the floor and listened. They discussed whether or not there'd be another war. They talked about people called Germans, and about a man named Adolf Hitler. I remember Mr. Tom saying, "We beat the shit out of the Kaiser and if we have to we'll beat the shit out of this bastard with a moustache."

Billy Bert and I listened, but we didn't understand. We paid more attention to the sound of crickets and to the flashing of lightning bugs that we saw in all directions. In rural Mississippi night was black as coal, and lightning bugs were everywhere, tiny beacons in the darkness. Flying vertically, flying horizontally, they called to one another with greenish-yellowish, blinking signals. We chased them, captured them, and kept them in fruit jars with holes punched in the lid.

And in the day Billy Bert, Booker T., and I walked down the gravel road past the Methodist Church, past the railroad tracks, past where Uncle Henry and Aunt Mandy lived—all the way down to Highway 80, which ran from Brandon to Pelahatchie. We'd sit on the ground under a sweetgum tree and watch a strange sight going by: miles and miles of trucks passing, one right after the other, all the trucks painted a dark brown.

Daddy explained there might someday be a war and the trucks, he said, were army convoys. These truck convoys headed down the highway toward Pelahatchie. Where they were going and what they were up to, Billy Bert, Booker T., and I didn't know. We just sat beside the road and watched the trucks pass by.

4

Jackson

THOSE HALCYON DAYS with Mr. Tom, Aunt Mandy, and Booker T. eventually ended. Why Mother and Daddy decided to leave Gulde, I never knew. Parents don't explain such decisions to a child. I do know my father and mother always remembered Brandon, Pelahatchie, and Gulde with affection.

From Gulde we moved to Columbia, a town in Southwest Mississippi. Mother and Daddy taught for a year at the Mississippi Industrial Training School, Mississippi's school for delinquents. We lived on the reformatory grounds in a three-room apartment located on the first floor of one of the girls' dormitories.

My memories of living in Columbia are disconnected. I remember it mainly as a town where a Mississippi patriarch named Hugh White lived. Hugh White was a man who had made a fortune in the lumber business, lived in a mansion on the edge of town, and had served a term as Mississippi's governor. He was a corpulent man who wore white suits and hung out in a barber shop on Main Street. When Daddy took me to the barber shop for a hair cut, I'd sit in the barber's chair and stare at Hugh White. To my boyish mind looking at Hugh White was like looking at God. I would observe silently as a stream of men dropped by the barber shop to discuss business with Hugh White—a man everyone addressed as "Governor."

Columbia I remember also as the place where I got my first bicycle—a blue Flying Arrow that was the prized possession of my boyhood. It was purchased from a store on Columbia's Main Street and was paid for by my father in monthly payments. For hours I'd ride my Flying Arrow over the roads and sidewalks of the Industrial School.

The Industrial School was a place where unwanted and disciplinary-problem boys and girls were sent by court order to attend school and to take vocational courses and to work in vegetable fields. Mother and Daddy didn't like their jobs at the Industrial School. In fact, Daddy began talking about getting out of school teaching. As he explained, there wasn't enough money in it to make a decent living.

From Columbia we moved to Greenwood, a cotton town on the Yazoo River in the Mississippi delta. For a few months Daddy had some kind of a job with the Works Progress Administration. While we were living in Greenwood, the Japanese bombed Pearl Harbor. The air became electric with excitement because our country declared war on Japan and Germany. Overnight defense plants and military bases started springing up across the South, bringing prosperity in their wake and an end to the Great Depression. Men by the thousands were drafted and civilian jobs became available.

Daddy, beyond draft age and choosing not to volunteer for military service, found a job with the Mississippi State Board of Health. The day he got this job was, I think, the happiest he ever knew. More than anything else my father wanted employment security. I remember him saying about his Health Department job, "This will give me a monthly pay check the rest of my life."

My father was of that generation for whom the Great Depression of the 1930s was life's decisive event. He never got over it. All during the Depression he'd held on by the skin of his teeth to one low-paying teaching job after another, living constantly in fear of losing his job. Time and again he had borrowed money from his brothers or from the White System, a small loan company in Jackson, to make ends meet.

For the remainder of their days my parents (haunted by insecurity) were frugal with money. They rarely spent money on travel or on luxuries like dining out. Their philosophy was to live as simply as possible and to save every dime they could. Even during the post-World War II boom I'd hear Daddy say, "It never pays to go in debt because someday the bottom might fall out again and we'll have another depression."

My father went to work in the Mississippi Health Department's venereal disease section. The war had brought new and expanded military installations to Mississippi—installations like Camp Shelby at Hattiesburg, the Air Force bases at Greenville and Columbus and Jackson, and Keesler Field on the Gulf Coast at Biloxi. These bases brought prostitutes, and the prostitutes brought syphilis and gonorrhea, diseases already acute among Mississippi's blacks. My father's job entailed traveling throughout the Mississippi delta and to army camps over the state searching for venereal disease carriers. I recall his remark, "I bet I've talked to more whores than any person who's ever lived."

In connection with Daddy's new job with the Health Department, we moved from Greenwood to Jackson. By this time I'd finished elementary school and was ready for junior high. From this point in my life my memory has fullness, clarity, continuity. Here I began to understand life and understand myself. In every person's life, I believe, a moment arrives when scales of innocence fall from our eyes and we begin to understand *for ourselves* the world around us and how we fit into it. We sense what people judge to be important. For the first time we view our fathers and mothers with objectivity, comparing our parents to other people and perceiving in them heretofore unrecognized limitations. And we see ourselves as others see us, intuiting our "place" or "station" in society. This encounter with self-understanding can be an occasion for joy or an occasion for sorrow.

I experienced for the first time this encounter with self-understanding the summer we moved from Greenwood to Jackson, and for me this encounter was unsettling. During the 1940s Jackson was not the booming minimetropolis it is today. Rather it was a stratified, ingrown Southern town, a place where you either belonged or didn't belong. You were either "in" or "out"—there was no in between. Those families that were "in" lived in North Jackson (in Woodland Hills and out on the Old Canton Road) in brick homes with winding driveways. They engaged in business or practiced law or medicine. They belonged to the country club and had Negro maids who wore white uniforms while preparing three meals a day. Their sons and daughters knew how to dance and to play golf, belonged to fraternities and sororities, drove Buick convertibles, and attended "Ole Miss." To them, everyone else who lived in Jackson was an outsider.

In my mind no doubt existed about which side of the "in" or "out" fence my folks and I were on. We were on the outside; we were hicks who had come to the city. When my parents and I moved to Jackson we, like dustbowl "Okies" moving west, brought everything we owned in a gray 1937 Chevrolet. I was ashamed of this car and I slumped down in the seat so I wouldn't be seen riding around Jackson in it. Mother and Daddy didn't have the money to buy a house or to rent an apartment; consequently, we moved into a downtown boarding house—Mrs. Anabelle Craft's boarding house at 630 North State Street. The house, known locally as the W. J. Davis home, was one of those "Southern mansions" built around the turn of the century, white, two stories, with Corinthian columns across the front. Its rugs and furniture were threadbare and musty. The living room chandelier and the cut glass around the front door were evidences of departed elegance. The house was owned by Mrs. Webb Buie, an aristocratic, wealthy widow who lived next door in a more ornate "Southern mansion" with an observatory, spacious galleries, and stained glass windows. The Buie home, preserved as a house of historical interest, is still standing on North State Street in Jackson.

The boarding house was operated by Mrs. Craft, a hardworking woman who was short in stature and had snow-white hair and deep lines across her face. I admired Mrs. Craft, but Mrs. Craft's boarding house I loathed. God never intended for any of his children to live in boarding houses. There was no privacy, no sense of belonging. Boarders sat on the front porch in rocking chairs, on the outside smiling at each other while on the inside holding each other in contempt. Because of the war, housing was scarce, and people were tucked into every nook and cranny of Mrs. Craft's boarding house. There must have been twenty-five boarders, most of them unmarried women. My parents and I lived on the second floor. Mother and Daddy had a bedroom; I lived on a small screened porch. Living on a porch was nice in spring and summer but in winter it was cold as ice. To help keep out the wind and rain I hung blankets, suspended by wire, around my bed. This porch was on the back side of the house next to the second-floor bathroom.

Stella, a black woman, cooked the boarding house meals. When they were prepared Stella stood in the hallway and rang a bell. The moment the bell started ringing doors opened and everyone rushed for the dining room. There were three tables and I could never predict next to whom I'd be sitting. Dishes of food were passed around. Everyone pretended not to take too much or to select the best pieces of chicken, but if the platter got to me last I ended up with a wing or a back and there wasn't anything I could do about it.

I remember two of the boarders. One woman was a walking bottomless pit. I could never believe the amounts of food she ate. She cleaned every serving bowl on the table, downing gargantuan amounts of creamed potatoes, butter beans, and okra. I'll never forget this woman because of the noise she made while using the bathroom. The second-floor john was next to the porch I lived on, and I could hear when anyone went to the toilet. The door to my porch was partially glass and was covered with a curtain. I could, I discovered, peep out on the hall and keep up with who was using the john. This woman's bowels never moved gently. To the contrary, she always defecated with a roar. I'd be stretched out on my bed and I'd hear someone go into the bathroom. A moment of silence would be followed by a Vesuvian blast. Boom! I kept reconnaissance and with unfailing regularity the blast meant that woman was sitting on the john. Early one morning while defecating she emitted a particularly impressive roar. I was on my bed, half asleep, and just for the devil of it I yelled, "Bombs away!" That morning at breakfast she gave me a dirty look, signaling that she didn't appreciate my attempt at humor.

The other boarder I remember was a buxom woman in her midtwenties from Meridian. I was past puberty and she aroused my youthful libido. This young woman lived on the second floor toward the front. One night I was peeping out my door, checking on the john, keeping up with who was coming and going. The door to the young woman's room opened. She stuck her head out to see if the hall was clear. Seeing no one, she headed for the john to take her bath. To my surprise and youthful delight, she had no clothes on—not the first stitch! I could see everything, and it was the first time I'd seen a nude woman. From then on a set part of my daily routine was watching for this young woman. Night after night her door would open, she would check the hall, and then she would walk quickly to the bathroom in the buff. When eventually she moved away Mrs. Craft's boarding house became, at least for me, a less intriguing place.

The worst feature about living at Mrs. Craft's was not having a place to call my own. There was no sense of belonging. I remember one Saturday morning climbing a pecan tree in the back yard of the boarding house. No sooner had I perched on a limb than Mrs. Craft charged out the back door yelling at me, "Clayton, get out of that tree! Get down right now!" Mrs. Buie, the wealthy lady next door who owned the property, had looked out her window and spotted me climbing the tree. She had phoned over a command to Mrs. Craft for me to get down.

To my knowledge this was my first personal encounter with the Mississippi aristocracy. In Jackson, Mrs. Buie was of the social elite. Her husband had been one of the founders of the First National Bank. Mrs. Buie had a chauffeur and invited ladies to her house for afternoon tea. And here she was ordering me to get down out of her pecan tree. This order made me angry. What harm was I doing? What difference did it make if I sat in the sunshine on a tree limb? Yet the tree belonged to Mrs. Buie and if she ordered me to get down there was nothing I could do. My only recourse was to mutter to myself, "Mrs. Buie, go hang it up!"

Maybe because I despised being around Mrs. Craft's boarding house, maybe because I knew my folks were poor and if I was going to have anything I'd have to make it on my own—whatever the reason, I decided to go to work. At twelve or thirteen years old, I may have been a hick, but I was a hick willing to hustle and to make a buck on the streets of Jackson.

My first job was selling and delivering newspapers—the *Clarion Ledger* and the *Jackson Daily News*. As long as I could remember Daddy had subscribed to the *Clarion Ledger* and the *Jackson Daily News* so he could read its daily column by Fred Sullens, the editor, entitled "Low Down on the Higher Ups." Today the *Clarion Ledger* and the *Jackson Daily News*, Jackson's two newspapers, are under common ownership. But in the 1940s they were separately owned. In the morning I'd get up and deliver a *Clarion Ledger* route in downtown Jackson, picking my papers up at the plant on Amite Street. In the afternoon, after going to school at Bailey Junior High, I'd deliver a *Jackson Daily*

News route that ran out North State Street from the Old Capitol to the Baptist Hospital.

On Sunday morning when the papers were large my daddy got up early with me and helped me carry my routes. After all the Sunday papers were delivered, we'd go to the Toddle House on North State and eat breakfast together. Toddle House restaurants, with their counters and stools, have now disappeared from Southern cities. They were similar to today's Waffle Houses. Toddle House cooks prepared omelettes—a way of cooking eggs that was new to me. They'd beat the eggs in a mixer and then cook them—while aerated—with cheese in an omelette skillet, producing a fluffy spectacle that was a marvel to my eyes. Every Sunday morning Daddy and I ordered omelettes with ham or bacon. Then we'd order an omelette to go and carry it back to Mother at Mrs. Craft's boarding house. Every Sunday morning I took pride in serving Mother a Toddle House omelette in bed.

I gave my paper route customers the best of service, throwing their papers on porches or putting them behind screen doors. I don't remember a single customer being rude or attempting to "rip me off." Instead they were fair and courteous, paying punctually for their papers. My most courteous customer was Mr. Sam McRae who owned McRae's Clothing Store on Capitol Street near the Illinois Central depot. When I went to his home on North State Street to collect for the paper he always came to the door in suit and tie and tipped me twenty-five cents. After the Second World War, Mr. McRae's sons expanded the business, and today McRae's is one of the South's regional department store chains.

While the war was on, newspapers printed "Extras" to announce important wartime developments. I remember walking out North State the day Germany surrendered, selling extras while yelling at the top of my voice, "Extra! Extra! Germany surrenders!" People poured out of houses, buying papers as if they were five-cent hamburgers.

Picking up my papers at the *Clarion Ledger* and *Jackson Daily News* offices was my earliest exposure to the adult world outside the boarding house. Another fellow my age who sold papers was Chester McKee. He was more on his own than I was, since his father was dead. Chester financially supported his mother, a wheelchair invalid.

One morning the presses at the *Clarion Ledger* had broken down and we were all loafing around, waiting for the papers to be printed. Out of the blue one of the pressroom employees suggested, "Let's give old Chester here a nigger dick." To give someone a "nigger dick" meant to paint his penis with printer's ink. Several pressroom employees agreed that this was a laudable idea. They made a dash for Chester and Chester in turn made a dash for the door.

On his way to the exit, Chester grabbed a piece of lead pipe. By the time his pursuers got out the door Chester had taken a Stonewall Jackson stance in the middle of Amite Street. There Chester was, standing in the middle of the street with that piece of lead pipe drawn back ready to strike. His pursuers came to a halt at the curb. Chester, alone in the early morning light, his teeth clenched, said, "The first one of you bastards who puts a hand on me is gonna get the shit knocked out of him!" Chester and his tormenters glared at each other, and Chester continued to taunt them: "Come on, you sons of bitches! I'll knock the shit out of you!"

Awkward moments passed, and one by one the men who wanted to give Chester a "nigger dick" faded away. All my life I've hated bullies, and whenever I meet one I remember Chester's encounter with bullies that morning outside the *Clarion Ledger* office in the middle of Amite Street.

Delivering *Clarion Ledger* and *Jackson Daily News* routes and selling papers on the streets of Jackson gave me money to spend. I used this money to buy clothes and to buy hamburgers at the Krystal located at the corner of Capitol Street and North President. I spent money going to movies at the Paramount and Majestic theaters on Capitol Street and going to wrestling matches on Saturday nights at the City Auditorium. To me—a teenager with pimples—watching wrestling matches was a superb thrill. I enjoyed seeing the wrestling Curtis brothers from Vicksburg taking on "thugs" like the "Masked Monster" or the "Dirty Devil."

We moved to Jackson in the summer and when the fall of the year came around I enrolled as a seventh grader at Bailey Junior High. Today the public schools in Jackson are racially integrated, but when I was a student they were segregated. Hence, Bailey Junior High—

located at the intersection of Woodrow Wilson Drive and North State—was all white and a microcosm of Jackson's white population.

There were "insiders" and there were "outsiders." The "outsiders" were students who like me lived close to downtown or over on Bailey Avenue. The "insiders" were sons and daughters of North Jackson families. In classes at Bailey Junior High School (and later at Central High School) I was exposed to these "insiders" and, to my mind, they seemed the ultimate in sophistication. They were the last word in urbanity. On weekends in the fall of the year they traveled with parents to "Ole Miss" football games and in class on Monday talked knowingly about the quarterbacking skills of Charley Conerly. In summer they vacationed in the Smokies or in Florida. They danced, belonged to sororities and fraternities, and attended parties where they wore evening dresses and tuxedos. Those North Jackson girls, I thought, were beautiful beyond description. To me they seemed ethereal, unreal, as awesome as goddesses on Mt. Olympus. Some of them never wore the same dress to school twice. Everyday they wore a different outfit. When they passed me in the hall between classes at Bailey Junior High they looked straight ahead and didn't speak. They spoke only to one another and to fellows who (like them) lived in North Jackson in brick colonials with winding driveways. Oh, to be admitted to that charmed circle! What nobler dream than to be "one of them," within the circle of North Jackson aristocracy! My exclusion from that circle gave me a sense of rejection, a sense of being inferior. When you're young, your "place" is determined largely by who your parents are. I had no control over my present (that I lived on a screened porch in a boarding house, listened to the other boarders' bowel movements, and rode around Jackson in a 1937 Chevrolet). But I felt that I did control my future. Thus in the seventh grade I hammered out my life's goal: to become rich, to live in North Jackson, which in my adolescent thinking was comparable to living in Palm Springs or Newport, and to drive around town in a Cadillac. In a word, I decided to work until someday I amounted to something, becoming a person who mattered. I had no desire to remain a pimply-faced boarding-house hick.

5

Work

STRUGGLING TO BECOME SOMEBODY WHO MATTERED,
I had the good fortune while in junior high and high school to work
for a series of admirable employers whom I remember to this day with
respect. In the eighth grade, in addition to selling papers, I went to
work for Mr. Kelly Patterson, a Jackson businessman who owned a
chain of drug stores. One of Mr. Patterson's stores was in the Lamar
Life Building on Capitol Street across from the governor's mansion.
Another store was around the corner in what was then called the
Lampton Building, located diagonally behind the post office. Both
stores had soda fountains with tables and booths. Mr. Patterson gave
me a job waiting on tables, working some shifts in the Lampton
Building store, other shifts in the Lamar Life store. Throughout the
day office workers would descend on Mr. Patterson's soda fountains
for sandwiches, coffee, and Pepsi Colas. As on my paper routes, I
prided myself on giving these customers superior service. No sooner
would customers sit down than I was there to take their orders.

Mr. Patterson promoted me from waiter to soda jerk. I learned
to prepare butterscotch sundaes, chocolate malts, and ice cream
floats. I mastered the sandwich board, learning to garnish hamburgers and to prepare potato salad. My club sandwiches were masterpieces: three pieces of bread, ham and cheese with lettuce and
tomato, all quartered in triangular shapes with toothpicks inserted to
hold the pieces together, this delicacy in turn covered with potato
chips and garnished with pickles. During the noon rush I hustled from
one end of the soda fountain to the other, drawing coffee, mixing
malts, finishing off a strawberry sundae with whipped cream and

cherry, turning out pimento cheese sandwiches with lightning dex-
terity. The more business there was the better I liked it. After the
noon rush I'd wash dishes, police the soda fountain, and sweep the
floor. I made certain I was always on time for work, arriving at the
store a half hour before opening. In short, I like to think I was one
of the best soda jerks Mr. Patterson ever employed.

Inwardly I longed to be Mr. Patterson's son. Much of my adolescent life was spent longing for an ideal father, for somebody to
look up to and to lean on and to learn from. I wanted a father to run
interference for me. My father had commendable qualities and as a
boy I loved him. Yet in adolescence this relationship of love became
something of a love-hate relationship. For as Daddy grew older he
changed. Or was it I who changed? Adolescents can be cruel, lacking in compassion and void of empathy. Observing the world around
me, I sensed people in Jackson were judged by what they were
"worth." People were valued by what they owned. The more you
owned, the more people respected you. My daddy, the one who
drove a 1937 Chevrolet, the one who sat at night in a bedroom at
Mrs. Craft's boarding house, wearing an undershirt and spitting
chewing-tobacco juice into a Maxwell House coffee can, didn't own
much. In my thoughts I compared my father to other adults his age.
I resented what I perceived as my father's lack of achievement, his
failure "to succeed" and to accumulate. At the time I didn't understand that he was right off a Smith County cotton farm and that he
was a person bred to be a field hand and was driven out of Smith
County and Sullivan's Hollow by the boll weevil and by the soil's
infertility and by lack of economic opportunity.

Moreover, relating to my father was complicated by his Irish
temper. He prided himself on "telling people off." He had a tongue
that on occasion could be sharp as a razor. From time to time I was
on the receiving end of his razor tongue and his hot anger. His displays of temper, I now sense, were eruptions of personal frustration.
For in retrospect, I suspect my daddy didn't like living at Mrs. Craft's
boarding house any more than I did. Nor can I believe he enjoyed
traveling from one end of Mississippi to the other, chasing down
Negro whores with gonorrhea. But my father's philosophy was: "Get
a secure, salaried job and hold on to it for dear life. If there's another
depression you'll have an income coming in." By contrast, Mr. Pat-

terson was an entrepreneur—a man who got things done, owning real estate and operating a chain of drug stores. And so I longed to be his son. At times I imagined myself as a druggist standing behind the prescription counter and filling prescriptions as Mr. Patterson did.

My admiration for Kelly Patterson was shared by Oscar, the black porter who mopped the floor and delivered prescriptions around town on a bicycle. I recall Oscar's remark, "There ain't nothing under the sun Mr. Kelly Patterson don't know."

Behind the soda fountain in the Lamar Life store were steps going down into a basement storage room where we stored boxes of Kleenex and cosmetics and soda-fountain supplies. During rest breaks Oscar and I, along with other soda-fountain employees, went down into this basement room and shot craps. I conceived myself to be a keen crap shooter. I knew how to shake dice and to roll them with a wrist flip and finger snap while uttering, "Come to me, baby, and give me what I need!" Usually I won, but one afternoon I hit a losing streak and Oscar, the black porter, won all the money I had. Confident my crap-shooting luck would return, I went upstairs and borrowed ten dollars from one of the druggists (and to me at the time ten dollars was an astronomical sum). Back to the basement I went to take on Oscar in craps. My losing streak continued and Oscar smilingly relieved me of my borrowed ten dollars. From that moment to this I've never again had a desire to gamble.

Eventually I left my soda fountain job with Patterson's Drug Stores for a job in the shoe department of the Emporium. In the 1940s there were two main department stores in Jackson: Kenington's and the Emporium. These two stores, each some five or six floors in height, faced each other on Capitol Street and were the most fashionable stores in town—with carpets on the floor, illuminated display cases, clerks who wore black dresses and tried to look like aristocrats, and porters who wore bow ties. People drove from all over Mississippi to shop at Kenington's and the Emporium.

The opportunity to work at the Emporium came to me because the Merrill Lynch stockbroker's office was located on the first floor of the Lampton Building, adjacent to Patterson's Drug Store where I worked as soda jerk. A Merrill Lynch customer who patronized the soda fountain was Mr. Howard Walker, manager of the shoe department at the Emporium. One morning I was behind the soda fountain scrambling eggs when Mr. Walker, always impeccably dressed, said to me, "Young man, I've been watching you work here for some time and I'm wondering if you'd like to go to work for me over at the Emporium?" He told me he was manager of the shoe department and he explained what my job would involve: unpacking shoe cartons, checking invoices, stamping prices on shoe boxes, keeping the shelves in order, sweeping the floor and dusting—in other words, I was to be a general flunky.

I mulled the offer over for a day or two and concluded that working at the Emporium, Jackson's fanciest store (owned—so it was reported—by Jews), would be an upward move in the world. So off to the Emporium I, by then a tenth grader, went to work for Mr. Walker.

Shoes were Mr. Walker's passion. He breathed, he ate, and he dreamed shoes. Three or four times a year he'd go to market in New York. When he came back, he'd tell me about shoes he had ordered. His favorite brand was I. Miller. When a shoe shipment arrived I'd unpack the carton (with Mr. Walker hovering over my shoulders). Mr. Walker would open one of the boxes and hold the shoe up in the air and mutter, "Beautiful! Simply magnificent! The ladies will buy these like crazy!" He was right about the way shoes sold. The war had created a lingering clothing shortage and people were shoe hungry. Mr. Walker would run an ad in the newspaper announcing a shipment of I. Millers. The next morning by opening time a crowd of shoppers would be standing outside the Emporium's doors, and when the store opened for business shoppers would dash to the shoe department, begging to buy those I. Millers.

Mr. Walker was a study in perpetual motion. He walked in a trot, repeatedly adjusting his tie. One of my responsibilities was to have a copy of the morning *Clarion Ledger* on his desk by the time he arrived for work. Mr. Walker's routine never varied. He would rush to his desk, pick up the *Clarion Ledger* and turn to the stock market page. If he liked what he read, he purred, "Nice! Real nice!" If he didn't like what he saw, he inevitably exclaimed, "Hell's bells!" Whereupon he would dash out the door and head for the Merrill Lynch office two blocks away.

Mr. Walker was demanding—a perfectionist. He didn't get along with the shoe clerks who worked under him. His recurrent label for them was, "Slobs and ingrates!" But Mr. Walker and I got along. His wife was a superb cook and every Christmas while I worked at the Emporium Mr. Walker brought me a box filled with his wife's kitchen delicacies.

While I was working for Mr. Walker at the Emporium we moved out of Mrs. Craft's boarding house. Mother and Daddy had saved dimes and dollars and were able to make the down payment on a new home located out in West Jackson. In design this home was simple, less than two thousand square feet with one bathroom and three bedrooms, one of hundreds of those nondescript, asbestos-shingled houses built during the late 1940s in the postwar building boom. Yet in my mind this house compared favorably to Vanderbilt's Biltmore Estate. One of the happiest days in my life was the afternoon when I got off work at the Emporium and—instead of going to Mrs. Craft's boarding house—caught the Number Four bus and rode out to our new home on Claiborne Avenue. To have a room of my own to sleep in, to have access to a refrigerator, to eat in privacy with my father and mother, to have a back yard to sit in: these amenities I experienced for the first time since we'd moved to Jackson.

By the time we moved out on Claiborne Avenue I was in high school. In the morning I'd catch the Number Four bus and ride to Central High School in downtown Jackson. After school I'd work for Mr. Walker at the Emporium and, after I got off from work, I'd catch the Number Four for a ride back home. The street buses in Jackson were, like everything else, segregated. White people sat at the front; black people sat at the back. Running down the middle of the bus's ceiling was an iron rod on which was a sliding metal sign. On one side of the sign the word "Whites" was painted, while on the other side was painted the word "Blacks." When I got on the bus I had to make certain I sat on the proper side of this "white-black" sign, which could be pushed back and forth on the rod. If I got on the bus and all the seats toward the front were occupied, I'd push the sign backward past an empty seat and then sit down. If a Negro got on the bus and all the seats toward the rear were taken, he'd push the sign forward past an empty seat and then sit down. If I sat on the wrong side of the sign, the bus driver would make me move.

I didn't develop sensitivity to the race issue until I moved away from Mississippi. Yet on the Number Four bus I witnessed episodes that troubled me. The drivers—all white—on occasion deliberately passed by blacks waiting for rides at bus stops. I remember one Number Four bus driver who exhibited red-neck hostility toward Negroes. A black passenger would board the bus and as the Negro walked toward the rear, where blacks were required to sit, the driver would alternately step on the bus's accelerator and brake, creating a jerking motion, in turn causing the black passenger to lose balance and to stagger in the aisle. Seeing the Negro falter, this bus driver would laugh and say, "Rock, nigger, rock!" He called this "rocking a coon." I didn't think it was funny, yet it never crossed my mind to protest.

Blacks got raw treatment in the South of my youth. That's the way life was. They were abused not only by bus drivers but were abused also by politicians and by the police. All during the 1940s and 1950s Mississippi politicians tried to "out-nigger" each other, creating a tone of antagonism that became a dimension of the South's race problem. During my high school days, prior to television's heyday, political rallies at which candidates for office spoke were a feature of Mississippi politics. I went with Daddy to a political rally in Smith Park in downtown Jackson. The principal speaker was Theodore G. Bilbo, once Mississippi's governor, then its United States Senator. Bilbo was a short man who wore a white suit with red necktie and red suspenders. Bilbo's speech that night was a harangue against Negroes. I remember his shouting, "The best way to keep a nigger from voting on Tuesday is to beat the hell out of him on Monday night!" The crowd responded with laughs and cheers.

I also remember as a high school student going on one occasion with my father to the Jackson police station. Daddy had received a parking ticket and went to the police station to pay his fine. While we were in the station, a police officer brought in a black man who was under arrest. The black man made some remark that infuriated the officer. The policeman shouted at him, "What did you say, you burrhead bastard?" In anger the white officer started kicking the Negro between his legs. Screaming with pain, the black man fell to the floor, clutching his scrotum. After we had left the police station my father said to me, "Son, I wish you hadn't seen that. Someday this kick-a-nigger business is going to backfire on us." In retrospect my father's remark was prophetic.

I plugged through three years at Central High, taking the usual courses high school students take—algebra, history, physics. By the time I got to high school, I'd developed an interest in music. I played a clarinet in the Central High School band, which was the best high school band in Mississippi. Time and again at state band contests we won superior ratings in all categories—concert, marching, sight reading. We performed at high school football games, playing our trombone-featuring specialty—"Tiger Rag"—in support of the Central High School Tigers. Several times a year we'd march in parades down Capitol Street, dressed in maroon uniforms, playing John Philip Sousa marches. Our band director was Mr. Louis Pullo, a native of Italy. Mr. Pullo, who spoke English with an Italian accent, fascinated me. If we didn't play the way he wanted us to play, he'd shout at us, sometimes throwing his baton on the floor and walking out of the band room in disgust. I felt that he was a misplaced talent, a round peg in a square hole, for Mr. Pullo was a superb cellist. Instead of being a high school band director he should have been playing cello with the New York Philharmonic or the London Symphony. One afternoon after classes I went by the band room to pick up my clarinet. Mr. Pullo was in the band room alone. He was sitting in a corner, his back to the door, playing his cello, evoking tones suggestive of the poignant music one hears in a synagogue service. I stood transfixed, listening to the music. When Mr. Pullo had finished playing, he turned toward me and tears were streaming down his face. I've wondered about those tears. What did they mean? I'll never know.

Moreover, as a high school student I struggled, as all youngsters do, with the issue of how I was going to make a living. I liked to work. Indeed, I prided myself in love of work. Drawing on my experience in the shoe department of the Emporium, I thought about going into the shoe business. I toyed with the idea of becoming an attorney. I fantasized about the possibility of someday—as a lawyer—going into politics. The state capitol building was a stone's throw from Central High, and from time to time I'd go over to the capitol and sit in the visitor's gallery and watch the legislators at work, arguing over bills and voting on issues.

Because of my interest in law and politics I joined the high school debate team. Our debating coach was Mrs. Avis Russell, an English teacher. For three years in a row our team made it to state debating contest finals. We debated issues like national health insurance and compulsory arbitration of labor disputes. I spent hours studying these subjects, learning to argue both sides of an issue. In debating contests, you never knew whether you were going to be "pro" or "con" on an issue until right before the debate began. Our nemesis was the debating team from McComb, a town in Southwest Mississippi, which year after year clobbered us in state debating finals.

During the summer after my junior year in high school I quit my job in the shoe department of the Emporium. Arranging shoe boxes month after month had become tedious. I landed a food service job at the Heidelberg Hotel on Capitol Street. During the 1940s the Heidelberg, now demolished, was the Waldorf-Astoria of Mississippi. It was the hotel where couples honeymooned and Shriners held conventions and the Jackson Rotary Club met for its weekly noon meeting. The Heidelberg did a land-office business in its cafeteria, coffee shop, and catering. There were scores of banquets every week, and the hotel's top floor was "The Roof," a nightclub with orchestra and dance floor. All these food services were under the direction of the catering manager, Mr. Amos Lipham, a gentleman I knew. Since I'd toyed also with the possibility of someday going into the food business, I asked Mr. Lipham for a job and he gave me one working in the hotel's kitchen. When I asked Mr. Lipham for a job I had no way of foreseeing that in the Heidelberg kitchen I'd make a decision that would shape the rest of my life.

My responsibilities in the Heidelberg kitchen were multiple: stocking supplies, keeping beer iced, washing pots and pans, scrubbing floors, and cleaning out walk-in freezers. A hotel kitchen, I discovered, is a world unto itself: perpetual frenzy, banging pots and pans, yelling cooks, waitresses on the go. The air was always filled with steam and odors. The Heidelberg kitchen was for me a source of culinary delights. The cooks slipped me fried chicken and the baker always cooked extra pastries that I'd sample while standing in the walk-in cooler.

Some of the people I encountered in the Heidelberg kitchen were like characters out of a Charles Dickens novel. There was Henrietta, a wrinkled black woman in her seventies who arrived early each morning and spent the day sitting in a corner by herself peeling shrimp. That's all she did. Six days a week from sunrise to sunset Henrietta peeled shrimp that were used for making gumbo and shrimp cocktails. There was a black man named "Memphis," so called because for a time he had lived up in Memphis, Tennessee. "Memphis" was deformed. He was around four and a half feet tall with a grotesque hump on his back. He was the kitchen's vegetable man. All day long he worked in a cubicle of sinks and tables where he peeled potatoes, cleaned lettuce, and chopped onions and celery. "Memphis" was constantly making passes at the black girls who worked at the Heidelberg. Yet because of his deformity he was repeatedly rebuffed. And there was a waitress named Magnolia. Magnolia fancied she was wealthy. Her fingers were lined with "diamond" rings which she talked about constantly, boasting of how much they were worth and where she'd bought them. I always figured Magnolia's "diamonds" were phony, but they made her feel "rich," and that's all that mattered.

6

Called to Preach

TO THIS DAY I REMEMBER with pleasure my employment at the Heidelberg. Yet while I was working there something unexpected and unsought happened to me. That event has made all the difference in the world as far as my life is concerned, for I experienced what is commonly referred to as a "call" into the Christian ministry.

Inside me a "voice," to use Socrates' term, started saying, "Clayton, you are to be a preacher, a Southern Baptist pastor. That's what you are to do with your life." These inner urgings started slowly, quietly, intermittently, but with the passing of time they became stronger, more insistent, like a crescendo in a musical composition. I'd be riding to work on a Number Four bus or I'd be mopping the floor in the Heidelberg kitchen and the impulse would hit me, "You are to be a preacher." Weeks went by and these intuitions, as undeniable as they were unwelcome, became an inner ache. They hurt, and I tried denying or sublimating them.

This inner impulse was baffling. I didn't know what to do with it. I want to be believed when I say that I didn't welcome this inner voice. I had no desire to be a preacher. Not that I had anything against preachers, but the clergy, I felt, was not my cup of tea. That's why I found these lurings toward the ministry puzzling.

Why me?

To be sure, I'd always attended church. My fate was to be born into a lower-middle-class family that took religion seriously. I recall my father spending hours studying the notes of his *Scofield Reference Bible*. My parents were Southern Baptists, and the Southern Baptist denomination was to them what the Mormon Church is to Mormons out in Utah: an encompassing institution serving both religious and social roles that provided a context in which to live, as important as the home, if not more so. When Mother and Daddy were school teachers at Gulde we had driven into Brandon every other Sunday to attend a Southern Baptist church. And we'd belonged to Baptist churches in Columbia and Greenwood.

When we moved to Jackson my parents discovered that Mrs. Craft's boarding house was three blocks from the First Baptist Church on North President Street. Jackson's First Baptist Church was the largest Baptist congregation in Mississippi. It was located across the street from the state capitol. The first week we lived at Mrs. Craft's boarding house we visited this church and to my eyes it was the most beautiful structure I'd ever seen. I had not known that such churches existed. There were stained glass windows, magnificent pews (not crude benches like I'd seen in rural churches), carpeted floors, Gothic (I learned later) details, an organ, and a balcony from which I could look down on the congregation below!

The First Baptist Church had influential people in its membership. People like the Hedermans who at the time owned the *Clarion Ledger*. And people like Owen Cooper, the agricultural industrialist; Ross Barnett, the state's most prominent damage suit lawyer, later to be elected governor, who always sat with his family on the front pew; Leland Speed, Jackson's mayor; N. W. Overstreet, the architect; D. C. Simmons, a wealthy businessman. These names could go on and on—names of people composing Jackson's power structure. Yet the church's membership was complex. Alongside the power brokers were scores of ordinary folk: telephone operators and secretaries and store clerks.

My Mother and Daddy and I joined this congregation and every Sunday we were at church. I attended Sunday School classes and participated in youth and choir organizations. Yet my motivation for attending was not, I confess, religious. Instead, this large downtown church gave me a place, particularly on weekends, to get away from Mrs. Craft's boarding house, which I loathed. For me the First Baptist Church was a social outlet, a place to be with others my own age, a place for hayrides and Halloween parties. Best of all, I felt accepted there. I felt I was among friends. This happens in the lives of Sears

Roebuck and J. C. Penney Southerners. The church pays attention and accepts them when no one else will.

Over the years at the First Baptist Church I had listened to dozens of sermons, some by the pastor—a gentleman named Dr. Douglas Hudgins—some by "big name" preachers who visited this Jackson congregation. Preachers like Hyman Appleman, the converted Jew, and R. G. Lee, a minister from Memphis who looked like a banker and delivered sermons having titles like "Payday Someday" and "The Menace of Mediocrity." But through it all I never remotely considered being a preacher myself. In fact, preachers made me feel ill at ease. They never cursed or told a bawdy story or drank a rum and cola. Somehow, so I thought then, they were "different" from other people. As Sydney Smith said, there are three sexes: men, women, and clergymen.

And most of the preachers I knew were men of limited financial means. They were men who, to quote Sinclair Lewis, lived lives of dignified poverty. I didn't want dignified poverty; I wanted wealth. I craved financial security. My heroes were not Hyman Appleman and R. G. Lee but Jackson businessmen like the ones I worked for— Mr. Patterson with his drug stores and Mr. Walker at the Emporium and Mr. Lipham at the Heidelberg. I reveled in streetcorner talk about an entrepreneur in Jackson named Dumas Milner who had the city's Chevrolet franchise and was making a fortune in real estate. These men were my heroes and I wanted to be like them. I wanted to be another Dumas Milner! I wanted to show those North Jackson city slickers who wouldn't speak to me in the halls of Bailey Junior High or Central High School that I, Clayton Sullivan, could make a bundle of money and was as sharp as they were.

Yet time passed in the Heidelberg kitchen and the compulsion to become a preacher became disturbingly intense. I couldn't get away from it no matter how hard I tried. To this day I remember that *gnawing on my innards*, sickening and bewildering in intensity, grinding in force! This was not a "call" to a contemplative life, nor was it a "call" to quest for insight into the human role in the cosmos (at the time I was certainly unaware of that enigmatic issue). It was a "call" specific and limited: *a "call" to be a Southern Baptist preacher*, a "call" so real to me that I began to dread the consequences of not capitulating to it. I felt I was in the grip of a Power that I could not resist.

One of my daily chores in the Heidelberg kitchen was to slice and squeeze a crate of oranges so there would be orange juice on the cafeteria line for breakfast. One morning I was performing this chore. With my hands I was slicing and squeezing oranges but on the inside I was a civil war—struggling with this "call" into the ministry. Seeing no way out, I put down the knife with which I was slicing oranges and in the kitchen of the Heidelberg Hotel I, a high school student, closed my eyes and inwardly prayed a prayer from which I'll never escape. The gist of the prayer was: "Dear God, if you want me to be a preacher, I'll be one." This simple prayer was sincere. My decision to become a minister was, I emphasize, *not my idea.* Instead, this decision was my response to an imposed, unsought compulsion. I've met people who believe that men become preachers because they think they're "better" than others or because they have an abundance of religion. I, for one, had no abundance of religion and I, who lusted for the prostitutes who hung around the Heidelberg, did not think of myself as morally superior to anyone. To the contrary, I was coping with life as I experienced it. Life was one thing after another— all the way from watching Mother churn butter at Gulde to living in Mrs. Craft's boarding house on North State Street to encountering a compulsion toward the Christian clergy while working at the Heidelberg.

This decision to be a preacher I made early in the summer between my junior and senior years in high school. For a time I kept this decision to myself. Later that summer I went on a bus with a church group to Ridgecrest, a church retreat that Southern Baptists maintain out from Asheville in the mountains of North Carolina. At the close of one of the worship services at this retreat I "surrendered" to be a preacher. I "went public" with my decision.

My mother approved of this decision. My daddy didn't. He'd always wanted me to be a medical doctor like my first cousin Wayne, Uncle Kailey's son, who was practicing in radiology over in Meridian. Daddy had encouraged me toward a medical career by giving me a stethoscope and by taking me to have conversations with doctors like Dr. J. B. Wall, a member of the First Baptist Church. But in Dr. Wall's office in the Standard Life Building, I found myself fascinated not by needles and test tubes but by a picture on the wall portraying (so Dr. Wall explained) Faustus talking with Mephistopheles.

So when Daddy heard about my decision to be a preacher he got me aside and asked, "Son, are you sure you know what you're doing?" He had reason to ask that question. Three of his brothers were Southern Baptist preachers and some of them, I now perceive, lived turbulent lives. I remember one of my clergy uncles sitting on the back porch of our home on Claiborne Avenue, drinking coffee, and saying to my Daddy, "Clay, when I decided to make a preacher I didn't know it meant spending all my life kissing Baptist butts." He added, "All I'm doing now is bitching for time, waiting for sixty-five and Social Security." I'd seen another uncle—Uncle Jim—leave the Baptist ministry to go to work for the post office. Thus my Father had reason to ask, "Son, are you sure you know what you're doing?"

At the time I thought I did. Was this "call" to be a preacher authentic? Was it the voice of God? Or was it a bizarre aberration of my late-adolescent mind, or a trick played on me by some malevolent power? These questions are irrelevant. For in life we make decisions on the basis of present insights, feelings, convictions, without benefit of clarity provided by hindsight. Moreover, we stumble through life ignorantly, not always understanding the import of our decisions. When I started taking those first steps toward a ministerial career I thought I was doing the right thing. Yet at the time I'd never read a serious book. The history of ideas was beyond me. I didn't know disciplines like theology and philosophy existed. For all I knew David Hume was a quarterback for the University of Alabama. I had only the foggiest notion of what was involved in being a member of the clergy. To my mind being a preacher meant being a public speaker. That being a minister could involve frustration, suffering, and defeat were possibilities I didn't consider.

At the time my conception of the Christian faith was amorphous: a potpourri of unexamined clichés like "God is love," "All men are sinners," "The Bible is the Word of God." I believed you became a Christian by accepting what Southern Baptists call the "Plan of Salvation," giving assent to a series of selected statements found in the Bible. I had accepted the "Plan of Salvation" when we were living in Gulde, when I was eight or nine years old. Every other Sunday we attended the Baptist church in Brandon. One day my Daddy and the preacher—who had a bald head and whose name I don't remember—got me aside and "explained" to me the "Plan of Salvation." At the time I wasn't certain that I understood the logic of this "Plan of Salvation" but neither could I resist the overtures of my Father and the bald-headed preacher. They urged me to confess my sins so that I could be saved. I thought of two sins to confess. I had once shot a woodpecker with a BB gun. In my boyish mind to shoot a squirrel that might be eaten was morally acceptable but to shoot a woodpecker—a senseless act—was indefensible. My second sin was stealing the homemade candy that belonged to the 4-H Club and was destined for sale between acts of the senior play at the Gulde school. I told the preacher about the woodpecker and the candy, and he assured me that God would forgive me of these sins. The following Sunday I was baptized. That I felt no differently after baptism bothered me. I felt something was missing, but there was nothing I knew to do, and I decided to let the matter slide by.

I talked over my decision about becoming a preacher with Dr. Douglas Hudgins, the pastor of the First Baptist Church. Dr. Hudgins I admired. He was a man of manners and suaveness, not at all a "goody-goody" clergyman. He dressed like a Philadelphia lawyer, a characteristic I liked. He encouraged me, and it wasn't long before I became known around the First Baptist Church in Jackson as "the young man who's going to be a preacher." With this designation I was uncomfortable. It made me feel ill at ease. Yet I felt I was doing what I had to do.

My final year at Central High School passed quickly. I edited the high school annual, continued debating, and worked at the Heidelberg. During that final year of high school my feet were still on the ground. Living for years in Mrs. Craft's boarding house and selling newspapers on the streets of Jackson and working in the Heidelberg kitchen had given me some practical insights into life. Yet I would be less than honest if I didn't admit that during that final year at Central High I started taking steps down the slippery slope into religious fanaticism. Every morning before classes at Central High, a group of students gathered in one of the classrooms for prayer. I started attending these morning prayer meetings.

I also started attending "Youth for Christ" services. "Youth for Christ" is an interdenominational youth movement promoted by Billy

Graham, and in the late 1940s in Jackson "Youth for Christ" services were held on Saturday nights in the Central High School auditorium. Songs were sung, "testimonies" were given, and young men who were graduates of Bob Jones University in Greenville, South Carolina, frequently spoke. These young "Bob Jones" men smiled and wore white shoes, pink shirts, and yellow sport coats. They waved their arms and pointed their fingers while preaching a "demanding" version of the Christian religion centering around slogans like "Let Go and Let God" and "Turn Your Eyes upon Jesus." These young "Bob Jones" men argued against cosmetics, movies, cigarettes, and kissing in the moonlight. They fired Bible bullets on all questions and issues, and they walked up to strangers to ask, out of the blue, "Have you been born again?" Based on my observation, I was impressed with these young men from Bob Jones University. I thought they knew what they were talking about.

I started leaving religious tracts in the men's washroom at the Greyhound bus station. When walking down the street, I whistled hymns. In my shirt pocket I carried a copy of the New Testament. I missed none of the services at the First Baptist Church. Late adolescence became for me a time of religious fervor. My conduct in this regard wasn't anomalous, for in many people's lives late adolescence is the golden age of religion, a time when idealism is in the saddle. At this point in life I had not lived long enough to become cynical or to recognize the value of skepticism. Instead, I was swept away by the religious impulse. People so swept away are like inhabitants of Jonathan Swift's Laputa, where theory reigns supreme. They construct for themselves artificial worlds of words and fancies that do not correspond to the world as it is.

As a late teenager I began constructing for myself an artificial world—based on fragile assumptions—within which I was to live for years. I started downplaying the importance of the economic side of life. Wealth accumulation, I decided, would no longer be my goal. Instead, I wanted to be "completely dedicated to Jesus." My life's aim became "to do the will of God."

In this artificial world that I constructed the problem of evil did not exist. The world was beautiful, and people were good. I held to Pippa's view, "God's in his heaven—all's right with the world!" I knew how to dream, but I did not yet know how to suffer. I knew how to believe, not how to doubt. I knew how to laugh, not how to cry.

In my artificial world I assumed that the Christian religion was "true" and devoid of intellectual difficulties. And I assumed there was an "obvious" Christian message that could be grasped intellectually. Lacking the ability to transcend and to evaluate the culture in which I was raised, I assumed Southern society was "Christian." Indeed, I believed that the states of the Old Confederacy constituted the geographical center of Christendom, and I believed that the Southern Baptist Convention embodied quintessential Christianity. In my mind, the Southern Baptist Convention was an organization in which I invested undiluted trust and which increasingly became the source of my identity.

In my artificial world I designed a scenario for my life. I'd go to college and then to a seminary and spend my adult years pastoring and preaching to Southern Baptists, a people I saw as gracious, combining Christian virtues with Southern hospitality.

7

Mississippi College

THERE WAS NEVER A QUESTION about where I'd go to college. Many of my Sullivan relatives had gone to Mississippi College in Clinton, a town seven miles west of Jackson. Mississippi College is a denominational school owned by Mississippi Baptists. It is one of scores of church-related colleges founded in the last century, before the golden age of state universities. The campus is a complex of red brick buildings—a library, a student center, a gymnasium, dormitories, classroom buildings—sitting on both sides of the highway— U.S. 80, which has since been superseded by Interstate 20—that runs between Jackson and Vicksburg. The most impressive structure on campus is an antebellum chapel used by Union and Confederate soldiers as a barracks and hospital during the Civil War. My mother and father and his brothers had attended Mississippi College. One of my clergy uncles was chairman of its board of trustees. So in the fall of 1948 I enrolled as a student, enduring the absurdities of freshman hazing then a part of college life. Most of the students were, like me, sons and daughters of Baptist families, products of the small towns and rural communities of Mississippi.

During the 1940s and 1950s to have confused Mississippi College with Harvard or the University of Chicago would have been difficult. The campus reflected Mississippi's lack of wealth. The dormitories were Spartan—concrete floors, metal furniture, showers and toilets void of partitions. The cafeteria was reminiscent of a World War I mess hall. Laboratory and library facilities were inadequate, a feature none of us who were students recognized at the time. The intellectual atmosphere was as stimulating as the cold, saltless grits that were served in the dining hall. All faculty members were underpaid, few held doctor's degrees. Most members of the religion department, with the exception of Dr. Howard Spell, were retired Baptist ministers who in their classes refought the Protestant Reformation. Mentally they lived four hundred years in the past.

For me to suggest that all professors at Mississippi college were duds wouldn't be true. Some professors were superb. Mr. R. R. Pearce, a sociologist, tried to make us aware of how society molds us. Dr. H. P. James, a historian, made Alexander the Great and Charlemagne come alive. Dr. F. T. Walker, corpulent chairman of the English department, gave me a love for Nathaniel Hawthorne and Sinclair Lewis that I've never outgrown.

I settled in for a four-year stay at Mississippi College, rooming all four years in Crestman Hall, the largest men's dormitory on campus. I didn't care for the cafeteria food. I ate most of my meals either at the Owl, a stool-and-counter cafe right off campus, or at Major's Truck Stop on the edge of town.

One of the first things I noticed on enrolling at Mississippi College.was an absence of vending machines on campus. This absence provoked my entrepreneurial spirit. I got permission to place vending machines in the dormitories. Then I worked a deal with a vending company in Jackson whereby they provided the vending machines and I kept them stocked with candy bars, potato chips, and peanuts. I partially paid my way through college by working these vending machines—selling snack foods to my classmates.

Mississippi College had an atmosphere of contrived piety. Prayer meetings assembled always and everywhere. There were dormitory prayer meetings, noonday prayer meetings, sunset prayer meetings. In the Student Center building were prayer rooms where students could go and pray any hour of day or night. Five days a week chapel services were conducted in the main auditorium and everyone was required to attend.

The college's president was Dr. D. M. Nelson, a man who conceived of himself as an orator in the Demosthenes tradition. Twice a year in chapel services the student body was privileged to hear one of his orations, sprinkled with quotations from Cicero and Shakespeare. One morning some of the campus Philistines took steps to enliven one of Dr. Nelson's oratorical masterpieces. They slipped into the auditorium before the chapel service began and hid firecrackers with delayed fuses. They hid firecrackers above ceiling tiles, in the ventilation system, and behind the stage. They timed them to explode during the chapel service. Dr. Nelson began delivering to the student body an embroidered address replete with Ciceronian and Shakespearean quotations. We were getting the full D. M. Nelson oratorical treatment. All the faculty members, listening attentively, were sitting on the stage behind Dr. Nelson. And then—BOOM!— all over the place firecrackers started exploding! Dozens of them! No one knew what was happening. I didn't know whether to duck under my seat or to get up and run. Through the exploding pandemonium Dr. Nelson didn't bat an eye or miss a word. He continued his memorized oration as though nothing was happening. The ringleader of the firecracker Philistines turned out to be the son of a Baptist preacher. For this antic, he and his cohorts were expelled from college.

On the whole my first year at Mississippi College was uneventful. I went to pep rallies and football games. I worked my vending machines. I joined the Ministerial Club and hitchhiked back and forth between Clinton and Jackson. I took the usual freshman courses— Survey of World Civilization, Zoology (a subject I came within a whisper of flunking), and American Literature. I was still struggling to come to terms with being a minister. That encounter with a Power in the Heidelberg kitchen had made a profound impression on me. Yet I still wasn't entirely comfortable with my decision to be a preacher.

My second year was anything but uneventful. I encountered that year a Texan from Dallas who turned my life around.

Once a year at Mississippi College the institution conducted what was called Religious Emphasis Week. During this week a prominent Baptist clergyman came to Clinton and preached in a campus revival. He'd preach at the morning chapel services and at night he'd hold services in the sanctuary of Clinton's First Baptist Church adjacent to the campus. During the early 1950s at Mississippi College the annual Religious Emphasis Week was a pivotal event. Preparatory prayer meetings gathered all over the place. In prayer rooms in the Student Center more zealous members of the student body organized around-the-clock prayer meetings "to prepare the soil" for a "genuine" revival. By the time a Religious Emphasis Week began the campus atmosphere would be electric with excitement. "Great things are going to happen!"

During my sophomore year the visiting minister for this annual event was a gentleman named Dr. W. A. Criswell, the pastor of the First Baptist Church way out in Dallas, Texas. Dr. Criswell was in his prime and was known as "the prince of Southern Baptist preachers." As a wet-behind-the-ears sophomore, I'd never heard of Dr. Criswell. I didn't know what to expect.

Dr. Criswell hit the campus of Mississippi College like a hurricane crashing into the Mississippi Gulf Coast. Never before had I heard a pulpit spokesman like him. He was enthusiastic, humorous, bubbling over with jokes about Texans, convincing and entertaining! Dr. Criswell packed the people in. Night after night the sanctuary of the First Baptist Church in Clinton was overflowing with people, standing room only.

Most of the sermons I'd listened to over the years had been boring, and I kept looking at my watch, wondering when they would be over. By contrast, Dr. Criswell's sermons kept me on the edge of my seat. I soaked up his words as a sponge soaks up water. I laughed at his jokes about Texas. I noted his pulpit mannerisms. While preaching Dr. Criswell closed his eyes, conveying concentration and sincerity. He constantly held in his hands a New Testament, thin in size with gold edging and leather covers.

In one of the services Dr. Criswell preached a sermon entitled "Bearing the Brandmarks of Jesus." This sermon had a staggering impact upon me, evoking religious ecstasy, instilling within me a desire "to dedicate myself absolutely to Jesus." When Dr. Criswell came to the end of that service and extended an "invitation" for members of the congregation to make religious decisions all kinds of things happened. In the student body of Mississippi College was a generous sprinkling of World War II veterans, fellows who'd fought in Europe and in the Pacific. By the rest of the students they were viewed with respect, as a breed apart. These veterans looked at girlie magazines and drank beer in their dormitory rooms. Yet at the conclusion of Dr. Criswell's sermon many of them came forward, tears in their eyes, to confess their sins and "to get right" with God. And college students—I was one of them—flocked en masse to the front of the First

Baptist Church "to dedicate our lives completely to the service of Jesus."

At Mississippi College people talked about this Criswell revival for months. Much of my adolescent life had been spent searching for a father figure, a model to fashion myself after. Overnight Dr. Criswell (who didn't know I existed) became my father surrogate. He turned my life around in the sense that doubts about being a preacher vanished. I now knew what I wanted to do with my life. I wanted to be another W. A. Criswell. What higher ambition! What nobler dream! To walk in W. A. Criswell's footsteps! To be pastor of a big city congregation, to stand behind a pulpit and sway crowds, to fly on airplanes to speaking engagements, to tell funny stories, and to convert people to the Christian faith! I, who had listened to visits to the john at Mrs. Craft's boarding house, who had packed around all my life an inferiority complex, who was ashamed of my upbringing, now knew beyond a shadow of a doubt what I wanted to be—a Southern Baptist preacher in the mold of a Texan like W. A. Criswell. Overnight my life, up to that point a soiled rag, was invested with a glow and purpose which heretofore it had not had! My calling: to be a gospel star!

In the aftermath of the Criswell revival my slide down the slope into religious fanaticism accelerated. I became one of the most "religious" students on the college campus. I attempted to live by the dictum: "Pray without ceasing." Repeatedly I visited prayer cubicles in the Student Center where I got down on my knees and spent hours begging God to take control of my life. In afternoons I took walks on gravel roads leading into the surrounding countryside. I found isolated groves of trees where I knelt and prayed, importuning God to use me in his service.

My classwork at Mississippi College began to suffer. Religious commitment became my justification for academic mediocrity. Instead of studying history or the physical sciences I spent my time discussing "theological issues" in bull sessions with fellow ministerial students. I preferred chasing religious questions while drinking coffee to studying Chaucer. I viewed premedical students who studied around the clock as oddities.

By assuming all the world was like Mississippi College, I allowed my thinking, values, and goals to be molded by the religious euphoria of a small, church-related college campus. I forgot the down-to-earth world I'd experienced while selling papers on the streets of Jackson and while scrubbing floors in the kitchen of the Heidelberg. I preferred the heady atmosphere of Mississippi College where people sang, loved each other, and prayed for Japan's conversion.

During his week's stay in Clinton Dr. Criswell had remarked to a group of ministerial students, "The only way you fellows will ever learn to preach will be to get out and preach." I took this observation to heart. I felt I had to start preaching in order to learn how to preach. In the Southern Baptist Convention, which has no structure of bishops, a local congregaton (by voting) "calls" or "invites" a person to be its pastor. With the help of friends I received a "call" to become the pastor of a small Baptist congregation at Fannin, a one-store community in the Pearl River swamp about ten or fifteen miles east of Jackson. On receiving this "call" I was ordained into the Southern Baptist ministry by my home church, the First Baptist Church in Jackson.

As a neophyte preacher I gave myself with enthusiasm to pastoring (on weekends) this minuscule rural congregation. With regularity I visited my congregants, conducted devotionals in their homes, and spent hours agonizing over sermons. My library for sermon preparation consisted of a *Scofield Reference Bible* (given to me by my father) and a *Cruden's Concordance*. The church building at Fannin was a one-room structure, covered with asbestos shingles and surrounded by a cemetery. The dominant member of the congregation was Mr. Monroe Swilley, an elderly, compassionate gentleman. Practically everyone in the congregation was either Mr. Swilley's son or daughter or son-in-law or daughter-in-law or grandchild. He owned hundreds of acres of land and he owned the community's cotton gin. Indeed Mr. Swilley had lost one of his arms in a cotton gin accident.

I remember Mr. Swilley with gratitude because he shielded me from my stupidity, coming to my defense after I preached my sermon against the lawnmower. Some members of the congregation wanted to purchase a lawnmower to use for cutting the grass around the church building. In rashness of youth I decided this eminently practical idea was no good. I preached a sermon denouncing the lawnmower, arguing that the money for its acquisition ought to be spent on other causes. At the sermon's climax I struck the pulpit with my fist and shouted, "To hang with this idea of buying a church lawnmower!"

My jeremiad against the lawnmower (indicative of the profundity of my theology) upset my Fannin parishioners. A majority wanted to give me the axe, a fate I richly deserved. Mr. Swilley, as I learned years later, intervened, contending that dismissal would scar me in my attitude toward the ministry. To his sons and sons-in-law who were after my scalp he said, "We're going to overlook the young preacher's mistakes."

Among Southern Baptists during the 1950s the "Youth Revival Movement," an off-shoot of the postwar boom in religion, enlisted college students to form "teams" and conduct revivals with an emphasis on youth. During my last two years at Mississippi College I became active in this movement, forming my own team and conducting dozens of revivals in rural and town churches across Mississippi. I was the team preacher, while other students led the singing, another played the piano, and a fourth was a chalk board artist. The chalk artist, using colored crayons that glowed when illuminated, drew pictures and diagrams illustrating various Christian beliefs. He knew how (in ten minutes time!) to diagram the history of mankind from creation to the end of time, while in the process expounding the purpose of the universe and of human existence.

When my revival team went to a community—like New Hebron in Lawrence County—to conduct a revival, we plastered the place with posters. On occasion I'd mount a public address speaker on my car and drive up and down streets and roads inviting people, over the public address system, to attend the revival services. As the team preacher I wore white shoes, pink shirts, and a yellow sport coat while conducting revival services. I prided myself on what I thought was a flashy city-slicker appearance. None of my sermons were original. Instead, they were all secondhand. Like a Charlie McCarthy, I repeated what I had heard other preachers preach. I always carried pad and pencil so when listening to sermons by others I could write down illustrations and sermon outlines. These sermons I plagiarized, delivering them later as my own. My favorite sermon was entitled "Bearing the Brandmarks of Jesus."

People complimented me on my sermons. A man in Yazoo City wrote me a letter in which he told me I preached like the Apostle Paul. Not being streetwise, I took such compliments seriously. They confirmed my emerging conviction that I had a "glowing future" in the Southern Baptist Convention. I had not yet learned that people could compliment me to my face and laugh at me behind my back.

While delivering my sermons I shouted and banged on the pulpit with my fist. In my thinking loudness was evidence of conviction of belief. Imitating W. A. Criswell, my clergy hero, I closed my eyes while preaching. Constantly I held in my hands a New Testament, leather bound with gilt-edge pages. Moreover, I equated perspiration with inspiration. If at the end of a revival service I was dripping with sweat I judged the service to be successful.

I mastered techniques for extending an "invitation" to a congregation when a worship service came to a close. I always closed services with hymns like "Just As I Am" and "Jesus Is Tenderly Calling You Home." As these hymns were sung, I urged people to come down to the front and to shake my hand, accepting Jesus as their savior or dedicating their lives to God. Being instrumental in leading people to make these decisions gave me a heady sense of power. I liked to see 'em move!

I believed what I preached. In my thinking every revival service was an encounter with eternity. Momentous events took place! Lost souls were either saved or turned their backs on God! Angels rejoiced and demons wept! The foundations of heaven and hell shook while eternal destinies were decided!

The years have gone by and from the vantage point of my mature years I look back upon my college career as a boy wonder preacher and I don't know whether to laugh or cry. I'd entered the clergy but I'd started off on the wrong foot. I was trying (like a fool) to be a little W. A. Criswell. I was becoming too big for my pants. Because I was able at Mississippi College to buy a car with revival earnings I thought of myself as a "big man on campus."

I was a cultural oddity and didn't know it. For any church to allow a college student without professional training to conduct "revivals" and to pastor a congregation is a crime. Yet this happens in the rural and small town South. Within the Southern Baptist Con-

vention (with its exaggerated emphasis on the local church) there is
an absence of ministerial control and guidance.

Saddest of all, I was an ingrate. I didn't know how to say "thank
you." I took for granted what others did for me, inviting me to
churches and into homes for meals and hospitality. Increasingly I
conceived of the ministry as an ego trip. I thought the ministry was
fortunate to have me in its ranks (instead of thinking of participation
in the ministry as being itself a privilege).

I was a study in ideological superficiality. I used words like "God"
and "sin" and "eternal life" without pausing to reflect on what these
words meant. To my shallow mind the supreme sin of the universe
was masturbation. After all, my father had told me masturbation was
not only "sinful" but would drive a person insane.

As a boy wonder preacher was I a complete phony? The answer
is no. I could not help being born into a corn pone culture that encouraged teenagers to preach. At the time in spite of my weird mixture of egotism and religiosity, I thought I was doing the right thing.
God had called me from the kitchen of the Heidelberg Hotel to be
a preacher—an anchor experience I couldn't escape. I'd been told the
only way to learn to preach was to preach. Before conducting one of
those youth revival services I spent hours on my knees in prayer. In
the naiveté of my Mississippi youth I believed that God heard prayers and I believed that I was functioning in tandem with God. I
thought of myself as an instrument through which he touched the
lives of others. A presumptuous idea, but a presumptuous idea that I
took seriously.

In the midst of it all were troubling aspects. If I believed the
Christian religion as I pretended why did I find it difficult to discuss
religious matters in a one-on-one encounter? I could stand behind a
pulpit and speak to crowds but I shied away from individual, personal conversations concerning religion. I preached only when paid.
On occasion I read the Bible but found it baffling. I recall spending
one afternoon on my knees in a gravel pit, reading the Revelation of
St. John from beginning to end. To me its content was mumbo-
jumbo. The "message" of the Bible as understood by the Old Time
Religion and the "Plan of Salvation" was not self-evident when I took
the time to read the Bible for myself. If I were certain the clergy was
"God's will" for my life, why was I reluctant to admit to strangers that

I was a minister? Why did I inwardly grimace when people called me "Brother Sullivan" or "the preacher"? And why was I more at ease with campus "pagans" at Mississippi College than with the campus saints?

One of the last revivals I conducted as a college student was at Inverness, a town in the Mississippi delta, that agricultural wonderland formed over millions of years by the flooding and receding of the Mississippi River. Delta people are different from hill folk. Delta planters farm thousands of acres of cotton, soy beans, and rice and move in realms of finance beyond the imagination of hill farmers. They live in palatial homes, read the *Wall Street Journal* and say what they think. If you don't like what they say, that's too bad.

I spent a week in Inverness conducting—along with two other college students—youth revival services at the Baptist church there. After each of the night services we'd have a social hour in one of the homes. We'd get together with a group of folk and talk and drink Cokes and eat peanuts. During one of these social hours I encountered a young delta planter whose name I never knew. I wish I knew his name because he influenced my life. His face was covered with lines of skepticism suggesting he had been around and knew the facts of life and knew how to see through people. In the midst of the Cokes we were drinking and the peanuts we were munching, this suntanned planter came up to me and said, "Young fellow, I want you to know I think you're a two-bit Jesus jockey." Having expressed this opinion, he turned and walked away. I never saw the man again.

This remark stunned me, yet it harmonized with my intuitions. I had sensed my superficiality, my lack of understanding. I was weary of being an echo. That's why toward the end of my stay at Mississippi College I made an inner resolve. Academically I had misused my college years. I had not studied and I knew it. I had preached revivals, operated vending machines, and engaged in bull sessions. But seminary was around the corner and I resolved to go to seminary and to study my heart out in order to acquire a deeper understanding of the Christian religion. I didn't want to go through life as a "two-bit Jesus jockey." Maybe that's what I was, but I didn't have to stay that way for the rest of my life.

PART II

Looking for God in Louisville

8

Southern Seminary

A SEMINARY IS A SCHOOL where people study to become preachers. The Southern Baptist Convention maintains six seminaries scattered across the country from the Carolinas to California. Just as there was never a question about where I'd go to college, there was never a question about where I'd go to seminary. All my life I'd heard about the Southern Baptist Theological Seminary in Louisville, Kentucky. This Louisville school, the oldest of Southern Baptist seminaries, is called the "mother seminary." One of my preacher uncles was an alumnus—Dr. W. A. Sullivan, who for a quarter of a century was pastor of the First Baptist Church in Natchez, Mississippi. He was the one I called "Uncle Wib." Everyone in the family was proud of "Uncle Wib" and looked up to him because he was one Sullivan who had "made a name for himself." Before him his brothers felt intimidated because "Uncle Wib" was chairman of the board of trustees of Mississippi College and pastor of a city congregation. He owned Natchez real estate and was considered rich. Uncle Wib, who smoked King Edward cigars, didn't come to see us; we went to see him. His home in Natchez was crammed with books, antique furniture, and prescription bottles. One day he asked me, "Clayton, do you think a preacher ought to make money on the side in business deals?" When I answered, "Yes," he said, "So do I. That's why you and I can't preach worth a damn."

I'd heard Uncle Wib talk about his Louisville seminary days and relate episodes about a professor named A. T. Robertson, a name that at the time meant nothing to me. For me it was foreordained: If I was going to be a preacher I was to go to the seminary Uncle Wib had attended. The possibility of going to a school like Yale or Duke never entered my mind. I was a Southern Baptist and Southern Baptists (like Mormons and Roman Catholics) stay within institutions they own and control.

So in the summer of 1952 my wife and I—during my senior year at Mississippi College, I'd married my high school sweetheart— moved from Jackson to Louisville. We left Jackson for Louisville early on a Tuesday morning in June. Having already packed our car with clothes, bedding, kitchen utensils, and household gear, my wife and I spent the night before leaving with my parents in their home on Claiborne Avenue. We all got up that Tuesday morning before sunrise. Mother fixed breakfast and fried two chickens for us to carry— fried chicken that she lovingly packed in a shoe box.

After breakfast, with a shoe box of fried chicken on the car seat between us, my wife and I backed out of my father's driveway, leaving Mississippi for Kentucky and leaving home for seminary. I had a lump in my throat. And in my stomach was a feeling of bewilderment because I didn't know what the future held. I remember the last words my father said that morning, standing beside the driveway waving goodby as I was pulling away from the house into the morning light: "Son, whatever happens, don't let 'em change you."

I'm not sure I know what Daddy meant by those words, "Son, whatever happens, don't let 'em change you." Change is inevitable. It's part of life. Not only was I going to change, but my fate was to spend almost nine years in Louisville, Kentucky, during a time of unprecedented change across the South. A storm cloud of social unrest was hanging over states of the Old Confederacy, and everyone knew it was hanging there except us white Southerners. The 1954 Supreme Court decision on school desegregation, Martin Luther King, the Selma march, the Birmingham riots, the freedom rides, and the collapse of Jim Crow—all were around the corner. The postwar boom in religion (the golden age of Billy Graham) ended, and the South's secularization accelerated. The South's leaders would no longer be preachers like R. G. Lee in Memphis and politicians like Eugene Talmadge in Georgia but Houston oil men, Dallas bankers, and Atlanta merchants. As St. Patrick's Cathedral in New York is dominated by Fifth Avenue skyscrapers, church steeples across Dixie soon would be overshadowed by oil derricks, chemical plants, and revolving cocktail lounges atop downtown skyscrapers. And for many on Main Street, the attaché case would replace the Bible as the symbol of significance.

All these changes were on the way, but I didn't know it on that Tuesday morning in June 1952 as I, then twenty-one years old and still green, drove northward out of Jackson on U.S. 51. For almost a decade I would live the life of a married monk, becoming a Baptist bookworm; my life would revolve around a seminary campus, where seminarians study religion as medical students study cadavers.

Other men my age, having graduated from college, were getting out of the academic sphere and were entering the rough-and-tumble world of work. They were becoming streetwise and were developing into street fighters, learning to put deals together and to write contracts and to multiply dollars. I was going in the opposite direction, becoming less streetwise, viewing the world more and more through stained glass spectacles, drifting ever higher and higher into the land of Laputa.

Before heading out for Louisville on that June morning I'd never, for all practical purposes, been outside Mississippi. Thus as I drove to Louisville everything I saw fascinated me. I drove up U.S. 51 through Grenada and Batesville and Hernando to Memphis. From Memphis I drove to Nashville and then on up through Bowling Green and Elizabethtown to Louisville. To me driving through Memphis was as exciting as driving through London. And traveling through the Kentucky-Tennessee hills was as stimulating as going through the Alps.

Shortly after leaving Mississippi I developed wanderlust, a love for travel. Outside Mississippi, I discovered, was a world to see and experience. The insight hit me: *I'd never been anywhere.* I was a land-locked Mississippian, unaware of the world around me. My world had been delimited by Meridian on the east, Vicksburg on the west, Greenwood on the north, and the Gulf Coast on the south. A cultural captive, I knew about cotton fields, about county-seat towns with Confederate monuments, and about pinelands with armadillos that roam around at night. But that was all I knew. I found myself trying to make up for lost time and for having lived the first twenty-one years of my life without going places and seeing things. Louisville is within driving distance of numerous cities—Cincinnati, Lexington, Indianapolis, Chicago, Columbus, Evansville, Paducah. I visited these and dozens more. I'd drive to a city like Cincinnati and park my car in a downtown parking garage and then I'd start walking. I'd walk for miles, looking at people and parks and monuments and buildings. I tried to see what there was to see. If something existed, I wanted to see it. I drove to Hazard in Eastern Kentucky and looked at the coal country; I drove to Lexington and looked at the blue grass area; I drove to Hodgenville and saw the cabin in which Abraham Lincoln was born.

That first time I drove to Louisville, in the summer of 1952, I arrived there on a Wednesday. The Southern Baptist Theological Seminary is located on Lexington Road near sections of Louisville called the Highlands, Cherokee Park, and St. Matthew's. When I drove on the seminary campus that first time I was spellbound. The beauty—the loveliness—of Southern Seminary overwhelmed me. Stately brick buildings! Massive beech trees! Acres of rolling lawn! Brick sidewalks and brick terraces reminded me of pictures I'd seen of Williamsburg. The church-related campuses I'd seen in Mississippi, like Mississippi College in Clinton and Clarke College in Newton, had been second-class in design and appearance. That's why I was surprised by Southern Seminary's campus. I didn't know Southern Baptists owned anything so elegant. In my mind the campus's beauty has never eroded. To this day I think the Southern Baptist Theological Seminary—so far as physical appearance is concerned—is one of the loveliest institutions of higher learning to be found anywhere in the country.

My wife and I settled in, renting an apartment on Brownsboro Road a few blocks from the seminary campus. My wife got a job teaching in the Louisville Public Schools. Her salary was our primary source of income.

Seminary students go out of their way to help each other, and from fellow seminarians (particularly students from Mississippi) I began learning the ropes about living in Louisville—where to shop, where to go, what to see. Louisville, Kentucky's largest city with a metropolitan population approaching one million, lies on the Ohio River with Indiana across the way. Located at a waterfall on the Ohio, it is sometimes called Falls City. Founded in 1778 by George Rogers Clark, Louisville has become the world's largest tobacco manufacturing center and a leading producer of gin and whiskey. It's an industrial city where Ford automobiles are assembled and General Electric appliances are manufactured. It is a river city of barges, row houses, mansions, slums and awesome parks bearing Indian names like Seneca and Cherokee with trees that in the fall of the year are a red-yellow-orange fire. In this city, named for a French king, I was to experience a series of "firsts" in my life. In Louisville I for the first time ate pizza—then a novelty food that we redundantly called "pizza pie"—watched television (in the early 1950s, television had not yet come to central Mississippi), drove on snow, sledded, ate chestnuts, worked in a manufacturing plant and a funeral home, joined a labor union, participated in a union strike, ate fried clams, visited a Unitarian church, had an automobile accident, went to a Broadway musical (*South Pacific*), saw presidential candidates (Eisenhower, Nixon, Kennedy, and Stevenson—with whom my wife and I shook hands), patronized a Big Boy restaurant, went to a horse race (the Kentucky Derby at Churchill Downs), flew on an airplane, rode a passenger train (realizing my boyhood dream of eating in a diner), ate strawberry pie, and watched an airplane fall from the sky and crash, illuminating the night with an orange-reddish glow.

September 1952 rolled around and seminary classes began. My goal was to earn what was called a Bachelor of Divinity degree, which—so I'm told—is now called a Master of Divinity. This degree required three years of study and course work. On one issue my mind was made up: I was determined to be a conscientious student, not the academic mediocrity I'd been at Mississippi College. As a neophyte seminarian I was dominated by a passion to prepare myself academically to be a Southern Baptist preacher. I had this desire to study because to me, a product of Deep South Protestantism, religion was something conceptual and propositional. In the understanding of religion that I had at that point in my life there was no real place for mystery or awe. Instead, the emphasis was on knowledge and right doctrine. To me religion was a complex of beliefs, intellectually analyzable, that I could take apart, understand, and put back together again, as one would tear down and put back together an engine in a Ford truck. I was certain that the Christian religion was "true" and that it was devoid of intellectual puzzles. I was sure that there was an obvious Christian message that I could grasp with my mind. I en-

tered seminary assuming that the "harder" I studied (studying—I pre-
sumed—the Bible and the "Plan of Salvation") and the more I learned,
the "clearer" the Christian religion would become to me and the
"better" preacher I'd be. Knowledge, I believed, led to understanding. And that's what I was looking for—clarity of insight. I wanted
to see *for myself.* I didn't want to be a preacher who was a Little Sir
Echo, a parrot for other people's views.

Thus with a sense of purpose and without reservation I gave myself to my seminary studies. I was able to do this because I had the
support of my wife, who was teaching school so I could devote my
energies to studying. No matter what the weather was or how I felt,
I never missed a lecture. I made it a point to sit on the front row of
my classes, as close to the professors as possible. In my class notes I
tried to write down every idea and fact my teachers expressed in their
lectures. I got up in the morning at 4:30 to study Greek grammar and
Hebrew syntax. I worked at my books until 10 or 11 o'clock at night.

As a seminarian I was fortunate because in the 1950s a remarkable cluster of teachers composed Southern Seminary's faculty, persons of intelligence and ability. Duke McCall was the seminary's
president. T. C. Smith, Henry Turlington, and Heber Peacock were
professors of New Testament. Estill ("Pistol Pete") Jones taught Greek
and T. D. Price and Hugh Wamble lectured in church history.
Wayne Ward, Dale Moody, and Eric Rust were professors of theology. Henlee Barnette and Guy Ranson taught ethics. Bill Morton
and Morris Ashcraft were in archaeology, while Clyde Francisco and
J. J. Owens were professors of Old Testament. Wayne Oates ex-
celled in psychology of religion. There were others.

By all these professors I was mesmerized and swept off my feet!
To me they were the smartest people I'd ever met. Some had written
books and I'd never before been around people who had written
books. In lectures they used words like *Heilsgeschichte* and talked about
the theology of Paul Tillich and Emil Brunner.

I sensed in my professors a total commitment to their academic
specialties. Because of personal enthusiasm they "made" their courses.
Although years have gone by I can still see "Pistol Pete" Jones standing before a class of first-year seminarians, trying to hammer Greek
verbs through thick skulls. I can hear T. D. Price describing Martin
Luther standing before the Holy Roman Emperor at Worms. I can

hear Wayne Oates, his leg propped on the lecture desk, explaining Buber to our Alabama and Tennessee and Mississippi ears. And I can hear Bill Morton keeping us on the edge of our seats while describing the excavation of mounds in Iraq.

Because of my undiluted admiration for them, my seminary teachers became my new father substitutes, replacing earlier father surrogates like Kelly Patterson, the druggist, and W. A. Criswell, the Dallas preacher. I was confident that my professors knew what they were talking about and would give me what I was looking for. Under Southern Seminary's faculty I took courses in biblical and language subjects, and courses in psychology of religion, church history, textual criticism, ethics, and the development of dogma. Surprisingly the subject that intrigued me most was Near Eastern archaeology. Bill Morton and Morris Ashcraft, the seminary's two archaeology professors, were superb. Through them I learned about tells and manuscripts and cuneiform inscriptions and esoteric goodies only archaeologists know about.

My wife and I spent the summer between my second and third years at Louisville traveling with these two archaeology professors, a trip made possible for us by the generosity of my father-in-law, a gentle and good man who worked in the printing business every day of his life until he was almost eighty, a man who never spent a dollar on himself but gave money profligately to members of his family. We traveled across North Africa and up and down the Levant, going to Egypt, Syria, Lebanon, Jordan, and Israel. And we traveled across Europe through Greece, Italy, Switzerland, France, and England. We saw temples at Luxor, caves at Petra, pyramids near Cairo, mosques in Damascus, catacombs in Rome, the Louvre in Paris. As a result of this travel, biblical history, heretofore obscure to me, assumed an astonishing solidity in my mind.

Every semester at Southern Seminary visiting lecturers came—people like William Manson from the University of Edinburgh and H. H. Rowley from the University of Manchester. I recall a series of lectures delivered by the late W. F. Albright, the Johns Hopkins archaeologist. In part these lectures dealt with the Dead Sea scrolls, the sensation of the academic world during the 1950s. Professor Albright talked about numismatics and ceramic chronology and Middle Eastern excavations. I find it impossible to describe my reaction to Albright—such encyclopedic knowledge! Such expertise! In Albright I caught a glimpse of true scholarship, and my encounter at Southern with people like him intensified my feelings of inadequacy and provincialism, making me want to study all the harder.

I spent hours in the seminary library and in the campus book store (an institution ruled imperiously by a woman whose first name was Evelyn) thumbing through books—the place where I thought the answers were. Indeed, the acquiring and reading of books became a passion for me. I wrote down titles of books my professors recommended in lectures and did my best to buy and to read them—everything from Gibbon's *Decline and Fall of the Roman Empire* to Dostoyevsky's *The Brothers Karamazov*.

At Southern Seminary my world expanded. I traveled, read, listened, and learned. I experienced an intellectual awakening. Up to that point I had been sleeping. Southern Baptist Theological Seminary was to me what Hume was to Kant: it aroused me from my mental slumber.

Southern Seminary, I concede, was not then and is not now in the "blue chip" academic league with the Harvard Divinity Schools and the Oxford Universities. But during the 1950s Southern served to liberate and illuminate scores of seminarians from the South. We, as isolated sons of Dixie, were unaware that the Christian faith *could* be studied historically, scientifically, academically. Many of us had lived our lives in a conservative jar, inhaling and exhaling a fetid fundamentalism. Our approach to the Christian faith was embarrassingly simplistic—lifted, in my case, from the pages of my father's *Scofield Reference Bible*, the radio sermons of Charles E. Fuller, and a miscellany of Baptist evangelistic tracts. Many of us assumed that our task as young ministers was to master the content of an infallible Bible and then "induct" and "deduct" from this inerrant source what the Christian religion was all about. The Bible, bound in leather and printed on onionskin paper, was our fetish. It functioned in our understanding as the Koran does in Islam. In our reasoning we entered the seminary as de facto Muslims.

At Southern Seminary we were introduced to new ideas and new ways of thinking. We learned of a mutation in biblical studies that had occurred about 150 years earlier as a byproduct of the Enlightenment. Then for the first time the Bible had been studied in a "scientific" manner. Biblical materials had been critically examined against their historical and ideological backgrounds, using an approach called the historical-critical method. Associated today with names like Julius Wellhausen and Rudolf Bultmann, this method was first used in Europe and has come to dominate biblical studies in schools like Cambridge, Oxford, Tübingen, Göttingen, Marburg, Harvard, Yale, and Chicago. While interpreting biblical materials in the light of the cultural milieu that produced them, users of the historical-critical method emphasize intellectual honesty and open-ended inquiry. One may not engage in pious fudging, but must follow the evidence wherever it leads. My professors at Southern made statements in almost every lecture that would have embroiled them in controversy with the Ministerial Club back at Mississippi College.

For years Southern Baptists, isolated in the Deep South and practicing ideological inbreeding, seemed unaware of the historical-critical method. Yet by mid-century a vanguard of Baptist scholars had absorbed the method at Edinburgh, Yale, and Tübingen and had begun to employ it at institutions like Southern Seminary. These professors played a creative, pioneering role in leading scores of seminarians into the thought world of the twentieth century.

Some people give to this historical-critical method the loaded label "liberalism" and contend that it destroys a person's faith. That wasn't my experience. To the contrary, at Louisville my faith was strengthened and undergirded. So much of the religion I'd been exposed to prior to Seminary had been, I now sensed, sentimental mush like cotton candy at the Mississippi State Fair—all sweetness and air but no substance and structure. In the "Old Time Religion" I'd been reared on there was no place for sustained and open intellectual inquiry. Rather one thought little and filled in the gaps with emotion and oratory. By contrast the material and the approach I encountered in my courses at Southern had about them a plausibility I found convincing. My reaction to the historical-critical method was similar to the reaction of Harry Emerson Fosdick: I discovered that I could be a Christian without committing intellectual suicide.

In my religious pilgrimage my encounter with Southern Seminary was a continental divide. I don't remember hearing terms like "liberalism" and "fundamentalism" before going to Louisville. I picked these words up after a semester or two at Southern. When I left Mississippi for seminary I was a fundamentalist, although I was unaware of it. Study at Louisville led me to see the Bible as a document with a human side and as a sprawling anthology of Jewish and Christian writings, reflecting in part views and speculations of those who wrote it. Undergirding the Jewish-Christian religion, I came to see, is a substructure of historical events that cannot be doubted. And although (after three years' study at Southern) I still didn't have things in focus, I intuited that there *really was* something to the Christian religion.

After three years in Louisville I received at the spring commencement of 1955 a Bachelor of Divinity degree. Mother and Daddy drove up from Mississippi for the graduation exercises. I celebrated earning this degree—a framed diploma that hangs today on my office wall—by stuffing myself with fried clams at a Howard Johnson's restaurant.

Those first three years in Louisville were rewarding. In some ways they were the best years of my life, and memories from them stick in my mind like mental thumbtacks.

Memories:

Of kicking red, orange, and yellow leaves with my feet while walking across campus in the fall of the year.

Of feeling snow blowing in my face while going to classes on January and February mornings.

Of listening to the striking of the steeple chimes.

Of seeing the Ohio River frozen over in mid-winter.

Memories:

Of going into downtown Louisville and eating apple pie at Kunz's Restaurant.

Of watching the annual Ptolemy-Seleucid touch football game in which faculty and students played.

Of having conversations with professors in the student grill.

And memories of hearing the Seminary students singing hymns at morning worship in Alumni Chapel. I can hear them now, hundreds of voices singing together.

Holy, holy, holy! Lord God Almighty!
Early in the morning our song shall rise to Thee;

Holy, holy, holy! Merciful and mighty;
God in three persons, blessed Trinity.

You've never heard a hymn sung until you've heard it sung at a Southern Seminary chapel service.

9

Graduate Study

EARNING A BACHELOR OF DIVINITY degree didn't end my seminary studies. I decided to stay on at Southern and to enter its graduate school and to work for a doctor's degree, a task that would take me almost five more years to accomplish.

In part my decision to earn a doctorate was an exercise in egotism. I say that because some of us who were students at Louisville in the 1950s were young men who were full of ourselves. In fact, we were too full of ego, our vanity masking our lower-middle-class roots. We thought of ourselves as future "First Baptist Church" pastors and as seminarians we related to each other with an unloving, intellectual competitiveness. We were ambitious, we were confident of what the future held, and we wanted to be called "doctor" like the professor-theologians on Southern's faculty. I was one of those unloving students, full of myself. I didn't want to spend the next forty years of my life being called "Brother Sullivan" or "Reverend." I wanted to be called *Dr. Sullivan*. And I thought that earning a doctorate, particularly from Southern, would "insure my success" in the Southern Baptist Convention, and I thought it would endow what I preached with an aura of authority.

But vestry vanity wasn't the entire story. While earning my basic divinity degree I'd caught a glimpse of the sweep and grandeur of contemporary biblical studies, viewed through historical-critical spectacles. There was so much I didn't know, and the more I learned the more I wanted to know. As a de facto Gnostic I was still functioning on the premise that knowledge led to insight, and during my first three years at Southern I'd learned many things. I'd learned all the way from an aleph to an iota subscript to the Gilgamesh Epic to the Wellhausen hypothesis to the synoptic problem to the puzzles of Pauline chronology. But this newly-acquired information did not constitute a "gospel" or a "message." Only later in life would I perceive that information accumulation—the piling up of facts, data, knowledge—does not give a preacher a "message" relevant to people's religious needs. Moreover, I was still young, and when one is young one's abilities to analyze surpass one's abilities to synthesize. One is better at tearing down than at building up.

As a seminarian, still in my mid-twenties, I found myself baffled. I was more certain of what I *didn't* believe than I was of what I *did* believe. Southern Seminary had destroyed my biblical fundamentalism but it had not given me anything viable to take its place. That's the weakness of the historical-critical method: its power to destroy exceeds its power to construct. The historical-critical method can give you facts and hypotheses but it cannot give you a vision. In a word, I didn't have my act together. I had not (to my satisfaction) "grasped" or "understood" the Christian faith. I felt additional study was necessary before I could be the trained, informed preacher I wanted to be, and I felt doctoral studies would meet that need.

So in the fall of 1955 I entered the seminary's graduate school. In the 1950s the graduate program at Southern was patterned after graduate programs in English universities. First of all, we chose an area in which to specialize, an area like theology or church history. Then, under the guidance of a faculty committee, we read books and attended seminars to prepare for doctoral examinations in our fields of specialization. After we'd passed these doctoral exams, which were the crucial requirement, we then completed our graduate program by writing a doctoral dissertation.

By the time I entered graduate school I'd developed an intense love for Greek. I had particular admiration for T. C. Smith and Heber Peacock—two of Southern's New Testament professors. For these reasons I chose to read for my doctorate in New Testament studies. I set for myself an unrealistic goal: to learn everything there was to know about the Greek New Testament. I wanted to master its language and thought. Particularly did I want to have a detailed knowledge of Jesus' life and teachings. I believed that such knowledge would help me understand the "essence" of the Christian religion.

Toward that end I dove into my graduate studies, taking seminars and working away on my reading list, which was a mile long. The approach to New Testament studies at Southern in those years can be symbolized by names of scholars like David Friedrich Strauss, Johannes Weiss, Morton Scott Enslin, Maurice Goguel, Alfred Loisy, and Adolf Deissmann. These authors (and a thousand more) I was required to study.

The first book I dug my mental teeth into as a graduate student was Albert Schweitzer's *The Quest of the Historical Jesus.* For weeks I gnawed on this book like a dog gnaws on a bone.

I moved back and forth through A. T. Robertson's *A Grammar of the Greek New Testament in the Light of Historical Research.* I read and reread this book, underlining its pages with pen and red pencil. I studied all 1,454 pages of Robertson's tome, and to this day I keep it—for sentimental reasons—on my desk.

I wore out two copies of *Nestle's Greek New Testament*—so that I could read a Greek New Testament as easily as a morning newspaper.

I participated in seminars on the demythologizing controversy and the Qumran materials and redaction criticism, seminars in which we liked to think we were on the "cutting edge" of contemporary biblical scholarship.

One year of graduate study went by.

A second year of graduate study went by.

From memory I could diagram Herod the Great's family and draw maps of first-century Corinth and Rome. I could describe all coins struck by the Hasmoneans and discuss in detail textual dislocations in the Fourth Gospel. I could write essays on Eusebius of Caesarea, on the development of the canon, and on differences between classical and Koine Greek.

Into a third year of doctoral study I plunged. My wife was still teaching to provide the family income. Like a medieval Talmudist, I sat from early morning until late at night at my carrel in the seminary library, developing hemorrhoids in the process. I read and read and read still more. I neglected exercise. I drank hundreds of cups of coffee, as my father had. My body became soft and flabby. My skin became white like milk. The lenses in my glasses got thicker and thicker.

On two different occasions while a graduate student I had opportunity to become pastor of small Kentucky churches. Both opportunities I unwisely refused. I wanted nothing to interfere with my doctoral studies.

By this time, the cart was before the horse. The means had become the end. When I first enrolled in seminary I'd looked upon study as a means by which to prepare to be a preacher. And I'd viewed Southern Seminary as a temporary dwelling place on my way to the pastorate. But to me, an overcooked graduate student, study by now had become an end within itself. In J. D. Salinger's *Franny and Zooey* one character remarks that the pursuit of knowledge can be a form of laying up treasures on earth. Knowledge had become my treasure on earth and I had become a ministerial Humpty Dumpty, all head and no heart. Southern Seminary had become for me a terminal womb—a place where I wanted to spend the rest of my life. An isolated, warm, secure world of scholarship, with lectures, seminars, monographs, journals, books, manuscripts.

I, who once sold papers on street corners in Jackson and scrubbed pots and pans in the Heidelberg Hotel kitchen, had become an institutionalized person. I had become a Southern Seminary parasite with exaggerated, unhealthy feelings of dependency upon the goodwill and approbation of my seminary professors. When my professors said "frog" I jumped. When they told a joke, I laughed. Psychologically I was a eunuch, no longer knowing how to function outside the seminary campus. For the "outside world" had become forbidding, like a cypress swamp at night in Southeast Mississippi.

10

"The Battle of Lexington Road"

AND THEN IT ALL EXPLODED, going up in fire and smoke just like Alex's and Melissa's house in Gulde went up in fire and smoke on that January morning when a spark from the fireplace ignited newspapers nailed to the walls for insulation. The roof fell in on my protected world on Lexington Road in Louisville where I'd been hiding and watching it all go by. A war broke out between Southern Seminary's faculty and Southern Seminary's administration. Among some Southern Baptists it is still known as the "Battle of Lexington Road."

From the vantage point of my mature years, I now perceive that seminaries are human institutions and, because they're human, they can experience controversies. Indeed, a seminary (where egos are grand, salaries are small, and feelings are intense) can erupt like a volcano. All hell can break loose between sunrise and breakfast. Presbyterian seminaries have erupted. Lutheran seminaries have exploded. So it was not a unique event when an old-fashioned, no-holds-barred, brass-knuckled Baptist brawl shattered Southern Seminary toward the end of the 1950s.

On one side of this Baptist imbroglio was Dr. Duke McCall, the seminary's president, and those who supported him. On the other side were thirteen seminary professors, not from the School of Music, not from the School of Religious Education, but from the School of Theology. Many were faculty "heavyweights." They were men of established reputations with cadres of disciples in the student body and alumni. These thirteen professors banded together and decreed that Dr. Duke McCall was a knave who ought to be fired from his position as president of Southern Seminary. Why this administration-faculty controversy took place I never knew for a certainty. Theories about the controversy, all unsubstantiated, abound.

One theory contends that this Baptist brawl was a byproduct of personality conflicts. Some of the folks involved "just didn't like each other." So it was all a matter of bad blood between brother Baptists. While a graduate student I sensed that some faculty members didn't like Dr. McCall. Behind his back they called him a "featherweight theologian." They said he was "a professional Southern Baptist." I also perceived jealousy. Some people said that Dr. McCall had been born with a silver spoon in his mouth. He lived in the Norton Mansion overlooking Cherokee Park and he drove late model Oldsmobiles. Some professors even cracked jokes about the way Dr. McCall walked.

Duke McCall was not a scholar with a *curriculum vitae* listing dozens of "scholarly" publications. He did not lecture on obscure German monographs about the "demythologizing" controversy. Rather, he was a shrewd denominational functionary, a man with organizational expertise, a salesman who understood the territory. At one time Dr. McCall had been executive secretary of the Executive Committee of the Southern Baptist Convention. He was a pragmatist, one who knew how to get things done. But he was disliked by some members of the Southern Seminary faculty, who regarded him as a denominational hack. Thus the brawl between Dr. McCall and the faculty took place, it was suggested, because the parties involved didn't care for each other.

Rivaling this "personality conflict" theory is what might be called the "power" theory. This explanation contended that at the roots of the administration-faculty conflict was a power struggle for control of the seminary. In the past, during the age of denominational patriarchs like E. Y. Mullins and James P. Boyce, the faculty—so some said—controlled Southern Seminary (determining policy, making personnel decisions, functioning as a committee of the whole). And the Board of Trustees had manifested a "hands off" attitude (deferring to the faculty) while the Seminary's president, not having executive power, had been merely "first among equals". This arrangement had prevailed from the seminary's founding down through the early 1940s. But the seminary had grown to become one of the largest theological institutions in the country. The "let's-all-sit-around-the-table-and-talk-it-over" procedure would no longer work. When the bylaw structure of the seminary was changed, placing administrative responsibility in the hands of the president rather than in the hands of the faculty, there was a shift from a trustee-faculty operation to a trustee-president administration. No longer was the president "first among equals." Now he was a person with clout.

During the 1950s (so it was reported) some seminary trustees wanted the president, Dr. McCall, to use that clout. They wanted him to keep a tighter rein on what was going on. They wanted Dr. McCall to exercise authority and control to keep the "mother seminary" *closer to the denomination*, more in the middle of the theological spectrum, sensitive to the feelings and beliefs of grassroots Southern Baptists. This desire to keep the Louisville seminary closer to the Southern Baptist denomination created "problems," because many members of Southern's faculty were devotees of the historical-critical method. This method struck some Southern Baptists, particularly those at the forks of the creek, as "dangerous." This method rattled the "Old Time Religion" with its cornerstone belief in an infallible Bible.

Moreover, some of the seminary professors at Southern had a condescending attitude toward the Southern Baptist Convention and toward its agencies, its leaders, and its publishing house in Nashville. In seminary classrooms they cracked jokes about the denomination's promotionalism and aggressiveness—such quips as,

> Mary had a little lamb;
> He might have been a sheep;
> But he went and joined a Baptist church,
> And died for lack of sleep.

As a student, I found this antidenominational attitude baffling. A characteristic of some intellectuals, I've learned, is a tendency toward institutional alienation. Intellectuals—evidently by nature—are antiestablishment. They want water without the jug the water comes in.

More puzzling to me as a seminary student was the condescending attitude some of my Louisville professors had toward Baptist preachers and toward the pastorate. The purpose of a seminary is to train men to pastor congregations. That's why I'd gone to seminary: to prepare myself to be a preacher. Going to Louisville was my response to that unsought and disturbing experience I'd had in the kitchen of the Heidelberg Hotel back in my hometown. In that experience, beside a crate of oranges and surrounded by pots and pans, I'd bowed my head and accepted a "call" to be a preacher. It was an anchor experience from which I've never been able to escape, no matter how hard I've tried.

Yet my seminary professors tended to look upon preachers as hucksters, denominational drumbeaters, or dummies. That's why one of my seminary professors remarked, "The most brilliant Southern Baptist ministers become seminary professors and college teachers. The rest have to go into the pastorate." I remember another rolling his class on the floor with laughter while telling about "a corncob preacher" who innocently remarked to him, "Professor, I've got a book at my house which came all the way from New York City." My professors reserved their most acidic remarks for "successful" clergymen. When asked in class what he thought about Billy Graham, one of my teachers answered, "The call to be a Christian is a call to be crucified. Authentic Christians don't run after salvation as Graham's converts do, like hogs running after slop."

Probably the most "successful" Southern Baptist minister during the 1950s was Dr. W. A. Criswell, the Dallas minister who had made an impression on me when I was a college student. Dr. Criswell came to Louisville and spoke at a morning chapel service. One seminary faculty member, to the delight of us who were his student listeners, told of encountering Dr. Criswell on the campus and of pretending not to know who he was. With a smirk he related, "When I shook Criswell's hand I played dumb and said, 'Dr. Criswell? I don't believe I've heard your name before. What church do you pastor?'" The professor went on to tell of a puzzled expression on Criswell's face and those of us who were listening laughed, feeling sophisticated, and failing to perceive the snobbery implied in our laughter.

This anticlericalism was due, in part, to my professors' ignorance of what it means to be a preacher. Most professors under whom I studied at Southern had no prolonged experience in the pastorate. That was unfortunate because they had no appreciation of the role the church plays in the lives of common people. They had no real understanding of what ministers do in relating to folk in the crises of life when sickness, divorce, tragedy, and death come. Maybe if all my seminary teachers had each conducted a hundred funerals the administration-faculty conflict I am relating would never have taken place. But in any case, because of their anticlericalism and denominational hostility some members of the faculty were not primarily interested in Southern Seminary as a service to the Southern Baptist Convention, as a preparatory school for working pastors. They wanted it to be a divinity school—the Harvard of the evangelical world, with a hyperintellectual approach to the Christian faith. They placed it in a world somehow "above" the Southern Baptist Convention and its fried-chicken-eating churches, a Laputa for Protestants alienated from their roots.

But was this "divinity school" role a desirable destiny for the "mother" seminary? Some people felt it was not, and they wanted the seminary's president and trustees to exert their influence to keep the seminary under the denomination's control, not under the control of an autonomous faculty.

This faculty-administration controversy lasted in its roaring, volcanic phase for almost a year. And while it was going on it was high drama, like a shootout at high noon at the OK Corral! Thirteen professors—the cream of Southern Baptist scholarship, the denomination's intellectual aristocracy, men who had studied at schools like Yale and Edinburgh, threw down the gauntlet! All thirteen professors threatened to submit their resignations en masse to the Board of Trustees. To the trustees they said, "Either get rid of Duke McCall, the seminary's president, or risk receiving our resignations. For Duke McCall is an impure man. He is a pragmatist who has defiled Southern Seminary by bringing on campus efficiency experts from Booz, Allen, and Hamilton."

This action revealed depth of feelings and conviction. Like Martin Luther nailing his theses to the church door at Wittenberg, these thirteen professors were laying it on the line! Going for broke! Rolling the dice! They believed that they were indispensable, for in a moment of candor one of the thirteen professors remarked to me, "You know darn good and well the trustees won't get rid of all thirteen of us. Doing that would destroy the faculty." Thirteen professors forgot the danger always involved in challenging entrenched administrative power. They forgot that if you play in the woods you can get eaten by the wolf. They forgot that thirteen is an unlucky number, for you can roll a pair of dice from now until it snows at the Neshoba County Fair in Philadelphia, Mississippi, and you'll never roll a thirteen.

This administration-faculty controversy gave those of us who were students at Southern Seminary something to talk about. Somewhere Schopenhauer remarks that one of man's most repulsive features is *Schadenfreude*, a perverse fascination with the troubles of others. The student body of Southern Seminary fell victim to *Schadenfreude*. We followed and watched the controversy with eager eyes, like medieval peasants watching knights on horseback fighting with lances in the distance. We sat around tables in the student grill and exchanged tidbits of gossip about the controversy. Saying, "Have you heard? The faculty has decided to get rid of McCall." "They tell me they have the goods on him on a plagiarism charge." "I understand he's a dictator and runs over the faculty and they're fed up with it." We students wasted time keeping up with the intricacies and footnotes of the controversy. Who said what about whom? Who said what about what? Because we were naive and overly impressed with seminary affairs, we thought the controversy was comparable in significance to the Russian Revolution or to the decline and fall of the Roman Empire.

People chose sides. Some faculty members and students lined up on the side of the thirteen professors; others sided with Dr. McCall. Letters were written. Petitions were circulated. Conferences were held in faculty offices. Meetings were conducted at night in professors' homes. Long distance telephone calls were made. Seminary trustees were contacted. Stories about the controversy, written by Ora Spaid, appeared in the *Courier Journal*, Louisville's morning newspaper. Assemblies were held in Alumni Chapel at which charges leveled against Dr. McCall were reviewed and debated. Faculty members verbally sliced each other. They took students aside and "explained" what a "hollow man" Dr. McCall was. During the controversy the professors delivered their lectures with far-away looks in their eyes, their thoughts obviously elsewhere.

The pettiness of it all was symbolized by a sign that appeared on the first floor of Norton Hall, the seminary's administration building. On the office door of one of Dr. McCall's colleagues was a sign which read: "Special Assistant to the President." This sign was modified by an anti-McCall partisan to read: "Special ASS to the President." This ASS sign was significant, for during this administration-faculty controversy many people on both sides made asses of themselves.

Eventually the brawl and the campus hysteria came to an end. The seminary's Board of Trustees intervened. An investigating committee from the board appeared on campus. Closed hearings were conducted for almost a week. The testimony given before the trustees was tape recorded. The thirteen professors came before the trustees and spelled out their bill of particulars against Dr. McCall. The trustees, although not graduates of Yale or Edinburgh, were not fools. They may have sensed that perhaps the assault on Dr. McCall was a ploy by dissident faculty members to seize control of the seminary. One of the thirteen professors had remarked to me, "We feel control of theological education is our professional prerogative". The trustees knew that personal dislike can masquerade as moral outrage. They had heard reports about the faculty's "liberalism" and about its antidenominational bias. Suppose the trustees had capitulated to the thirteen professors—thus allowing the faculty "to control" the seminary's administration? What then? Would not that capitulation open the possibility of Southern Seminary becoming a runaway engine? Controlled by its theological faculty, responsible to no one but itself—a divinity school serving the Grove of Academe but with tenuous ties to the Southern Baptist Convention?

These issues the trustees mulled over. Conference followed conference, meeting followed meeting. Attempt after attempt was made to find a "solution" to what had become an impasse. Finally sensing that no "solution" was possible, the trustees delivered the *coup de grace*. At a midnight meeting in June 1958, on the eve of Friday the 13th (there again the "unlucky number" *thirteen*), the trustees dismissed the thirteen professors—with the proviso that if they would agree to work with the seminary's administration they would be rehired. A Solomonic move! Under the circumstances, it seems to me now, an act of compassion and decency! In substance the trustees told the thirteen professors, "We don't want you to run the ship; that's our responsibility. But neither do we want you to abandon ship or to be thrown overboard. Come back on deck and let's all see if we can't still work together."

Unfortunately, feelings were raw. Pride was at stake. Too much water had flowed under the bridge. Too many harsh words had been spoken. For the thirteen professors the whole episode was embarrassing. What had started out as a lark had ended as a disaster. Their criticisms of Dr. McCall, which to them seemed potent, had not convinced others. Collectively the thirteen professors discovered their dispensability. They were like Haman, adversary of Mordecai. The scaffold they had erected for Duke McCall became their own gallows.

One of the thirteen (Dr. J. J. Owens, professor of Hebrew) accepted the trustees' offer to return to the faculty. The other twelve refused. In the twinkling of an eye these men—good men, men of scholarship, with a century of teaching experience among them, the backbone of Southern's faculty—were out on the street. In a sense their fate was their own choosing. They refused (as they expressed it) to "compromise with wrongdoing." They became prisoners of commitments made to each other. Their names were taken off their office doors. Some went this way. Some went that way. Some left the denomination.

In Southern Baptist folklore they are referred to as the "dirty dozen" and the controversy in which they participated is called the "Battle of Lexington Road"—the classic academic Donnybrook Fair of the Southern Baptist Convention.

11

Dissertation

I HAD NOT MOVED FROM MISSISSIPPI to Kentucky to witness a Baptist brawl. I had come to Kentucky to learn how to be a Baptist preacher. So the "Battle of Lexington Road" was an episode I hadn't expected. To me the controversy was puzzling. On the one hand, the seminary professors involved in the conflict were my idols, my mentors in the faith. For years I'd sat at their feet and entrusted to them my preparation to become a preacher. For more than six years they had been the dominant influence in my life. I'd heard them lecture—and lecture eloquently—on the Christian tradition. I'd heard them preach sermons in Alumni Chapel. I hold them in high esteem to this day.

On the other hand, Dr. McCall, a gentleman I didn't know on a personal basis, was the personification of graciousness. He was a man who never allowed himself to become "one of the boys" by using profanity or telling off-color stories. He was a suave gentleman who understood the dynamics of Southern Baptist life. One day he said to a group of us standing in the corridor of Norton Hall, "In Southern Baptist circles, don't ever attack a cliché directly; let clichés die quiet, natural deaths."

Maybe the thirteen professors had a legitimate complaint against Dr. McCall; then again maybe they didn't. All I know about the "Battle of Lexington Road" is street-corner hearsay. After the "battle" was over the taped testimony given over several days before the trustees by the accusing professors was transcribed. After this transcript was made the tapes were destroyed. The transcript was placed in a vault in Louisville where, by decision of the Board of Trustees, it will remain until A.D. 2015. As an outsider I'll always suspect the controversy was somehow rooted in the faculty's economic frustration, for the salaries they received were inadequate.

For some of us who were graduate students this faculty-administration conflict could not have happened at a more inopportune time. Having spent three years in preparation, I was ready to take my doctoral examinations in New Testament studies. So were other graduate students. Yet most of the professors under whom we'd studied and prepared for our doctoral examinations had been fired from the faculty. A Rube Goldberg plan was devised. The seminary administration arranged for our doctoral examinations to be given by and to be graded by the dismissed professors (men technically no longer on Southern's faculty). For a week in the summer of 1958 I sat in a seminar room in Norton Hall taking doctoral examinations.

As soon as these exams were behind me I started making plans to get away from Louisville. I still had to write a dissertation—a doctoral thesis—as the final step in my graduate program. Since the theology faculty at Southern Seminary was in shambles I sensed I'd have to write this dissertation more or less on my own. To get this done I needed a place that was quiet and that was conducive to research and to writing. In this regard Southern Seminary didn't fill the bill. Hovering over the campus was a miasma of ill will and unhappiness, like the stench lingering over a battlefield after the shooting and killing have stopped. That's why I decided to pack up my bags and go to Harvard University. I supposed that if there was any place in the country where I'd be able to study and to write my thesis Harvard would be the place.

On money received from an Eli Lilly grant and on money borrowed from my father-in-law I left Louisville and headed for the Harvard campus in Cambridge, Massachusetts. My wife and I drove across country on the Pennsylvania Turnpike. We drove up the seaboard on the New Jersey and Connecticut turnpikes. In Cambridge we rented an efficiency apartment in the same building where Paul Tillich lived. Time and again I saw Dr. Tillich, wearing an overcoat that almost touched the ground, trudging between his apartment and Harvard's campus.

I spent hours in Andover-Harvard library, writing my doctoral dissertation, "A Critique of Realized Eschatology in the Writings of

C. H. Dodd." I had the good fortune to discuss my basic ideas and reasoning with Krister Stendahl, then professor of New Testament studies at Harvard Divinity School.

I was still afflicted with wanderlust, trying to see what there was to see. During the week I worked like a one-armed paper hanger on my dissertation. But on weekends my wife and I took in the Boston-Cambridge area. We saw Faneuil Hall, the Boston Common, Beacon Hill with its townhouses, and the Old North Church where lanterns ("two if by sea") started Paul Revere on his ride. We drove to Walden Pond and saw where Thoreau built his cabin and we drove out to Cape Cod to visit cape towns like Sandwich, Barnstable, Hyannis, and Provincetown with its reminders of Eugene O'Neill. We took the subway at Harvard Square and rode into downtown Boston to explore streets bearing names like Milk Street and Acorn Street. I saw Trinity Church with its memories of Phillips Brooks. I visited the homes of Ralph Waldo Emerson and the Alcotts and saw Nathaniel Hawthorne's "house of the seven gables." I spent hours exploring the bookstores and shops of Harvard Square and walking up and down the Charles River, passing repeatedly the home of Henry Wadsworth Longfellow. I experienced New England snowfalls, heard Robert Frost read his poetry on the campus of Boston University, and sat spellbound while listening to a lecture by Henry Cadbury, whose book *The Peril of Modernizing Jesus* had made an impression on me as a graduate student at Southern.

After almost a year in Cambridge, I had finished research on my dissertation and had written a first draft. I headed back across country (again driving the Pennsylvania Turnpike) for Louisville and Southern Seminary. I was eager to be done with school. I'd spent three years working on a Bachelor of Divinity degree. I'd invested an additional four years in my doctorate. Seven years beyond college I had given to preparing to be a Southern Baptist preacher. I felt this was long enough. I was up to my neck in debt and I needed to get out of school and to get to work.

I had a promise of a job. On the trip my wife and I took to the Middle East with my archaeology professors, after my second year in seminary, I'd met Dr. David Moore of William Jewell College, a Baptist school in Liberty, Missouri. Dr. Moore had talked to me about coming to William Jewell and joining its faculty in the religion department. Yet before I could negotiate seriously with William Jewell College I knew I had to finish my doctoral work.

Returning to Southern Seminary after a year's stay in New England was for me an odd experience. The campus on Lexington Road was as beautiful as ever. But other things were not the same. I felt I was a stranger. Coming back to Southern Seminary from Boston and Cambridge was like returning home and discovering I had parents different from the ones I'd always known. In the aftermath of the faculty-administration controversy more than half the theology faculty had been dismissed. The entire archaeology and church history departments had been wiped out. The New Testament department in which I'd done my graduate work had been decimated. Four of the five professors on my doctoral committee (Heber Peacock, Bill Morton, Estill Jones, and Henry Turlington) had been dismissed. The only professor on my doctoral committee still on the faculty was Dr. Wayne Ward, one of the most decent and gracious men I've ever known. As a lame-duck graduate student I was assigned to a five-member doctoral committee composed—with the exception of Dr. Wayne Ward—of professors I didn't really know and under whom I had not studied. The final step toward getting my doctorate—and getting out of seminary and getting a job (I hoped) at William Jewell—was to secure their approval of the dissertation I'd written about the work of C. H. Dodd, the English New Testament scholar of Manchester and Cambridge.

On this new doctoral committee I·encountered a man from Texas. At strategic junctures in my life I have met Texans who have left their fingerprints on me, so that after encountering them I was never the same again. At Mississippi College I'd been influenced by Dr. W. A. Criswell, the pastor of First Baptist Church in Dallas. The Texan I encountered on my doctoral committee was Dr. Ray Summers. Dr. Summers, a man in his fifties and distinguished in appearance, was a person I'd never met before. For years he'd been a member of the faculty of Southwestern Baptist Theological Seminary in Fort Worth. He'd published a commentary on the Revelation of St. John. In the aftermath of the "Battle of Lexington Road" he'd been hired by the Louisville seminary to be one of its new professors in New Testament studies. Dr. Summers was one of the five professors on my dissertation committee and he turned out to be a dominant member.

Because Dr. Summers was on my doctoral committee I went by his office, located on the second floor of Norton Hall's faculty wing, and left with him a copy of my dissertation. Several days passed and Dr. Summers sent for me to come to his office for a conference. He wanted (I learned) to discuss the dissertation I'd left with him. My encounter that day with Dr. Summers, the Texas theologian, was a meatgrinder experience.

Dr. Summers, with graying hair, sitting behind a desk and dressed in a blue suit, began his conference with me by talking about "liberalism." He explained to me that in recent years "liberalism" had influenced the faculty and student body of Southern Seminary. He told me he'd read my dissertation on C. H. Dodd and was convinced I'd been influenced by the "liberalism" of my former professors. As Dr. Summers continued talking I began feeling sick down in my stomach. He informed me that in order to get my dissertation approved I'd have to rewrite it. In the form I'd submitted it to him, he explained, it was "too liberal." I'd have to rewrite my thesis to reflect a theologically "conservative" viewpoint.

Having expressed his evaluation of my dissertation on C. H. Dodd, Dr. Summers then expressed his opinion about me. He looked me in the eye and said, "Mr. Sullivan, I've read your dissertation, and I have to tell you that I don't think you have a moral right to be a Southern Baptist preacher."

That's what the Texan in the blue suit said.

"Mr. Sullivan, I've read your dissertation, and I have to tell you that I don't think you have a moral right to be a Southern Baptist preacher."

Damn! How that hurt! When Dr. Summers spoke those words to me they felt like an ice pick jabbing into my eye. I sat there in Dr. Summer's office stunned, not knowing what to say or what to do. I felt like a person standing naked on a street corner as people walked by and looked at me and sneered.

What had I done to offend this man? Why did he feel about me the way he did? Why was he telling me I didn't have a moral right to be a Baptist preacher?

I was the one who when I was eight or nine years old had accepted the "Plan of Salvation" and confessed to stealing homemade candy belonging to the Gulde 4-H Club.

I was the one who for years rarely missed a meeting of the BYPU or the RAs, where I had memorized names of Southern Baptist missionaries to Brazil and Argentina.

I was the one who, like Jacob, had wrestled with God over a call to be a preacher—finally surrendering to that call in the kitchen of the Heidelberg Hotel.

I was the one who—when a college student—had knelt under Mississippi pine trees and begged God to use me in his service.

I was the one who had memorized (with supporting Scriptures) all seven dispensations of the *Scofield Reference Bible*.

I was the one for whom being a Southern Baptist was not just a religion but a way of life.

I was the one who for eight years had immersed himself in the Southern Baptist Theological Seminary, living on a shoe string, questing for religious insight, studying like a mole, even memorizing obscure Greek verb forms in 2 Peter, the most difficult part of the Greek New Testament.

Now I was being told by a Texan that I didn't belong because I'd been influenced by "liberalism."

Dr. Summers's assault devastated me at the time, because for too long my life had revolved around the Louisville seminary. Nothing was more important in my mind than the approval of seminary teachers, men I held in esteem and who—I felt—held my destiny in their hands. I had not yet hardened. Now I couldn't care less what a Baptist professor from Fort Worth, Texas, thinks. But when I encountered Dr. Summers that day in his office at Southern Seminary I was what I was then—an insecure graduate student with milk-bottle skin who had allowed himself to be castrated by years of graduate study.

In my encounter that day with Dr. Summers, feelings of estrangement toward the Southern Baptist Convention began to develop within me. This drifting toward estrangement was an unexpected development. All my life I'd been a Southern Baptist. My parents and my wife's people were Southern Baptists. The Southern Baptist denomination was the source of my identity. I'd always looked upon fellow Southern Baptists as friends, and my life's ambition was to work within the Southern Baptist denomination as a preacher.

Again I was encountering the unexpected. My decision to be a preacher had been unsought. Being branded a "liberal" was another unsought development that to me made no sense. I didn't think of myself as "liberal." I'd been too preoccupied with my studies to think of what I was or to give myself a label. But whatever I was I'd become because of Southern Seminary and all I'd learned there. Now Southern Seminary, in the person of Dr. Summers, was rejecting me for becoming what it had made me. This, to my mind, was Kafkaesque.

Sitting in Dr. Summers's office, I sensed danger. I felt I was skating on thin ice. This man from Texas was expressing disapproval of me and of my dissertation on which I'd worked for more than a year. Similar disapproval would be expressed by Dr. Joseph Callaway, another member of my doctoral committee, recently hired by the seminary as a new archaeology professor. I feared my degree would be denied, for both Dr. Summers and Dr. Callaway broached this possibility with me. I could see years of graduate study going down the drain.

Sensing peril, I decided to crawl. Intentionally I groveled. I disguised my feelings. I kissed boots as a contrived policy—sacrificing pride and self-respect. That's what I did. I kissed the boots of my professors. I groveled before Dr. Summers and the other professors on my thesis committee.

As Dr. Summers had suggested, I reworked my doctoral dissertation. I loaded it with references to "conservative" scholars like George Barker Stevens. I rewrote and revised around the clock. In the process I developed an excruciating rectal itch. To get relief from this rectal pain I had to sit several times every day in a tub of hot water. After what seemed like an eternity my dissertation assumed a form acceptable to my professors. I became a Doctor of Theology.

12

Dr. Sullivan

WHEN I ENROLLED IN GRADUATE SCHOOL I naively believed that if I earned a doctorate, people would come knocking on my door. A doctor's degree from the Southern Baptist Theological Seminary, I assumed, was a guarantee of a job in the Southern Baptist Convention. That wasn't the way it turned out. In Southern's 1960 spring commencement I received my degree. But I had no job. Earlier I'd been verbally promised a teaching job at William Jewell College. During closing months of my graduate studies I'd banked on that teaching job in Missouri. Much to my chagrin, Dr. Summers, the Texas theologian, communicated with the good folk at William Jewell and advised them to withdraw the teaching offer. They followed his advice. I'll never forget receiving a telegram from Dr. David Moore of William Jewell informing me that I had no job. It arrived early one morning in Louisville. As I opened the telegram and read it, I experienced a surge of psychological nausea. I wanted to vomit but I couldn't.

As my student days at Southern Seminary came to an end I felt my world was unraveling, falling apart. I'd witnessed the "Battle of Lexington Road" with all its pettiness and vicious virtue. I'd been branded a "liberal," for unwittingly I had taken on the ideological coloration of seminary professors I admired. I'd been told I didn't have a moral right to be a Southern Baptist preacher, and I'd had a job I'd counted on pulled out from under me.

I was bewildered. I felt I didn't have a friend anywhere. I found myself questioning whether I should have studied to be a preacher. My dream was becoming a question mark. Was it all a mistake?

Maybe God had not spoken to me in the kitchen of the Heidelberg Hotel. Maybe I'd been fooled or maybe I'd played a trick on myself. Yet these feelings I suppressed. Instead, I reasoned, "It's too late to turn back now. I've invested eight years beyond college studying to be a preacher. Turning around wouldn't make sense."

Yet there I was, thirty years old and a theological Humpty Dumpty. I had a doctor's degree, a pile of debts, a rectal itch, no job and no prospects for one. Lacking maturity, I made mountains out of molehills. Yet at the time my troubles seemed like mountains. It would be easy for me to blame those troubles on others. But that wouldn't be fair. *I brought my troubles on myself.* I had never taken the liberal-conservative conflict within Protestantism seriously. Before going to seminary *I didn't even know there was a liberal-conservative controversy.* To my mind this issue was remote—like the Great Wall of China—or an issue for jests. I'd heard Southern Seminary professors make cracks about "fundies" and "fundamaniacs" and "fun-DAMNmentalism." But these cracks had gone in one ear and out the other.

I didn't understand the chemistry of religious fundamentalism. I didn't know that ax-handle Baptists in Texas, with an urge to purge in their hearts, will destroy you if you don't believe as they believe. I didn't know about Ayatollah fundamentalists, endowed with vigilante mentalities, who insist that all Southern Baptists should be cookie cutter Christians, every one identical because every one has been cut out with the same doctrinal mold.

As a seminarian my attitude, foolishly, had been live and let live! From my seminary professors I'd absorbed a devotion to intellectual honesty and to openness of inquiry. That's why in my doctoral dissertation and in conversations with Dr. Summers I'd expressed admiration for scholars like Albert Schweitzer, Johannes Weiss, and Alfred Loisy. I had seen the plausibility of their contention that hovering around the ministry of Jesus and early Christianity were unfulfilled expectations. Jesus had appeared to the first-century Jewish world announcing the imminent arrival of the Kingdom of God, a golden age for Jews. The early disciples had fervently expected Jesus' return on clouds of glory. As Martin Dibelius of the University of Heidelberg expressed the matter, it seems that at the basis of the whole mission of Jesus was an expectation of "something immediately impending which actually never has come to pass." Like a fool, I expressed agreement with this "liberal" insight—an insight, incidentally, shared by the *Scofield Reference Bible*, the Magna Charta of conservative Protestantism. This—I now see—I should not have done. No law required me to say everything I believed. I should have kept my mouth shut. At times duplicity and compromise are in order. As the Bulgarian proverb teaches, "My child, one is allowed to walk with the devil until one has crossed over the bridge and is out of danger."

At the time I was afflicted with graduate school myopia and with tunnel vision. As a doctoral student I'd devoted years to studying Jesus' life against a first-century Palestinian milieu. I'd immersed my mind in English, German, and French scholarship. In the process I'd concluded that scholars like Albert Schweitzer, Morton Scott Enslin, and Charles Guignebert *made sense*—were coherent and intelligent—in their reconstructions of Jesus' life and thought, displaying *honesty* in their writings. I perceived in their life-of-Jesus research a *lucidity of inquiry* that contrasted with the obscurantist pap produced by "conservative scholars" who live under the illusion that Jesus—the one who was raised from the dead and who continues to exert an evocative influence on mankind—needs defending and delivering from the charge of historical relativism. Naively I expressed my agreement with the "liberals" of New Testament studies while failing to understand this agreement was a "kiss of death" in the eyes of "conservatives." I had not yet grasped Albert Schweitzer's dictum that religion is the only field of human inquiry where a premium is placed on intellectual dishonesty.

One thing I knew. I needed to get away from Louisville. Southern Seminary had changed. It was not the school I had known prior to the administration-faculty controversy. I wanted to go off somewhere by myself, lick my wounds and try to get my act back together. The week after graduation I loaded my belongings into my car and prepared to leave. I was following my feelings. I was acting on emotion, not on common sense. But I had a problem: although I didn't want to stay where I was, I didn't have any place to go. For me it was like living again in Mrs. Craft's boarding house—I had no place where I belonged.

I left Louisville early on a Thursday morning. When I got to the edge of town I didn't know whether to drive north or south, east or west. All directions were uninviting. I drove eastward. Why toward the east? I don't know. I had to go somewhere. So I drove eastward, drifting in the direction of the seaboard. I stopped at every Howard Johnson's I came to and drank coffee.

My wife and I spent nights in cheap motels. The cheaper they were the better. I sat for hours in motel bath tubs soaking my painful rectal itch. Night after night I stretched out on motel beds, finding sleep impossible. I'd toss and tumble all night, wondering from the time I lay down until sunrise the next morning: What am I going to do? Where do I go now that I'm an unemployed, "liberal" Southern Baptist preacher? I did not know the answer.

I drifted across Virginia and ended up eventually on the Baltimore Turnpike that runs between Baltimore and Washington, our nation's capital. I spent two days driving aimlessly up and down the Baltimore Turnpike. I'd drive north for a while and turn around and drive south. Then I'd go northward again—only to turn around and drive back southward. I recall seeing homes on both sides of the turnpike, homes that suggested security and a sense of place and belonging. These homes of stone and brick aroused within me the question: How do I find in this world a niche to fit into?

I needed a job, a peg to hang my hat on. Yet the world around me seemed impenetrable. Because of events at Louisville (being branded a "liberal" and being turned down by William Jewell College) I knew the door to teaching at a Baptist school was closed. An obvious alternative was to become the pastor of a congregation. After all, that's why I'd gone to seminary, to study to be a preacher. Yet becoming pastor of a Southern Baptist church isn't easy. A Baptist preacher who doesn't have a job is up against a problem. The Southern Baptist denomination is loosely organized. Each church stands alone, selecting ("calling") its own pastor. There are no bishops or district superintendents to assign a pastor to a church or to help and guide unemployed ministers. Southern Baptist ministers work within a helter-skelter system of "contacts" and "recommendations" and luck and fate—a system I never understood. You're more or less on your own.

A part of my difficulty was that during my seminary years I'd not "kept up my contacts." A reserved person, at heart an introvert, I hadn't kept my fences mended. My nose had been in books, theological journals and Greek grammars. This was a mistake. If you're going to be a Southern Baptist preacher you've got to "keep up your contacts." "He who would have friends must show himself friendly." You need to stay close to people who're in a position to help when help is needed, writing them letters, going by for visits, shaking their hands and letting them know what's going on. This I hadn't done. I cut my own throat by failing to do so.

My wandering up and down the Baltimore Turnpike ended in Washington. My wife and I rented a room on Massachusetts Avenue. I landed a job working as a dishwasher in a restaurant about six blocks from the White House. For weeks I floundered, washing dishes. Dr. Clayton Sullivan, B.A., B.D., Th.D., and dishwasher. I am certain I had the best theological training of any dishwasher in our nation's capital. How many other Washington dishwashers could recite the names and locations of the uncial manuscripts of the Greek Bible? Or spontaneously discuss Josephus's account of first-century sectarian Judaism?

Finally I seized on a plan. Whether it would work or not I didn't know. But it was the only course of action I could devise. I did not personally know Dr. Duke McCall, Southern Seminary's president and the man around whom the "battle of Lexington Road" had been fought. We'd spoken to each other and we'd had two or three conversations. But that was all. I decided to call Dr. McCall and to explain to him where I was, what my problem was, and how I needed help. Maybe he would help me get a job somewhere as a preacher.

Reluctantly I placed a long-distance call to Dr. McCall in Louisville. Over the phone I started explaining to him my predicament. In the middle of my explanation I lost control of my emotions. I broke down and started sobbing. I cried like a baby, something I hadn't done since I had cried while Daddy cleaned out my risin sockets with rubbing alcohol. I remember saying over and over with anguish, "Dr. McCall, I need help! Dr. McCall, I need help!"

I look back on that telephone call with embarrassment. My conduct was grotesque. Yet at the time I was up a tree and I didn't know how to get down. I, a ministerial Humpty Dumpty, was having a crash course in growing up.

Dr. McCall—a person I'd heard described by critics as a "hollow man"—could not have been more compassionate. He heard me out and then said, "Clayton, you stay by the phone. I'll be back in touch with you before the day is over." An hour later Dr. McCall called back. In substance he said, "You come on back to Louisville. We'll find something for you to do at the seminary, and I'll help you find a pastorate."

Back to Louisville I went. Dr. McCall gave me "make work" employment in the seminary library. I was "research librarian." In fact I was a seminary graduate without a job. I was a preacher without a pulpit. Scared of the faculty, ashamed of my status, I maintained a low profile. I stayed in my small office on the third floor of the James P. Boyce Library, performing chores assigned by Dr. Leo Crismon, seminary librarian. Several months went by and finally (thanks to Dr. Chester Quarles, a Baptist leader in Mississippi) I received a "call" to become pastor of the Baptist congregation in Tylertown, Mississippi.

The Southern Baptist Theological Seminary is now for me a fading memory. I spent eight years there. The first six were stimulating and enriching, a time of expanding mental horizons. The last two years were disasters. I received emotional wounds which have had difficulty healing. For years after leaving Louisville I had nightmares in which I'd be surrounded by seminary professors, taunting and threatening to deny me the doctor's degree for which I'd slaved. Time and again I've awakened from these nightmares, covered with sweat and haunted with a vision of Dr. Ray Summers, the Texas theologian, sneering and saying, "You do not have a moral right to be a Southern Baptist preacher."

At Southern Seminary I was exposed for the first time in my life to "professional" Christians. "Professional" Christians, I discovered, have a bewildering capacity to treat one another brutally. As the Texas proverb affirms, "There is no hatred like Christian hatred." No poison is as potent as the venom of the virtuous. During the "Battle of Lexington Road" I watched with puzzlement as professors I admired kicked each other as hard as they could. They "lectured eloquently" on the Christian tradition, "preached inspiring sermons" in alumni chapel, and then fought with one another like drunken thugs having a barroom brawl. I could not bridge the gap between what I heard them say and what I saw them do. Consequently, I began to doubt the Christian enterprise.

In the aftermath of the controversy I too practiced Christian hatred. I seethed as I rewrote my thesis to satisfy the "conservative" tastes of Dr. Summers and his colleagues. I camouflaged my anger and kept my raw feelings buried. Then on graduation day, having in hand the framed diploma declaring me a Doctor of Theology, I went from the graduation ceremony to a telephone booth and called my two chief antagonists on my dissertation committee. Reverting to language I had used years before while selling newspapers on the streets of Jackson, I told each of them, "I want you to know I think you're a goddam dirty son of a bitch."

Bizarre is it not, repulsive is it not, that I invested years in Southern Seminary to learn what the Christian faith is all about, looked upon my professors as father surrogates and religious guides, and then ended my studies at Louisville in an eruption of bewildered anger? There is, I repeat, no hatred like Christian hatred.

When I left Southern Seminary, headed back to Mississippi, I took a final look at the campus. I looked at the beech trees and at the stately colonial buildings. I looked at Alumni Chapel with its white steeple pointing upward into the Kentucky sky, a symbol of the words "Our Father who art in heaven." The campus as a whole still seemed to me an aesthetic masterpiece, an architectural jewel!

Years earlier I had arrived on this campus a Mississippi fundamentalist looking for God. Clutching my *Scofield Reference Bible*, confident the world was my oyster, I entered Southern Seminary one person, but I came out another person. Years of study had taken me from Scofield to Streeter to Schweitzer to Strauss. From knowing nothing about the historical-critical method I had mastered at least the profile of historical-critical studies. I had gone from certainty rooted in ignorance to bafflement caused by being exposed to more information and theory than I knew how to assimilate. My debt to Southern Seminary is profound, and I will never escape its influence on my life.

PART III

Inside
the Cream Pitcher

13

Tylertown

AFTER NEGOTIATIONS with a pulpit committee and after preaching what in Southern Baptist circles is called a "trial sermon" I was "called" (invited) to become the pastor of a Baptist congregation in Tylertown, Mississippi. The good people of this church didn't know anything about what I'd been through up at Southern Seminary. They didn't know that, according to Dr. Ray Summers, I didn't "have a moral right to be a Baptist preacher" and that I'd been tarnished by "Louisville liberalism." For all they knew I was a respectable seminary graduate, not an unemployed preacher who had, among other things, washed dishes for a living in a restaurant in Washington, D.C. So in 1961 my wife and I moved from the ethereal atmosphere of Southern Seminary to Tylertown. I moved from a world of books, manuscripts and lectures to a world of Beulah Avenue merchants and dairy farmers.

Tylertown, a county seat in Southwest Mississippi and the trading center for Walthall County, isn't close to anywhere. It's ten miles from the Louisiana line. New Orleans is seventy-five miles to the south, on the other side of Lake Pontchartrain. Jackson is a hundred miles to the north. The closest place of size is McComb, a town twenty-three miles to the west. This geographic isolation works to Tylertown's economic advantage. Because no other towns are close by people from miles around must come to Tylertown to shop.

Tylertown and Walthall County belong to a stratum of society about which sophisticated urban America knows little. Walthall County is pastures, fences, fertilizers, silos, ponds, dipping vats, cattle barns, dairy herds, hogs, rye grass, tractors, combines, plows, soybeans, and milking sheds. All these agricultural devices are indispensable to our society, but they are unknown to people living in Chicago and Atlanta who patronize supermarkets, never reflecting on where food comes from. Food comes out of soil worked by farmers—farmers with faces made red by the sun, who drive pickup trucks and have dirt under their fingernails, who get up at 4:30 in the morning and go to work regardless of the weather. Farmers age prematurely because of manual labor. They are viewed patronizingly as "hayseeds" by people who eat steaks in fine restaurants and fail to understand that without tillers of the soil there would be no food.

Walthall County boasts of being "the cream pitcher of Mississippi." Walthall County is dairy country, a little Wisconsin. For miles in all directions are dairy and cattle farms that supply milk and meat to the New Orleans metropolitan area. I spent five years living in this "cream pitcher," and in the course of those five years I came to know Tylertown inside out. Tylertown sits astride U.S. 98, the blacktopped, two-lane highway running from Mobile, Alabama, across Mississippi over to Natchez on the Mississippi River. In the middle of Tylertown, where highways 98 and 27 intersect, there is a brick courthouse with a jail next door. Close by are the county library, the post office, and the health and welfare departments.

Beulah Avenue, with two traffic lights, is a potpourri of Pigott's Drugs, Walker's Five and Ten, Bill's Dollar Store, the *Tylertown Times* office, Hartman's Funeral Home, May's Cafe, Simmons's Department Store, Crawford's Clinic, Ball Hardware, Packwood's Dry Goods, Hudson's Bankrupt Store, Breland's Drugs, Pigott's Dry Goods, the Mississippi Power and Light Company office, the Tylertown cinema, the Sears catalog store, the Western Auto, Moore's Auto Parts, Jones Furniture, and the bank sitting across the street from the Tylertown Drug Store, above which Dr. Alcus Harvey, the town's retired physician, has his medical office.

South of Beulah Avenue, Tylertown's main street, are the railroad tracks bordered by the black residential section and tin-roofed warehouses once used for storing cotton. Scattered across town with no logic as to location—for across the years no zoning codes regulated Tylertown's growth—are churches and schools, shanties and feed mills, homes and beauty shops, groceries and service stations. Tylertown's one industry of size is the Haspel Clothing Factory (owned by entrepreneurs from New Orleans and New York) where men's suits are manufactured by housewives bending over rows of cacophonous needle machines.

Practically every white person in Walthall County and in Tylertown is a Southern Baptist, for in this part of the Deep South the Southern Baptist denomination enjoys a regional imperialism. To move into a place like Tylertown and to assume responsibility for the Baptist congregation—most of the white population, for all practical purposes—is no easy task, even for a newly minted Doctor of Theology. In the small towns of the South the Southern Baptist church is a pivotal institution, serving not only religious functions but also a social role as the white community's unifier. It is the place where rich and poor may intermingle, very nearly as equals. Constructed of yellow bricks and of colonial design, the building of the Tylertown Baptist Church was the town's handsomest structure. Over the years hundreds of thousands of dollars had been invested in the church's physical facilities.

I remember that day in 1961 when my wife and I made that move into the cream pitcher. Our furniture—much of it newly purchased—was loaded in a Mayflower moving van. I was apprehensive and nervous from head to toe. When I made that move I believed in prayer and I believed that a benevolent deity (a "Heavenly Father") directed my life. Ten miles from the edge of town, half-way between Tylertown and McComb, my wife and I pulled off the road and stopped beside an abandoned farm house. We got out of the car and we knelt on red dirt and we prayed together. We asked God to guide us in Tylertown as we became a pastor and a pastor's wife.

But I was not only apprehensive; I was also excited. I felt that, just maybe, things were finally falling into place. Maybe I was getting my act together. Now I had a job and an income, my first real income since marriage! I was about to become what I had for years longed to be—a Southern Baptist preacher.

Moving to Tylertown meant that I was to live again in Mississippi, the place where I wanted to live. I was coming back "home" after being away for eight years. Here I knew the territory. I was born and reared in Mississippi. It may be the poorest state in the Union, and many other things, but to me it's *home*. All of my grandparents are buried in South Mississippi's Piney Woods. I have always experienced a feeling of belonging when I have landed on a Delta flight at Thompson Field in Jackson or, when crossing the state line, I have seen beside the highway a sign, "You are now entering Mississippi: the Magnolia State."

With renewed vigor I gave myself to pastoring Tylertown's Baptist congregation—a congregation approaching a thousand members in a town of less than two thousand. I worked around the clock, making hospital calls and visiting "shut-ins." I conducted public worship services and performed weddings and officiated at funerals. I spent hours talking with people who wanted to mull over their problems with me. I massaged church organizations and I smoothed ruffled Baptist feathers. I prepared sermons and I studied late into the night in my office at the church. I'd brought to Tylertown boxes and boxes of books from Louisville. I subscribed to an array of theological journals. I kept up a rigorous reading schedule—hoping through study not to become intellectually "stale" as a working preacher.

I wanted to "know" the members of my church. I was determined to get inside the home of every person who was a member of the Tylertown Baptist Church, learning their names, learning who they were, learning what they were like and the lives they lived. To that end I kept in my car a list of members and I went over this list time and again—checking names off one by one as I visited and revisited people on the list. I went to see people who lived in elegant homes and I went to see people who lived in shacks. I visited church members who owned thousands of acres of land—looking at their barns and herds—and I visited church members who lived on welfare. With all of these people I carried on conversations and experienced their hospitality. From them I picked up insights about life: "Preacher, when you're down and out, quitting never solves anything." "Always do more than you're paid to do." "Don't ever say anything behind a man's back you wouldn't say to his face."

I did my best to become a part of the "cream pitcher." I deliberately spent time on Beulah Avenue talking to people. I went in and out of the stores on Beulah Avenue speaking to clerks and owners. I took time to drink coffee at the Tylertown Drug Store, at May's Restaurant, and at Hinson's Cafe. I went to basketball and football games. I attended Halloween carnivals and family reunions and I watched the annual Christmas parades as they came down Beulah

Avenue. I joined the Rotary Club and attended its weekly meetings in the dining hall of the Methodist Church. I went to Chamber of Commerce banquets and to school plays and to political rallies and to cattle sales.

In this way I learned how to be a preacher and a pastor, by being one. I went from house to house and I wore out my car driving up and down graveled roads. In the process I felt myself coming back down to earth after having lived eight years in an artificial world at the Louisville seminary. I began to get my feet on the ground again, slowly getting over having gone to a theological school. I discovered more to life beyond books and theological journals and Greek manuscripts.

Indeed, during the first year I lived in Tylertown I learned more about people and human nature than I'd learned during my previous thirty years. I discovered people in a small town are like pickles in a pickle barrel; they come in all shapes and sizes. "Small towns produce small minds," some may say, but with this aphorism I cannot agree. In Tylertown I encountered scores of knowledgeable people. I met people who traveled and read and had a wide range of interests. I also met people with small horizons, like the Walthall Countian who told me he'd never been outside Walthall County because he didn't "figure" there was anything outside Walthall County worth seeing.

After working in Tylertown for a year my wife and I took our first vacation. We drove down to Panama City on Florida's Gulf Coast where for two weeks we stayed in a beach cottage loaned to us by friends. When I got to that beach cottage the truth hit me: I was tired, "dog tired." I was physically and emotionally exhausted. For a year as a working pastor I'd pushed myself around the clock and I'd worn the leather off my shoes. I stretched out on a bed in that beach cottage, the Gulf breeze blowing through the windows, and I went to sleep. For three days my wife and I slept around the clock, getting up only to eat. The life of a preacher, I was discovering, drains one's physical and emotional energies. The demands made upon you are many. You see and you hear much. You encounter the sick and the distressed. You bury the dead. You have an uninterrupted view of what happens to people in the rough and tumble of life. You're exposed to people's insides and their psychic innards, at times soaking up their emotional turmoils as a sponge soaks up water.

14

Fallen Sparrows

A RESPONSIBLE MINISTER should be mature emotionally, wise in the ways of the world, and willing to live with ambiguities. Without preparation for the problems of real people in real life, a minister can be overwhelmed by what he sees and hears. Because I was unprepared for my clear view of events in the lives of other people, I found myself grappling as a preacher with what I came to think of as my "coherence problem." Exactly when this grappling began I don't know. Some problems don't spring out like a jack-in-the-box; rather, they move in slowly, like the coming of dusk, or like springtime grass turning green. They arrive, and one is not aware of the precise moment of arrival. At some point in time—unrecognized by me—I found myself struggling in Tylertown with my coherence problem. This problem was peculiarly mine because I was the *preacher*.

My coherence problem involved "getting it all to fit together and to make sense." It had to do with life as experienced by people in Tylertown and Walthall County and with my role as a preacher. Did the Christian faith make sense—and indeed, was it "relevant"?—when I related it to the way most people lived inside the cream pitcher? Did what I said and did as the preacher make sense? Or was being a Baptist preacher in a Mississippi town like "shoveling smoke"? I am not alone in this kind of struggle. Scores of preachers in the towns and country crossroads of Mississippi, Alabama, and Georgia have encountered the problem of coherence, rooted as it is in the ways of the South and the ways of the world.

I hadn't gotten my shoes and socks unpacked in Tylertown before I realized that inside the cream pitcher a lot of hurting was going on. As I had driven through a two-traffic-light Mississippi town, with its church steeples, and with dogs sleeping under chinaberry trees, everything appeared to be peaceful. But once I knew the folk who lived there I discovered there was hurting in living.

There was a woman whom I'll call Mrs. Howard, in her late sixties, a member of my congregation. She lived right off Beulah Avenue in a frame house behind a gasoline station. She was a good woman and a widow whose life revolved around her son, Johnny Fred. Johnny Fred, then in his thirties, was physically deformed, his body twisted like a gnarled tree; he was mentally retarded and his speech was garbled. Every day Mrs. Howard parched and boiled peanuts and sacked them in brown paper bags. In turn, Johnny Fred would maneuver his convoluted body up and down Tylertown's Main Street, selling those peanuts to passersby.

Time and again I visited Mrs. Howard, Johnny Fred's mother, in her house behind the gas station. We'd sit and talk and in our conversations she would worry aloud to me about what was going to happen to Johnny Fred when she was dead. One day she asked me a question I didn't know how to answer: "Preacher, why did God let Johnny Fred be born the way he is?" Her bluntness jarred me. I saw the anguish in her eyes, and I didn't know what to say. How can a preacher, who explains and defends God's ways in his dealings with human beings, "explain" or "justify" to a mother her deformed, mentally-deficient son?

I could have answered Mrs. Howard with "preacher talk." I could have spoken "pretty words." Mississippi religion lives not out of systematic reflection but out of emotion, a religion of clichés. One of those stock phrases is "God loves us." At revival meetings we often join our voices and sing,

> Could we with ink the ocean fill,
> And were the skies of parchment made;
> Were every stalk on earth a quill,
> And every man a scribe by trade;
> To write the love of God above
> Would drain the ocean dry;

Nor could the scroll contain the whole,
Though stretched from sky to sky.

Surely when Mrs. Howard asked, "Preacher, why did God let Johnny
Fred be born the way he is?" I could have answered her with what I
was "supposed" to say. I could have told her "Mrs. Howard, when it
comes to Johnny Fred and his condition we've got to remember that
all things work together for good for those who love the Lord. And
you've got to remember God loves Johnny Fred and God loves you."
But would those words have made sense? Is there any way to rec-
oncile human tragedy with a view of God as compassionate? What
would my "pretty words" have done to whatever "integrity" I pos-
sessed? How could I say to this baffled mother: "God loves you. And
this God of love has 'blessed' you with a deformed, mentally-deficient son who hobbles down Beulah Avenue selling peanuts while
truck drivers frighten him by blasting their horns."

I think I would have made some sense if I'd said, "Mrs. Howard,
I don't know the answer to your question. Here you are a widow with
a deformed son, living in a shack behind a gas station, supporting
yourself and Johnny Fred on parched peanuts. Frankly, Mrs. Howard, I think you're eating chicken shit." That's an expression out of
Sullivan's Hollow where my Daddy grew up. When they said about
a person—"He's eating chicken shit"—that meant he was experiencing troubles, particularly troubles undeserved and irrational. A farmer's barn burns down, or lightning kills his hog, or there's not enough
rain and the crops don't make—these troubles are troubles one lives
with; one has no choice in the matter. When troubles like these came
in Sullivan's Hollow, they said, "He's eating chicken shit." Cut down
to the bone, that's what Mrs. Howard was doing. No one in Tylertown would have chosen voluntarily to exchange places with her or
with her son. Both of them were eating chicken shit.

Since I didn't know what to say to Mrs. Howard's question, I
failed her. I sat there in the room and said nothing, avoiding her eyes.
Yet my encounter that day with Johnny Fred's mother was a paradigm for what was to come. Repeatedly I met people in the cream
pitcher who were hurting, experiencing a flood of irrational sorrow.

The first week I lived in Tylertown a middle-aged woman came
to my office at the church and for more than two hours poured her

heart out in a verbal Niagara. At times she trembled as she talked. Her self-image was crushed because she'd been dumped in a divorce, abandoned by her husband for a younger woman. There she sat in my presence licking her emotional wounds. She told me of the impact the divorce had made on her and on her children. In the course of it all she said, "Dr. Sullivan, there's honorable sorrow and there's dishonorable sorrow. And what makes my sorrow hard to bear is my feeling it's dishonorable. You'll never know my feelings of shame and embarrassment over the collapse of my marriage."

I sat listening, again not knowing what to say. For I sensed that her life was broken and would never be mended. She saw herself as a dumped divorcée and a rejected wife; yet she was an admirable woman, a working mother who poured her life out for others as a school teacher. She was a church member. But she was going through life eating chicken shit.

I saw hurting in the face of Mrs. Hattie Pittman the day she saw her husband killed by an automobile. Mr. and Mrs. Pittman, he in his eighties, she in her sixties, whose son Paul edited the local newspaper, were walking side by side down Highway 27 north of town, a stone's throw from their home. They were talking to each other about their children and grandchildren and Mr. Pittman was saying over and over to his wife, "God has been good to us." Down the road a car came and veered into Mr. Pittman, knocking him through the air, mangling him before Miss Hattie's eyes. The Tylertown Volunteer Fire Department came out with a water hose and washed Mr. Pittman's flesh and blood off Highway 27. In the aftermath I saw the anguish in Mrs. Pittman and in the four Pittman children, but what could I say?

I perceived suffering in Elton Moore's wife as she watched her husband's body wither away because of a muscular disease no medicines or therapies could stop—a withering process lasting for months before death came.

I sensed pain in Ellen Winn the morning her husband, T. O., was killed south of town—bludgeoned in his pickup truck by a drunk from Louisiana who was speeding up Highway 27 on the wrong side of the road.

As Tylertown's preacher, living an uncloistered life, I confronted a prevalence of pain among my people. My "coherence problem" has never gone away. I've never escaped from the shadowy side of life. I've seen children wasting away from leukemia. I've watched living bodies rot from lupus and cancer and cystic fibrosis. I've been with parents moments after a child has been killed by lightning. I've stood in a hospital room and listened to the sobs of a woman raped by a black man, hearing her anguish and cries of terror, hearing her say, "For the rest of my life I'll be dirty! Unclean! Every time people look at me they'll think 'There goes the woman who was screwed by a nigger.' "

I've encountered people locked into deformed bodies, bodies twisted from birth—thus going through life in wheelchairs. I've encountered folk with defective and twisted minds. I've listened to a wife whose husband moments before had committed suicide by blowing his brains out with a shotgun. I've sat beside a mother who held in her hand a telegram which read, "We regret to inform you your son has been killed in the line of duty" in Vietnam. And I've seen people existing into a senile and pointless old age, nature's final insult. I recognized these absurdities of life for the first time in Tylertown, where I was the preacher. Most of this human suffering— it seemed to me—was undeserved and served no purpose. This suffering that I encountered in the cream pitcher is a microcosm of suffering on a broader scale, a microcosm of the natural and moral evils that have erupted in this century. So the coherence problem doesn't exist in small Mississippi towns alone; the shadowy side of life is universal. Sooner or later every person with eyes to see and ears to hear stumbles into what theologians call "the problem of evil."

As a neophyte minister in Tylertown, I experienced reality shock. My seminary training, for which I am still appreciative, hadn't prepared me for life's rawness and pain. Indeed, I began to think that much of what I'd learned in Louisville was not relevant to the pastorate. I had moved back to Mississippi able—at the drop of a hat— to discuss "the Persian background of Deutero-Isaiah." I knew fourteen reasons why the last chapter of Romans was a misplaced letter of Paul to the church in Ephesus. But when you're talking to a woman whose husband has been killed in a head-on collision with a logging truck, issues like the authorship of Deutero-Isaiah are beside the point.

So after I became a working pastor in the cream pitcher my religious quest assumed a different shape. Before I moved to Tylertown, my search had been self-centered and self-motivated. *I* asked the questions. *I* searched for answers and played intellectual games with religion. A prisoner of ego, *I* quested for "religious insights." That's why I'd gone to the Southern Baptist Theological Seminary. I'd assumed that study and accumulation of knowledge, piling facts on top of facts, led to "understanding." By reading books and by attending lectures and by earning theological degrees I had thought that I would "understand" life's mysteries and "share" my "illumination" with others, as I would share with friends a cake won in a bingo game.

After living for a time in Tylertown I no longer asked the questions, but life forced questions on me—questions I had never asked. If God is a heavenly father who loves his children, why does he give some of them chicken shit to eat, sending them leukemia and twisted bodies and broken hearts? Did not Jesus teach, "What man of you, if his son asks him for a loaf, will give him a stone? Or if he asks for a fish, will give him a serpent? If you then, who are evil, know how to give good gifts to your children, how much more will your Father who is in heaven give good things to those who ask him?"

I found myself often contemplating another curious saying of Jesus: "Are not two sparrows sold for a penny? And not one of them will fall to the ground without your Father's will." What an enigmatic remark! Jesus did not mention flying sparrows or singing sparrows, but falling sparrows, and he said that their falling was God's will. Why is it God's will for sparrows to fall to the ground?

Because I could not solve the problem of fallen sparrows, I felt on occasion like a farce while talking to bereaved parishioners. I did not always remain silent as I did the day Mrs. Howard asked me, "Dr. Sullivan, why did God let Johnny Fred be born the way he is?" To have remained always silent would have constituted curious behavior. From time to time I used "preacher talk." I spoke pretty words. I spoke "charity at the expense of clarity," dispensing verbal placebos. With my outer self, while conducting funerals and counseling congregants, I discoursed with surface certainty about "all things working together for good for those who love the Lord." I appropriated Leslie Weatherhead's distinctions concerning the "intentional" and "circumstantial" and "ultimate" wills of God as they pertain to life's tragedies. But to my inner self my words at times sounded like mumbo-jumbo. And in the presence of undeserved suffering I saw the point of Robert Frost's couplet.

> Forgive, O Lord, my little jokes on Thee,
> And I'll forgive Thy great big one on me.

My grappling with the dilemma of human suffering drove me to a study of theology. Before becoming a working pastor I'd viewed theology as a waste of mental energy. Indeed, while in seminary I looked upon those who read theology as folk too lazy to study Greek grammar or Hebrew syntax. But in Tylertown, confronted by my coherence problem, I started reading theologians, those thinkers who take a comprehensive view of the Christian religion, "systematically" explaining what it's all about.

But I discovered in Christian theology no entrenched tradition of reflection on tragedy. In Christian thought there is no recognized role for undeserved suffering. The "Old Time Religion"—and its ci-tified relative, "neo-orthodoxy"—has much to say about sin. And the dandy intellectualism—religion viewed through "historical-critical" spectacles—I encountered at Southern Seminary has much to say about morality. But both the "Old Time Religion" and the "histori-cal-critical method" skirt the questions, "Why was Johnny Fred born the way he was? Why are some people brought into this world to hobble down Beulah Avenue in grotesquely-twisted bodies and to devote their life's energies to peddling peanuts?" Questions like these Christian thinkers tend to avoid. They leave the sad dimension of life to the Siddhartha Gautamas and the Schopenhauers and to the Clarence Darrows and the Mark Twains.

But the tragic dimension of life (like Banquo's ghost) will not go away. It causes us from a human viewpoint—the only viewpoint we humans have—to question the nature of God. So I was able, at least, to understand why a Tylertown Baptist said to me, "Preacher, the greatest fear I have is when I die and pass over to the other side I'll discover God is the bastard I've sometimes feared him to be."

15

The Caste System

SUFFERING—RAW HURTING—was the first disorienting issue I encountered on moving into the cream pitcher. Yet as I continued to push myself day and night my coherence problem assumed new wrinkles. No longer was I a teenager or a college student; no longer was I a seminarian in my twenties. I was now in my thirties, and shadows of early middle age were beginning to fall on me. I was settling down for what James Baldwin called the long, hard winter of adulthood, and I discovered that middle age brings to the surface emotional and psychological longings that I hadn't known I had. When these emotional and psychological needs were not satisfied—indeed, when they were frustrated—I began to feel doubt and regret about being a preacher. These feelings became another element in my coherence problem.

The longer I lived among Walthall Countians the more clearly I sensed among them a class system—an almost Hindu-like caste structure. Some people were on top of the pyramid, others were in the middle, and still others were on the bottom. One's place in Walthall County's pyramid or caste system wasn't determined by religious devotion or by moral values; it was determined by whom you were "kin to" and by what you owned.

At the top was the cream pitcher's aristocracy—the people others envied and looked up to, who had power and money and didn't mind using them to get more. Foremost among this elite caste were the county's large landowners with thousands of acres of timber and farm land (some having producing oil and gas wells). They said time and again, "You'll never go wrong buying land; after all, they aren't making any more of it." They said, "Always buy land and never sell." About land, with its river bottoms, creeks, hills, and trees, there is a mystique. It's the ultimate source of wealth. In Mississippi owning land makes one a "somebody," endows someone with a significance that otherwise one would not possess.

Also in the elite caste were Tylertown's doctors, dentists, and attorneys, along with its bankers and Beulah Avenue merchants, some from mercantile families who once were in the "furnishing business"—providing on credit groceries, farm equipment, seed, and fertilizers to the county's farmers. These people, the large landowners and the business and professional class, and their wives and children, constituted the cream of the cream pitcher . . . Walthall County's elite. They belonged to the Tylertown Country Club, where they played golf in the mornings and in the afternoons. They belonged to bridge clubs and shopped in New Orleans (not in Tylertown or McComb or Hattiesburg). They drove Chryslers and Lincolns and lived in homes that in design and furnishings looked like they'd come out of *Better Homes and Gardens* or *Southern Living*.

This local aristocracy is composed of families that have lived in Walthall County for generations. Members of this elite caste pass wealth, homes, and land from one generation to the next. They pass on the "family jewels" from father to son and from mother to daughter, taking pride in family inheritances and family roots. Indeed, a prerequisite for full, unquestioned acceptance into the cream pitcher's caste system at any level was to have grandparents buried in one of the county's cemeteries. Having grandparents buried in Walthall County gave a person an aura of acceptability nothing else could match. Family clusters were as much a part of the landscape as the hills and the creeks and the rivers. Families like the Brumfields, Harveys, Grubbs, Dillons, Stogners, Holmeses, Ginns, Magees, Pigotts, Conerlys, Pittmans, Mitchells, Crawfords, McDonalds, Fortenberrys, and Simmonses. All these families have lived in the cream pitcher for generations. One could live in Walthall County for a quarter of a century, but if one hadn't been born there one was always an outsider and a newcomer.

Beneath the aristocratic upper crust of landed gentry and business and professional people was a subelite, amorphous class consisting of druggists, insurance agents, veterinarians, feed mill and wood yard operators, the Borden Company representative, the county agent, the postmaster, and county politicians—the sheriff, circuit clerk, chancery clerk, superintendent of education—along with their wives and children. These people were not among the upper crust, but they were vital to the cream pitcher's functioning.

The male members of these two top castes constituted Walthall County's power structure. They were the shakers and doers who decided what happened. They determined bond issues and local elections. They constituted the membership of the Tylertown Rotary Club. In Tylertown to be admitted to the Rotary Club was evidence that one had arrived; to be a Rotarian one had to own a business or be in a profession or have clout—like being the circuit clerk or postmaster. The postmaster could be a Rotarian; a mail carrier couldn't. Being a Rotarian gave one the privilege of attending the club's weekly meetings held in the dining hall of the Tylertown Methodist Church. The only two members of the Rotary Club without power or wealth were Tylertown's Baptist and Methodist preachers. They were allowed in so they could be the Rotary Club prayers who with regularity blessed the creamed potatoes and meat loaf prepared by the good ladies of the Missionary Society.

Further down the pyramid was an amorphous middle stratum consisting of government workers, postal employees, bank clerks, school teachers, secretaries, and the county's small businessmen like service station operators and owners of quick-stop grocery stores. Other members of this stratum were "middle-size" dairy and cattle farmers, owning not vast acreage but enough land to have "working farms." All these people were respected; they were known by everyone and were a part of the county's backbone. Yet they were not held in awe, for they did not have wealth. They drove Fords and Chevrolets and survived from paycheck to paycheck. They spent every dime they made pursuing an elusive prosperity.

Still further down Walthall County's pyramid was a submiddle caste: people clerking in Beulah Avenue stores, blue collar workers—like mechanics at the Ford agency—and hourly employees at Haspel's Clothing Factory, one of whom remarked to me, "Dr. Sullivan, when I'm working on a suit at Haspel's I always imagine I'm making it for my husband." Most of these people had reputations for being dependable employees, who gave a day's work for a day's pay.

This class included the county's smallest landowners, who did not have enough land to make a living from the soil. They were "part-time" farmers, who lived in the county while commuting to the shipyard in Pascagoula or to the oil fields over in Louisiana. This layer of society produced George Wallace voters and Elvis Presley fans. They felt ill at ease when "dressed up." The men owned one suit of clothes, worn only to church on Sunday mornings and to funerals at Hartman's Funeral Home. Many lived in Jim Walter houses or trailers. Most had no more than a high school education.

At the bottom of the pyramid were blacks and poor whites, otherwise known as niggers and red necks or as coons and white trash. They were the last residue of slavery and the sharecropper system, trapped in rural poverty and in dirt-road slums, living in house trailers and in shotgun shacks covered with tar paper with no screens over the windows. In their front yards petunia beds grew out of discarded, half-buried automobile tires, and fig trees were decorated with Milk of Magnesia bottles. Some avoided employment; some lacked employment; they sat on the front porch doing nothing because there was nothing for them to do. Some squeezed out a living doing "day work" on farms (fixing fences and mowing hay) and cutting pulp wood and hauling stumps to the Hercules plant in Hattiesburg. Poor blacks and red necks are the flotsam and jetsam of Southern society, not wanted because there's no place for them in the towns and on the farms of Dixie.

Those in the cream pitcher who drove Chryslers and cashed Texaco royalty checks paid to them from producing oil wells on inherited land said about poor blacks and red necks: "All they do is sit on their asses and live off of welfare. Why don't they get off their butts and go to work?" They failed to understand that there are only *so many* jobs in the cream pitcher. In fact, there are not enough jobs for those "higher up" in the pyramid: Haspel's Clothing Factory employs only *so many people*; Hudson's Bankrupt Store employs only *so many*. When all the jobs are taken—that's it. There are no more.

In Walthall County those with land and money didn't cotton to the idea of sharing their inherited land and money with "coons and white trash." Instead the rich took steps to exclude the poor from vital participation in the pyramid. One of Walthall County's largest landowners remarked to me about blacks, "Preacher, we're gonna keep those coons in their place—at the bottom of the tree. And the best way to keep a coon from climbing a tree is to clip his claws. Never let the bastards have a chance."

This caste system can be found (with variations) in scores of rural counties across Georgia, Alabama, and Mississippi. It's a structure permeated with veneration for wealth and ancestry, providing people with feelings of acceptance and with security. They often say, "The nice thing about living in Tylertown and Walthall County is that everyone knows everyone else. In Walthall County you'll never meet a stranger."

Walthall Countians, I observed, took the caste system for granted as part of the "givenness" of human existence. To them it was like the sun in the morning and the moon at night. No one questioned its distribution of this world's goods. About wealth they said, "That's the way life is; some people have it and some people don't."

The question of concern to me, since I was living in Walthall County, was, to what layer or to what caste did I belong? Where did I, the preacher, fit into the cream pitcher's pyramid? The answer was *I didn't.* I, as the Southern Baptist preacher, was *on* the pyramid, *not in* the pyramid. I was *around* the pyramid, *not of* the pyramid. In Southern towns, I discovered, preachers are like traveling salesmen or barkers at the county fair. They are not viewed as permanent residents, but as transients passing through. As Thelma Stallings, one of my church members, remarked to me, "Preachers are like football coaches. They're comers and goers." In Southern towns preachers are nomads with Bibles, riding through life on a smile, a shoe shine, and a three-point sermon outline.

The people of Tylertown were gracious to me and they were gracious to my wife. For in Southern towns people are "nice" to the preacher, treating him like the family's cocker spaniel. They extend to him a hospitality they extend to no one else. They open to him their homes. They feast him at their tables, stuffing him with roast beef and pecan pie. Indeed, I sometimes think Southerners are too "nice" to preachers. They send them holiday cards with ten-dollar bills at Christmas, and they give them boxes of candy at Easter. Week after week they brag about their sermons. They say, "Preacher, your sermon Sunday was the best sermon I've ever heard." Parishioners tell preachers "how much you mean to us" and pump ministerial egos

with compliments. "Preacher, you're the best pastor our congregation has ever had." Ministers naively accept these compliments as
valid, failing to perceive that compliments are not legal tender. Such
treatment gives some preachers a bloated sense of importance, transforming them into social cripples who expect privileges and hospi-
talities other people don't enjoy. They acquire an unrealistic,
exaggerated opinion of themselves.

Few people take time to dig beneath this veneer of privilege and
hospitality in order to analyze the psychodynamics of congregation-
minister relationships. They do not reflect on the ambiguities and
nuances of those relationships, thus failing to perceive how preachers in Southern towns are disposable and temporary (like wax-paper
wrappers for McDonald's hamburgers). The longer I lived in the
cream pitcher the more I understood my transitoriness. I had come
"home" to Mississippi, *but* I did not "belong" in Walthall County.

16

The Parsonage
and the Halo

MY TRANSITORINESS IN TYLERTOWN was symbolized by where I lived: in the parsonage, a house owned not by me but by the Tylertown Baptist Church. The parsonage was of nondescript design. It was a brick-veneer structure, painted white with a slate roof, with rooms having twelve-foot ceilings. The windows were oversized and the plumbing was antique. Impossible to warm in winter and equally impossible to cool in summer, the parsonage had been modified, added to, and remodeled. Which door was the front door? Which door was the back door? I never knew for certain.

Over the years churches in Mississippi towns have followed the curious custom of building parsonages right next door to churches. The Baptist parsonage was cheek-by-jowl with the church's sanctuary. From the bathtub to the baptistry was a distance of about fifty steps. The parsonage was surrounded by the church's partially graveled, partially paved parking lot. On Sundays and repeatedly during the week the house in which I lived was encircled by parked automobiles. Across the street from the parsonage was the Tylertown Elementary School where hundreds of students attended classes and played and yelled in the school yard.

Living in the Tylertown parsonage, located between the church and the school, was like living in the middle of a highway. Yellow school buses and automobiles were constantly coming and going and people were always walking by. Church members sporadically dropped by the parsonage for visits and chats. I appreciated these visits but they created problems. During the day I always had to be ready to go to the door and greet church members. I could never take my clothes off and stretch out and relax for at any moment the door bell might ring.

My reservations about living in an exposed parsonage may sound childish. But the parsonage's location meant that I was never off the job; I was "on duty" twenty-four hours a day. A preacher living in a parsonage located next door to a church is like a butcher living inside his butcher shop. Where a person lives has a bearing on his psychological well-being. Every middle-aged person, I believe, needs a home as a place of refuge, a place to go to at the end of the day to get away from it all, feel protected, and experience privacy. This psychological need for a place of refuge doesn't exist in one's teens or twenties, when home is where your hat is, whether it's in a dormitory room or a garage apartment.

By now I wanted a place to retreat, a place I owned and controlled. The biblical saying about birds having nests and foxes having holes went back and forth through my mind. That's what I wanted. I wanted a nest. I wanted a hole to go into where I could hide and prop my feet up and read a newspaper. I wanted a place where I could smoke a cigar and soak in a tub of hot water and say, "This home belongs to me. No one can run me out of here." But this is what I *didn't* have in Tylertown where I lived a hundred steps from the church organ. I could hear Mrs. Mangum, the organist, practicing on Saturday afternoon for Sunday's services. I lived within the shadow of the church steeple. The slate roof that kept the rain off my head and the walls that kept the cold air out on January nights belonged to others. This accentuated my feeling of rootlessness in Tylertown. I was a boarder who had come and would, someday, go. I felt vulnerable, *for when someone else controls the roof over your head, he also controls you.*

Not only did I live in the public parsonage, but I also wore a *halo*, another imputed characteristic excluding me from the fabric of Walthall County society and isolating me from fellow human beings. I use the term *halo* symbolically, to refer to the stereotyped image of preachers in the rural South. Southerners see preachers as "different," as sexless saints removed from the common lot of humankind.

As Sydney Smith said, there are three sexes: men, women, and clergymen.

Most preachers, especially those with professional training, detest the halo image. Others—a flamboyant minority—polish the halo regularly and wear it with conspicuous devotion. They interrupt the prayers of others with exclamations like "Amen!" and "Oh yes, God!" They exclaim spontaneously "Praise the Lord!" and "Thank you Jesus!" (pronounced JEEE-sus). They pretend not to be aroused when a shapely woman walks by. They never seem to curse or become angry (for to cuss or to get mad wouldn't be "nice"). They are perpetual reminders of "sin" and "salvation." They mount on their cars bumper stickers that read "Jesus Is Coming Soon" and "Are You Ready for the Judgment Day?" Secretly they hope their clergy bumper stickers will deliver them from traffic tickets and provide them with gasoline discounts. They use hyperbole while praying in public, shouting, "Oh dear God, send our way—we pray Thee—an earth-shaking, hell-moving, angel-singing, heaven-inspired, spirit-filled, sinner-saving, glory-hallelujah, bathed-in-the-blood revival meeting!" These preachers pretend to have no interest in the material side of life; they are waiting only for Jesus to return in glory! These preachers adopt artificial speaking styles, in whiny, nasal voices—like swarming mosquitos—with a "holy" pronunciation and inflection. On occasion they are so overcome with emotion that tears flow. At times they shout and hit the pulpit with Mosaic wrath, as I did when I was a "boy wonder preacher" at Mississippi College.

These preachers are quick to criticize, devoid of compassion, and prone to indignation. They lead campaigns to retain Sunday blue laws and to restrict beer sales. They always carry Bibles and always wear suits—even on hot days in August.

A friend of mine, on his way to California to attend the Southern Baptist Convention, had a flat tire in the desert. A Southern Baptist minister from Alabama—also on his way to the convention—stopped to be of assistance. When the Alabama clergyman got out of his car to help he was dressed in black shoes, a black suit, and a white dress shirt and black tie. No one was around for hundreds of miles! The weather was blistering hot! He was out in the middle of the New Mexico desert! Nonetheless he was dressed as though standing on the top of a wedding cake.

This halo tradition was constructed in part by generations of Southern clergymen, particularly those not professionally trained, who thought they were *supposed* to wear a halo. In their provincialism they thought they were "serving the gospel" by "being different." And this tradition was constructed in part by generations of Southerners who *wanted* to believe preachers are "different" from other people.

When I moved from Louisville into the cream pitcher the folk living there viewed me in terms of the rural South's ministerial stereotype. They looked upon me as the one wearing a halo, not as a sinner with a penis and frailties and feet of clay. Rather, I was the cream pitcher's hired saint, Tylertown's parson. *Parson:* a word of Latin derivation, from *persona:* the term for a mask worn by an actor. By derivation, the one playing an assigned role in a drama. Thus *parson:* the mask wearer who plays an assigned role. In Tylertown I played the role of the community's professional Christian.

The months went by and I discovered that *halos* become *heavy.* Halos are for angels, not humans. Halos isolate, separating the preacher from others. Halos cause many to feel "on edge" or ill at ease when the preacher is around. I recall going one afternoon into one of Tylertown's barber shops for a hair cut. Several men were sitting in the barber shop, and as I walked in the shop's owner blurted out, "Here's the preacher. Since he's here let's all watch our language." Who wants to go into a barber shop if it means being a killjoy for others, causing people to "watch their language"? After that episode I rarely patronized the barber shops in Tylertown. I'd drive over to McComb or over to Hattiesburg and get my hair cut where no one knew me. In that way I avoided being a barber shop sore thumb.

One of Tylertown's professionals was a gentleman whom I'll call Brass Marlin. He was the cream pitcher's lawyer par excellence, an attorney I repeatedly heard described as "crooked as a barrel of snakes." But when anyone in Tylertown needed legal representation Brass Marlin (crooked or not) was the person everyone went to for legal advice. He was a man of keen intellect, who said to me, "I'm glad I'm an attorney and not a preacher. When a preacher sees an injustice all he can do is look at it and talk about it. But when I see an injustice I can take it to court and see that justice is done."

One Tuesday Brass Marlin spoke to the Tylertown Rotary Club. He spiced his remarks with the word "hell." Yet every time he used the word "hell" he'd look over at me and say, "Excuse me, preacher." "Hell. Excuse me, preacher." "Hell. Excuse me, preacher." What Brass Marlin didn't know was that to me his "Excuse me, preacher" was embarrassing. I sat there in silence. My face was red like an apple. I wanted to stand up and protest: "Please, Mr. Marlin, don't make me feel like an oddity by saying, 'Excuse me, preacher.' Before I became a preacher I sold the *Clarion Ledger* on the streets of Jackson. I've worked on construction crews and in factories, in restaurants and in warehouses. I learned a long time ago what profanity is. Damn! Shit! Screw! Bastard! Asshole! I've heard 'em all. And they don't upset me. So please, Brass Marlin, don't say, 'Excuse me, preacher.' For when you say that you're cutting me off from the other men sitting in this room. And I don't want to be cut off. I want to be one of them."

I remember one Saturday afternoon dropping in unexpectedly to visit a church member who hadn't attended worship services for several Sundays. I wanted him to know I was missing him at church. He and some guests were sitting outside on a patio drinking beer. When they saw me walking up one might have thought I was the sheriff raiding a crap game. I heard one of the guests mutter, "Oh my God!" They started hiding beer cans behind newspapers and behind pot plants and behind the barbecue grill. By so doing they made me feel awkward. I wish they could have known that a can of Schlitz or Budweiser would not have offended me. Why couldn't they have done what Christians in Germany would have done? Why couldn't they say, "Pastor, sit down and enjoy a beer with us." Christians in Germany drink beer like Southerners drink coffee. Did not Martin Luther, the Protestant reformer, have the Apostle's Creed, the Lord's Prayer, and the Ten Commandments inscribed on his beer stein? But no! I found red faces, apologies, embarrassment, and grotesque behavior that caused me to wish I hadn't dropped by to visit a Baptist.

These were petty episodes, minor events, inconsequential in and of themselves. But when such episodes happened repeatedly, as they did in Tylertown, becoming a motif or a theme in my life, it made me feel like a walking wet blanket. I felt cut off from others, isolated.

After a time this sense of isolation rubbed on my emotions like sand-paper. It wore me down, contributing to a feeling of fatigue and making me wish I weren't a preacher.

17

"A Fine Little Preacher"

LIVING IN AN EXPOSED PARSONAGE and wearing a halo were fun and games in comparison to yet another issue that disturbed me. As a Baptist preacher in a Mississippi town, was I "pissing on a turtle"? "Pissing on a turtle" is another saying out of Sullivan's Hollow; it means "you're wasting your time." It's like "carrying coals to Newcastle." The longer I lived there, the more preaching in Walthall County seemed to be a similar exercise in futility.

Most Walthall Countians of my acquaintance were obsessed with the bread-and-butter side of life. They were devoted to the pursuit of material wealth and creature comfort. The men of Walthall County were, it seemed, particularly money hungry and devoid of religious concern. Their own net worth—and the net worth of others—was their chief topic of conversation. In my congregation, a cluster of women were devout; but for most of the people of the cream pitcher *things*—to quote Emerson—were in the saddle. Money, not the Lord of Abraham, Isaac, and Jacob, was the god that mattered.

People in Walthall County valued:

Land. "You never go wrong buying land. Land always has a use—if nothing more than keeping sunlight out of hell."

And oil wells.

And dairy herds.

And silos and barns.

And certificates of deposit.

And tractors and automobiles and combines and beef cattle.

And because things were in the saddle, riding mankind, then *ipso facto* religion was not. Rather religion was a matter of convention, something out on the edge, like a dessert is to a meal—an embellishment but not the main course. Religion's peripheral role made me—the preacher—feel peripheral, causing me at times to feel like a bumpkin pissing on a turtle. I was busy and making noise but accomplishing little of significance because the folks I pastored had their hearts and minds elsewhere.

By its very nature religion involves—at least in part—ideas. Religion entails an existential encounter with cosmic questions concerning God, evil, and humanity's origin and end. With religion goes a concern with motives and moral issues. In other words, religion entails, to some degree, reflective inquiry. And that's precisely the kind of "egghead" activity for which most rural and small-town Southerners have little use. For the typical Southerner is not a person who revels in abstract ideas and concerns. Indeed, I could number on fingers of my hands the people in Tylertown with an interest in serious reflection. One was Everett Crawford, a medical doctor who cared about history and his family's Virginia roots. Another was Dr. Alcus Harvey, the town's retired physician, who read books on top of books, who let me fish in his pond, and who said to me, "Always do more than you're paid to do." Another was Paul Pittman, editor of the *Tylertown Times*, who startled me the first time I met him by asking, "Clayton, have you read Albert Schweitzer's *The Quest of the Historical Jesus?*" And there were reflective women like Dawn Barrett, Carolyn Dillon, Vendetta Pigott and Betty Pittman.

But people like these were exceptions. The typical Southerner, rather than reveling in ideas, revels (as William Faulkner's novels illustrate) in *actions* and *things*. The Southerner builds a deer camp and goes deer hunting. He buys a boat and goes fishing. He trains bird dogs and hunts doves. He acquires land, builds up a farm, cuts timber, raises cattle, and slaughters hogs. He plants soybeans and repairs tractors and trades in commodity futures on the Chicago Board of Trade. He stocks a deep freeze with butchered meat. He is rarely concerned with history, ideas, or encompassing philosophical questions. Rather the Southerner is concerned primarily with *things*. The first week I was in Tylertown a member of my congregation asked me, "Preacher, what kind of bird dog do you have?" I told him I didn't own a bird dog. "That's too bad," he replied. "I always judge a preacher by his bird dog."

This emphasis on things—on wealth—explains why people were positioned in Walthall County's societal pyramid as they were. Those owning the least were at the bottom. Those owning the most were at the top. The ultimate compliment that could be paid to people was, "They have money." Maybe money accumulated years ago by mercantile families (in the furnishing business) who screwed blacks and poor white trash with Shylockian interest rates. But the significant issue was not how the family wealth was acquired. Rather the significant issue was, "They have money."

This emphasis on things explains why Tylertown Baptists *talked* as they did, for what people talk about reveals what they're thinking about. I recall street corner conversations in Tylertown about the comparative value of family holdings. "Preacher, have you ever stopped to figure up what the Harvey farm is worth? All that land, equipment, cattle? You put your pencil to it and it'll go over a million dollars before sunrise!" And excited talk about oil drilling activity. "Preacher, guess what I heard this morning? Texaco is going to drill a well on the Dillon place south of town!" And discussions of people's incomes. "Now you take the Fortenberrys. He has a good job with the government. She teaches school. On top of a double income they've got interest coming in from all that money her father left 'em. They've got to be pulling in fifty thousand a year or they're not making a dime." "Dr. Sullivan, have you seen the new Kelly home down at Dexter? Through the grapevine I've heard they've spent a hundred and twenty-five thousand on it. Looks like one of them houses out in Dallas. That's what two producing gas wells can do for you."

These conversations about things—about wealth—brought a gleam to the eye and a lilt to the voice. Emmett Dillon, the janitor of the Tylertown Baptist Church, told me that "people in Walthall County love money so much that when they look at a full moon they think about a silver dollar." Religion was equally pervasive, but secondary. Religion, like silos, was a part of Walthall County life. Church buildings dotted the countryside. Revival meetings were conducted. Christmas cantatas were sung. Particularly were religious activities provided for young people. But the attitude of most Walthall Countians toward religion was sentimental. Comparable, so Paul Pittman, Tylertown's newspaper editor, explained to me, to the attitude one has toward an old grandfather's clock, encased in mahogany, which has been in the family for years but doesn't work any more. For nothing in the world would one get rid of grandfather's clock. Indeed, it is polished and dusted regularly and has a place of honor in the living room. Yet no one expects grandfather's clock to tell time or to regulate life. Similarly in the cream pitcher religion was sentimentally valued. But no one expected the Christian faith to change the cream pitcher's love of wealth or to mold the underlying values by which people lived. Rather, *religion was a veneer for materialism.* Materialism is not exclusively a Wall Street phenomenon; it is a phenomenon found also in the hills of South Mississippi, where people who live in towns and on pig farms are influenced by what Germans call the *Zeitgeist*—the spirit of the times with its adoration of the dollar and what the dollar buys.

Walthall County's preoccupation with things and wealth wouldn't have bothered me if as an adult I'd chosen to live a "nonreligious" life. When I was in high school my life's goal was to be "rich"—to live in a brick colonial in North Jackson and to drive around town in a Cadillac. But in high school I was swept away by the religious impulse and I became convinced I'd been "called" to be a preacher. I attended a denominational college and was engulfed by its religious euphoria. I spent eight years at Southern Seminary in Louisville. All the way from high school through seminary I viewed the world through stained glass spectacles. I assumed that Southern society (with its church steeples) was unselfishly "Christian." And I assumed church members were de facto "Christians" in their values and life-styles. While an adolescent and seminarian I innocently saw no gap between profession and practice in Southern religion. Because of naiveté I underestimated human greed and the lure of possessions and the potency of entrenched power structures.

When I moved to Tylertown and started living in the cream pitcher, with its materialistic orientation, I was like a Trappist monk in a Las Vegas casino. Like any person encountering an alien environment, I experienced reality shock. I found the world *as it is,* not as it "ought" to be. Yet as I continued living in Tylertown and the cream pitcher I became less and less "bothered" by blatant materialism. The "shock" began to wear off. Just as Walthall Countians had been molded by the cream pitcher's veneration of wealth, I was similarly influenced. As the years passed I found the cream pitcher's values and emphases increasingly alluring. I didn't change Tylertown. Tylertown changed me.

In the congregation I pastored were people at the top of the cream pitcher's social pyramid—members who were large land owners, cattle and dairy farmers, Beulah Avenue merchants, and professional folk. They invited my wife and me into their homes—homes with shuttered windows, Baker furniture, carpeted floors, brick patios, and fireplaces where wood burned with fingerlike flames on winter nights. These homes (which conveyed feelings of privacy and "belonging-ness") were surrounded by lawns with magnolia and oak trees. In conversations these Baptists told me about their "deals" and their financial affairs, not boasting but simply stating facts.

Mentally I began comparing my situation as preacher to the situation of these Baptists who were at the top of the caste system. When I did this I didn't like what I saw. I began feeling sorry for myself and experiencing pangs of jealousy. My wife and I lived in the parsonage, which was like living in a barn in the middle of a highway. For pastoring the Tylertown congregation I was paid $600.00 a month. After taxes and retirement deductions and Social Security were taken out of my salary I had less than $500.00 a month to live on. This income was not adequate to cover my expenses; in fact, if my wife had not had a private income we could not have paid our bills every month. Resentfully, I thought to myself, "Here I am, scraping by on a preacher's salary. If I'd studied to be a lawyer or a doctor instead of a preacher I'd be making as much money as my church members tell me they make." Within me there was a collision between religious imperatives and human desires. I—charmed by the cream pitcher's value system—did what Demas, St. Paul's companion, did: *I fell in love with this present world.*

I craved its goodies. I wanted to live in a home with a brick patio where I could grill steaks over charcoal. I wanted to drive around in a Buick rather than the rusting Rambler I owned. I wanted to make enough money so that I would not feel pinched at the end of the month. I wanted my wife to be able to buy dresses at Godchaux's in New Orleans. Like St. Peter on the Sea of Galilee, I took my eyes off Jesus, and I wasted my energies and emotions comparing myself to others. As Peter found himself sinking beneath the Galilean waves, so I found myself sinking beneath waves of self-pity. I felt short-changed, convinced that I was pending my life holding the short end of the stick.

My discontent was intensified by the fiasco of my proposed pay raise. After I'd been pastoring the Tylertown congregation for two years some of the church members broached the possibility of a salary increase. I knew I needed one. I'd worked hard since moving to the cream pitcher. When I moved to Tylertown the Baptist congregation was in debt for more than one hundred thousand dollars for a building recently constructed. I'd led a financial campaign that had wiped out this indebtedness. I somewhat self-righteously felt I'd earned a salary increase. So when the church's finance committee proposed that my salary be raised from $600.00 to $650.00 a month I was elated. Fifty more dollars each month would help pay the bills.

A week before my salary increase was to be voted at a church business meeting I received a telephone call from a person I'll call Mr. John Edward Patrick, a member of the congregation who owned a dry goods store on Beulah Avenue. Mr. Patrick, a slender man in his seventies, had snow-white hair and a hearing aid. Mr. Patrick told me he wanted to come by the parsonage for a "heart to heart" talk.

That afternoon I met Mr. Patrick at the parsonage. With him was another member of the church whom I'll call Mr. Avery Mosley, a corpulent man who wore glasses. Mr. Mosley was a retired farmer who lived out from town on sixty acres of land. Mr. Patrick and Mr. Mosley were significant folk in the Tylertown congregation. Mrs. Mosley was president of the Missionary Society. Mr. Patrick was a patriarch of his clan, of which there were many members in the Tylertown Baptist Church. His brother, Davey Patrick, was the owner of a pharmacy and the father of two sons who were prominent members of the congregation.

I had no inkling why Mr. Mosley and Mr. Patrick had come by to see me. For several moments we sat in the parsonage living room, engaging in small talk. Finally Mr. Patrick cleared his throat and told me why he and Mr. Mosley had dropped by the parsonage. "Dr. Sullivan", he said, "Avery and I hear through the grapevine you're up for a salary raise."

I told him this report was true. The finance committee, I explained, was going to recommend at the next church business meeting that I be granted a salary increase of fifty dollars per month.

"Preacher, that's why Avery and I have come by." Mr. Patrick replied. "We want to talk to you about this raise. What we're going to say we're saying as your *friend* and as a *friend of the church*. We feel you ought to know there're some of us in the church who feel payin' a preacher $650.00 a month is too much. Way too much. And if this salary raise passes it's going to upset some folks and none of us want that to happen. What we want is harmony in the church."

Mr. Mosley joined the discussion. He looked at me and said, "Dr. Sullivan, please don't think there's anything personal in what John Edward and I are saying. As far as I can tell all the folks here in Tylertown like you. You're a fine little preacher and you have a fine little wife. And we feel you're doing a good job. But $650.00 a month is too much for a preacher to make, and if this pay raise goes through there're going to be hard feelings."

The conversation continued in this vein. Mr. Patrick got it all in focus when he said to me, "Preachers aren't used to nice things."

As the conversation progressed I felt my face turning red. My stomach got an "uptight" feeling. On the inside I was angry. I felt humiliated. I wanted to say to Mr. Patrick and to Mr. Mosley, "Look! As it is I'm not earning enough to make ends meet! What's wrong with me making enough money to pay my bills! Why should I live off my wife's private income? I want and need and deserve a raise! And if the two of you don't approve—that's too bad! Go hang it up."

But that's not what I said. Instead, I reacted with duplicity. I disguised my true feelings. I assured them I, too, didn't want "hard feelings." I thanked them for their time and advice. Inwardly I seethed with resentment, but outwardly I smiled at the dry-goods merchant, and I smiled at the retired farmer, whose funeral I eventually conducted. Late one afternoon, about three years later Mrs. Mosley drove from Tylertown back to the Mosley place north of town. Turning off the highway she saw her husband slumped in his chair on the front porch, his head oddly turned. He'd had a heart attack. Mrs. Mosley said to me, "Preacher, the moment I saw Avery slumped over in his chair I knew he was dead."

After their parsonage visit Mr. Mosley and Mr. Patrick used their influence to see that my pay raise was withdrawn. This confirmed my intuition that for many in the cream pitcher preachers had sentenced themselves, in Sinclair Lewis's phrase, to a life of dignified poverty. Pay the preacher with compliments, not with cash. Compliments are dandy. But in Tylertown, I discovered, compliments don't pay the dentist nor did they pay the grocery bill.

My behavior before Mr. Patrick and Mr. Mosley, opponents of my salary raise, revealed an emasculating process I perceived taking place within me. In Tylertown I constantly felt that I was living on the verge of bankruptcy. My bills were never completely paid. I survived from paycheck to paycheck. My financial situation stimulated feelings of insecurity that I had brought into adulthood from my lower-class upbringing. Emotionally I've never been able to get away from Mrs. Craft's boarding house. And my financial precariousness created within me a disturbing feeling of dependency on the congregation. I felt I *had* to get along with them. After all, they paid my salary, and they owned the roof that kept the rain off my head.

The longer I lived in Tylertown the more I went out of my way to develop an image of "being nice" in all my dealings with church members. Turtles "protect" themselves by developing hard shells; Baptist preachers in Southern towns "protect" themselves by becoming personified marshmallows and incarnate lollipops. They're always nice. They're always agreeable. They always smile at the Baptists. In the cream pitcher I never raised my voice or made a controversial statement. While walking down Tylertown's Beulah Avenue I spoke to everyone I met. I shook people's hands and slapped them on the back. While driving around town I waved at people, giving a "friendly toot" with my car horn.

My speech was always filtered through a process of "double think." Before making a remark to a church member I'd pause and mentally calculate "how" it would sound to the person to whom I was talking. If I sensed a statement would cause offense I'd either not make it or I'd modify it to make it palatable. In other words, I always thought twice before saying nothing.

I mastered the art of waffling. When members of the church confronted me with opinions and ideas with which I disagreed I employed evasive remarks such as, "You don't say!" "You've got a point there!" "How about that!" My sycophantic behavior created within me feelings of self-contempt, depriving me of a sense of masculinity. While attending Mississippi College I'd heard a fellow student remark, "I don't like preachers." When I asked her why she replied,

"Because they're so damn nice all the time." In Tylertown I came to appreciate this observation because, beneath my plastic veneer of conviviality, I didn't like myself.

18

Blacks and Whites

SHE WAS A PICTURESQUE MEMBER of the Baptist congregation in Tylertown, and she and I got along with each other superbly. Everyone called her Miss Carrie. Her full name was Mrs. Ab Hinson. She was in her seventies, physically spry, and mentally alert—as much a local institution as the courthouse on Beulah Avenue. Miss Carrie was the wife of Mr. Ab and the mother of two sons, Cliff and Jake, who operated Hinson's Grocery, the store where I bought most of my groceries. As she was of the old school, Miss Carrie didn't say "blacks." Or "Negroes." She said *niggers*. And the first week I was in Tylertown Miss Carrie came up to me and said, "Preacher, what *in the world* are we gonna do about the niggers?"

Miss Carrie's question ("What *in the world* are we gonna do about the niggers?") captures the frustration of Mississippi whites during the 1960s concerning the race issue. This frustration flowed from the disintegration of the South's Jim Crow system in the aftermath of the Supreme Court's *Brown v. Board of Education* decision.

From birth through my college years I'd lived cheek by jowl with Jim Crow. Segregation was all I knew. I remember when the J. C. Penney store on Capitol Street in Jackson had separate water fountains for blacks and for whites. Service stations had separate toilets for whites and Negroes. Throughout my youth in Mississippi I never saw a black person eating in a "white" restaurant or spending the night in a "white" hotel. In Mississippi society blacks were viewed as inferior. They rode at the back of the bus, went to separate schools, lived in shanties on the other side of town, and attended black churches (called "nigger churches"). Nor do I recall from my Mississippi youth hearing anyone question the justice or injustice of seg-regation. Jim Crow was a part of the givenness of human experience. For a white Southerner to question segregation would have seemed as surprising as to question the existence of God.

When I moved from Mississippi to Kentucky to attend the Southern Baptist Theological Seminary I carried my Jim Crow racial views with me. I was a bigot. As a boy wonder evangelist at Missis-sippi College I'd spiced my sermons with "nigger jokes." While a first-year seminary student at Louisville I recall driving one weekend to Indianapolis, Indiana. On the way to Indianapolis I came upon an automobile accident. A car had flipped off a bridge and had over-turned into a shallow river. As one of the first to arrive at the acci-dent scene, I stopped my car and joined two or three other spectators who were standing on the bridge and who were gaping at the over-turned car, which was submerged in the water below. The sight was macabre. The automobile's occupants were drowning. A man stand-ing beside me remarked, "It's a car full of niggers." Immediately I ex-perienced a feeling of "relief." To my Mississippi mind a car full of drowning blacks was somehow "less terrible" than a car full of drowning whites.

Yet in the course of my eight-year stay in Louisville my racial views changed. During my Mississippi youth I'd been exposed mainly to "cornfield niggers," like the blacks I'd seen on Saturday afternoons on Main Street in Brandon and Pelahatchie. Those blacks wore dirty overalls, worked in corn and cotton fields, ate pig's feet, guffawed rather than laughed, and spoke the kind of dialect that Mark Twain placed on the lips of his fictional black characters. I'd also been ex-posed to "zoot suit niggers," for in Jackson during the 1940s black men had made themselves look ridiculous to me by strutting down Farish Street dressed in what were called "zoot suits"—garish clothes with broad lapels, lengthy coats, bulging pants—while sporting walking canes, sunglasses, wide-brimmed hats, and watch chains that almost touched the ground.

While living in Louisville I was exposed for the first time to blacks who were not "cornfield" or "zoot suit niggers." In this regard I re-member a detail of my first trip to New York. All my life I'd heard about the Empire State Building, and I was determined to go to its top floor and to view New York from the Empire State Building's observatory. The gentleman selling the observatory tickets was a Negro. While purchasing my ticket from him I noted that *he didn't speak with a "black dialect."* This jarred me. I couldn't believe my ears. The Negro ticket vendor pronounced English as white people speak the language. Without "yassuhs" and "sho nuffs." I was nonplussed by the Negro vendor because I *didn't know Negroes could speak without using "black dialect."*

All of my professors at the Louisville seminary were vocal in criticizing the South's traditional racial views. Indeed, during the 1950s, after *Brown v. Board of Education,* the civil rights issue became "the righteous cause" of the academic world. I remember Eric Rust, my theology professor, affirming that "You men must remember Jesus was not a white man." Professor Rust added, "If Jesus tried to join a First Baptist Church in Alabama he would be denied admission."

Louisville seminary was the place where I first heard Jim Crow openly challenged. On the campus of the Southern Baptist Theological Seminary (where—for all practical purposes—there were no Negroes; the student body was more than ninety-nine percent white) I experienced a "reversal" of my racial views. I became "enlightened." I became an admirer of Dr. Martin Luther King and a believer in integration. I became "ashamed" of Southern segregationists.

During the 1950s all of us who were Louisville seminarians from Mississippi and from Georgia prided ourselves on our newly acquired racial views. We were (we liked to think) no longer "prejudiced." We openly associated with the two black students at Southern Seminary (they were from Nigeria; there were no black students from Georgia or Mississippi). We sat in the student grill and—with expressions of concern on our faces—talked to one another about "going back home and devoting our lives to solving the race problem." We conceived of ourselves as prophets of social justice (walking in the footsteps of Amos and Elijah). Clarence Jordan of Americus, Georgia, whose Koinonia Farm was nationally famous, was our hero, and we winced when Dr. W. A. Criswell of First Baptist Church in Dallas spoke to the seminary students in Alumni Chapel and said, "Fellows, things are changing down home. You used to be able to say 'chiggers.' But now you have to say 'CHEE-groes.'"

On occasional visits from Louisville back to Mississippi I paraded my newly acquired views on integration before my relatives (much to their chagrin). "The South has no choice!" I would say. "Justice must prevail! Integration is going to come whether white Southerners want it to come or not." I felt righteous and noble as I dropped these moralistic opinions.

But during my first week in Tylertown when Miss Carrie stopped me in front of Hinson's Grocery and looked me in the eye and asked her question—"Preacher, what *in the world* are we gonna do about the niggers?"—I decided right then and there I'd better be cautious about what I said. One of the first discoveries I made after moving back to Mississippi was that people were uptight over the race question. They were tense and on edge. The 1950s and 1960s, decades of controversy, were difficult decades for Mississippians. Not since Reconstruction had the state passed through a time of such radical social change and political upheaval.

Now Mississippi blacks were getting ideas. They were thinking unthinkable thoughts. Television was the conduit for these new ideas and unthinkable thoughts. Nearly every shack in Mississippi sprouted a television antenna, and on their television sets Mississippi blacks heard the voices of Hubert Humphrey and Roy Wilkins and Martin Luther King—voices proclaiming a new era in racial relationships. Beginning in the summer of 1954, the year of *Brown v. Board of Education*, NAACP groups in Vicksburg, Jackson, Clarksdale, Natchez, and Yazoo City filed petitions asking local school boards to comply with this Supreme Court decision. The unthinkable was being thought—that blacks and whites could attend the same schools, that Jim Crow could be dismantled.

To this challenge Mississippi whites responded by organizing the Citizens' Council movement, a Ku Klux Klan in a tuxedo. This movement was fathered by Robert Patterson, a planter from Ita Bena in the delta. The first Citizens' Council was established in Indianola, a delta town to the east of Greenville. From Indianola the Citizens' Council movement spread across Mississippi like a broomsage fire. More than a hundred chapters were formed in the state. There was a Citizens' Council in every county. The movement drew thousands into its ranks—businessmen, farmers, editors, lawyers, doctors, bankers—and it established in Mississippi a reign of suspicion and terror. In every town a solid white middle-class and upper-class front was built to oppose integration on any level. The Citizens' Councils

were to be feared. Their members had clout. They could hurt you—
bringing economic ruin and social ostracism upon anyone who got
out of line on the race question.

The Mississippi state legislature established the State Sovereignty Commission, Mississippi's version of the Gestapo. This
Commission, supported with tax revenues, sought to preserve segregation by hiring secret investigators to inquire into the "subversive
activities" of Mississippians who questioned the status quo.

Despite all the valiant efforts of the Citizens' Councils and of the
State Sovereignty Commission and despite the pronouncements of
the politicians things got "worse" for segregationists, not better.
Pandora's Box had been opened. Blacks would no longer "stay in their
place." As one Walthall Countian, "Slim" Crawford by name, expressed it to me, "The niggers is swellin' up." They were doing things
they'd never done before, and going places they'd never gone before.

They were even walking on sand on the Mississippi Gulf Coast.
Extending from Gulfport to Biloxi is what we Mississippians describe
as the "world's largest man-made beach"—twenty-eight miles of sand
for sunbathing, walking, and picnics. This beach was a government
project of the Depression. From the beginning in the 1930s, when
the beach was completed, blacks had never been allowed on the sand.
The police kept them off. I remember spending three days during
the 1950s at a Gulf Coast motel not far from the Friendship House
restaurant. The motel's manager pointed at the sandy beach across
U. S. 90 and remarked to me, "If I ever see a nigger on that sand I'll
take a two-by-four and beat his nigger brains out." Yet in April 1960
fifty Negroes walked out on that sandy beach. They were assaulted
by a white mob that beat them with sticks and chains. This episode
provoked a riot in Biloxi in which eight blacks and two whites were
shot.

Not only were Negroes thinking about going to white schools
and thinking about walking on sand, they were also agitating to vote.
In Mississippi prior to the Second Reconstruction blacks didn't vote.
They were kept away from the ballot box by poll taxes and by voter
examinations (given by circuit clerks) in which they were asked to
copy and to explain sections of the Constitution. No black could explain the Constitution satisfactorily for a circuit court clerk. Many

black leaders felt the key to social change was seizing and using the right to vote. Thus agitation for the ballot moved into the forefront of the civil rights movement.

This agitation over the ballot brought the civil rights issue to the cream pitcher, where I was living, placing at my doorstep what at the Louisville seminary had been a theoretical issue. Tylertown is slightly more than twenty miles from McComb, county seat of Pike County, and McComb became a hotbed of civil rights activities during the 1960s. To McComb had come civil rights workers from the North, who were connected with the Student Nonviolent Coordinating Committee (SNCC). Young blacks and whites arrived from New York and Massachusetts and conducted voter registration campaigns, teaching blacks how to fill out voter registration forms and delivering fiery speeches at night in "nigger churches." Black churches became the vehicle par excellence of the black struggle for social justice.

One day one of those black out-of-state civil rights workers came to Tylertown, went to the courthouse, and walked into the circuit clerk's office to make inquiry about blacks voting. In the circuit clerk's office he came face to face with the circuit clerk, a man named John Q. Wood, who was a member of my congregation. John Q. Wood was a man in his sixties who Sunday by Sunday sang bass in the choir of the Tylertown Baptist Church. He was one of Walthall County's most seasoned politicians, with relatives behind every pine tree and with camp followers all over the county. Everybody called him by his first name and middle initial: *John Q.* John Q. specialized in helping people with their "guv-ment" problems. John Q. was the man to see if you had troubles with your veteran's benefits or with your Social Security check.

John Q. and the "New York nigger" confronted each other in the circuit clerk's office. One was a courthouse politician out of a Faulkner novel. The other was a New York Negro. They were two men with conceptual and experiential backgrounds as different as those of a Newport aristocrat and a bayou Cajun. Exactly what happened I don't know. John Q. and the "New York nigger" talked for a few moments. Everyone agrees they talked about whether or not blacks could vote in Walthall County. And everyone agrees the "New York nigger" made some remark that caused John Q. to lose his temper.

But at this point the accounts diverge. Some said (the way they heard it) that John Q. slapped the Negro. Others said (the way they heard it) that John Q. hit the Negro with his fist. A more elaborate version affirmed that John Q. pulled open a desk drawer, took out his revolver, and hit the Negro on the head with his pistol. The confrontation became the talk of Tylertown: "John Q. knocked the shit out of a nigger at the courthouse."

The day after the fracas I went by the circuit clerk's office to see John Q. He was ebullient. Overnight among his camp followers he had become a champion. When John Q. saw me walking into the circuit clerk's office he boomed, "Come on in preacher! It's good to see you! Have you heard my new nickname?" Before I could answer he continued, "Everybody's calling me John Q. 'the nigger-knocker.' " He then launched into an account of the preceding day's episode. "Preacher, you should have been here yesterday cause all hell broke loose."

Looking at me quizzically, John Q. bantered, "Preacher, have you ever seen a grown nigger dressed in short pants? I'm here to tell you I saw one yesterday. Right into this office walked a grown darkie with a mustache and with a little straw hat on. And he was dressed in short pants and—can you believe this?—he was carrying a walking cane!"

"He was one of these out-of-state darkies," John Q. continued. "Coming in here wantin' to know if I was gonna let the niggers vote." Pausing, he said, "Preacher, I listened for a few moments and then I let that smart-aleck nigger have it. I hit him as hard as I could."

"You know," John Q. mused as an aside, "if I could knock the hell out of enough of these niggers I'd be elected sheriff next time." During the 1950s and 1960s many Southerners in rural counties ran for the sheriff's office on a promise "to keep the niggers in line." To this end they cultivated a masculine image. The "tougher" they were the more likely they were to be elected sheriff. In the Tylertown Baptist Church were a number of men active in Walthall County politics. I remember asking one of them to consider teaching a Sunday School class. He refused and gave as his reason, "I'm thinking about running for sheriff next time, and if I taught a Sunday School class it'd be a strike against me. Folks would say I was getting soft."

John Q.'s musing continued. "Preacher, the niggers here in Walthall County are good niggers. They're quiet and humble. They know their place and stay there. I doubt if there's a single nigger in this county who wants to vote. But these out-of-state darkies come in here dressed in short pants and stir our niggers up. It makes me so mad I don't know what to do."

Not everyone in the cream pitcher agreed with John Q.'s views. For in Tylertown, I discovered, there was a "liberal" minority composed of people who read and traveled and had lived in other parts of the country. They perceived how anomalous Southern racial mores were. They were embarrassed about John Q. hitting the Negro, and they resented the Ku Klux Klan and the Citizens' Councils and high-decibel politicians who yelled *nigger, nigger, nigger*. Feeling compassion for blacks, they spoke with contempt of the "mad dogs"—their name for militant segregationists. Yet in Tylertown the "liberals" maintained a low profile. They whispered their views and shared their feelings only with those they trusted. For the worst fate a white citizen could experience in Mississippi during the 1960s was to be tagged a "nigger lover" or a "bleeding heart."

19

Competing Visions

AS THE MONTHS PASSED Mississippi's atmosphere became supercharged. Feelings were raw. Mississippi, which was not so much a state of the union as it was a state of obsession, was neurotically preoccupied with the race issue. There was a miasma of paranoia and a hysteria of hatred and frustration. As Paul Pittman, Tylertown's newspaper editor, expressed it to me, "The woods are on fire!"

On the morning of 1 October 1962, James Meredith, a black man and a veteran of nine years in the Air Force who described himself as an "American-Mississippi-Negro citizen," was enrolled by force as a student at the University of Mississippi in Oxford: *an event breaking for the first time Mississippi's ironclad segregated educational system.*

It was unbelievable and inconceivable—"a nigger at Ole Miss!" Ole Miss, the university where for generations Mississippi's aristocracy has sent its handsome sons and beautiful daughters. These sons and daughters were sent to Ole Miss in Buick convertibles to join fraternities and sororities—the same ones to which mama and papa had belonged—and to prepare to be the state's business and professional and political leaders. They were sent to Ole Miss to follow Johnny Vaught's football team, to wave Confederate flags when the Ole Miss band played "Dixie," and to learn to whoop the "Hotty Toddy" yell.

> Hotty Toddy, God Almighty!
> Who in the hell are we?
> Flim, blam, bim, bam,
> Ole Miss, by damn!

Into this academic bastion of Magnolia aristocracy, symbolized by the Lyceum with its white columns, came a black man who was enrolled after a night of rioting on the Ole Miss campus. Federal marshals had accompanied James Meredith to Ole Miss because Ross Barnett, Mississippi's governor, had vowed to keep Meredith from entering the university. A riot ensued in which federal marshals, ringing the Lyceum, battled a mob composed of Ole Miss students and die-hard segregationists from Mississippi and neighboring states. In this riot two persons were killed, scores were wounded, and the Ole Miss campus was left looking like a battlefield—littered with burned-out cars, broken window glass, and green chips from hundreds of smashed Coca-Cola bottles. The mob—two of its members were also members of the congregation I pastored in Tylertown—had thrown at the federal marshals stones, pieces of pipe, bricks gathered from nearby construction sites, and gasoline bombs made from Coca-Cola bottles. And the mob had attempted to dislodge the marshals with a bulldozer and with water hoses.

Yet federal power prevailed. Federal troops were ordered to Oxford by President Kennedy, and they were some of the toughest soldiers our national government had—soldiers from the 82d and the 101st Airborne Divisions. They were sent to Ole Miss from military bases at Fort Bragg, North Carolina, and Fort Benning, Georgia. Eventually twenty thousand federal troops poured into Oxford, more than the combined population of town and university. There was an overwhelming display of raw military power, more intimidating than all the sheriffs of Mississippi combined.

What was the world coming to? Black soldiers from Fort Benning with rifles and bayonets, marching down the Main Street of Oxford, the home town of William Faulkner! All for the purpose of getting a black man admitted to Ole Miss!

What happened in Oxford and on the Ole Miss campus was a reversal of reversals! A one-hundred-and-eighty-degree change in direction! We white Mississippians didn't know what to think or what to say. For here the fist of force was being used *for the nigger, not against the nigger*. We white Southerners were accustomed to the state's power being used *against* blacks. Police prohibited Negroes from going into restaurants and public libraries. Sheriffs with Red Man chewing to-

bacco in their mouths made certain Negroes "stayed in their place."
Circuit clerks, like John Q., kept Negroes from voting. They became local heroes for doing so. And if a Negro got "uppity" the police took care of him. But now Mississippi whites would be "taken
care of" by the 82d and 101st Airborne Divisions because a Mississippi Negro refused to "stay in his place." The impregnable wall of
magnolia segregation was breached, breached while Ross Barnett was
our governor. Ross Barnett had promised that no black would go to
school with whites while old Ross was sitting in the governor's chair.

It all happened, we white Mississippians said, because of the antics of a dictator in Washington named John F. Kennedy who had a
prissy wife (who wore her hair funny) and who had a niggerloving
brother named Robert. And we said it all happened because blacks
had been stirred up by a nigger preacher over in Atlanta named Martin Luther King. And we said it all happened because the federal
marshals ringing the Lyceum on the Ole Miss campus were trigger-
happy. *We white Mississippians blamed everyone but ourselves.* We cursed
the federal government and the Kennedys and the news media and
through sick humor gave vent to our anger.

In the wake of the Ole Miss-James Meredith fiasco Mississippi's
struggle over integration intensified—like a witch's brew becoming
even more troubled. The Deep South was on a roller-coaster ride of
social revolt—a roller-coaster ride that I witnessed from the vantage
point of Tylertown, right in the middle of Southwest Mississippi's
Ku Klux Klan country.

Competing visions were in collision. We white Mississippians
were longing for the good old days of Vardaman and Bilbo. "Our
niggers are good niggers," we said. "They're quiet and humble. They
don't want to integrate. They're happy like they are. Why, you've
never lived until you've been a nigger on Saturday night—getting
drunk and screwing every woman you want to. If only President
Kennedy and his prissy wife and his niggerloving brother would let
things alone then the dust would settle and everyone could be happy
again."

But the blacks had another vision. They no longer wanted to be
"quiet and humble." They wanted a larger slice of the pie. They
wanted to be treated with courtesy and respect. This desire we white
Mississippians found difficult to understand because we'd never

looked at blacks as *persons*, as people with *feelings*. We'd looked at blacks as fragments of persons. We'd called them *hands*—hands for picking cotton and sawing pulpwood. And because blacks wanted to be persons—not hands—they didn't stop. They conducted freedom rides and boycotts. There were sit-ins and demonstrations and marches and speeches and voter registration drives. In these activities blacks were joined by priests from Pennsylvania and nuns from New Jersey and clergymen from Chicago and rabbis from Rochester. And the frustration and anger of white Southerners grew white hot. This frustration and anger led to the burning of Ku Klux Klan crosses all over Southwest Mississippi. One Ku Klux Klan cross was burned at night on the lawn of the Tylertown Baptist Church, a stone's throw from the parsonage in which my wife and I were living. And "nigger churches" were dynamited and fired. McComb, right down the highway from Tylertown, became known as "the dynamite capital of the world"

Coiled around Mississippi like a water moccasin was a monster. During the day it hid in the Tallahatchie, Yazoo, Tombigbee, Chickasawhay, and Pearl River swamps. At nightfall the beast crawled out of the slime and did its evil work. Vernon Dahmer was burned alive, and Medgar Evers was riddled by bullets while standing in the carport of his home. In Jackson the rabbi's house and Temple Beth Israel's sanctuary were dynamited. The monster's work reached its climax in Mississippi's orgasm of hatred when President Kennedy was assassinated in Dallas and when Michael Schwerner, James Chaney, and Andrew Goodman, three civil rights workers, were murdered near Philadelphia and were buried beneath eighteen feet of Neshoba County clay. The community emotions surrounding these murders have been vividly described by Florence Mars, a Mississippi author from Neshoba County, in her book *Witness in Philadelphia*. When Schwerner, Chaney, and Goodman were murdered in Neshoba County, a member of the Tylertown Baptist Church remarked to me, "Preacher, those three little bastards got exactly what they deserved."

Some Mississippians rejoiced over Kennedy's assassination, particularly after it became clear that Kennedy had been shot not by a Southerner but by a "communist" named Lee Harvey Oswald. When the news of Kennedy's death was announced over the public address system in the Tylertown public schools some students clapped their hands and shouted their approval.

My father first heard about President Kennedy's assassination while stopped for a traffic light at the intersection of Robinson Road and Rose Street in Jackson. An unknown white man pulled up in a car beside my Father and yelled, "Have you heard? They've shot the son-of-a-bitch in Dallas!" At the moment of Kennedy's assassination my mother was at work in the office of Stribling Brothers Machinery Company in West Jackson. One of her coworkers, hearing of Kennedy's death, remarked, "The only regret I have is that I didn't pull the trigger."

20

The Tragedy of the South

ALMOST TWO DECADES HAVE PASSED since John F. Kennedy's assassination—two decades during which Mississippi and the rest of the Deep South have gone through a Second Reconstruction. Jim Crow has disappeared across Dixie and the blatant, public racism of Vardaman and Bilbo has largely evaporated. The "impregnable walls of segregation" that Ross Barnett and Jim Eastland talked about were not, so it turned out, impregnable at all. Rather those walls were like the "one-hoss shay" of Oliver Wendell Holmes fame. Oliver Wendell Holmes wrote a poem about a deacon's shay (a buggy) that was magnificently constructed; yet it collapsed in a heap one day—dumping a venerable descendant of the deacon to the ground. That's what happened to the "magnificently constructed" walls of Mississippi segregation. Like the deacon's shay they collapsed, with the ironic result that today Mississippi is the most racially integrated state in the Union. Mississippi now has the highest number of elected black officials of any state. Negroes patronize motels, restaurants, and libraries. The public schools have integrated and blacks compose the backbone of the Ole Miss football team. The only institutions left segregated are churches, funeral homes, country clubs, and chapters of the Daughters of the Confederacy.

From the vantage point of where we are today we can see that when we white Mississippians rioted on the Ole Miss campus and when we buried Schwerner, Chaney, and Goodman in an earthen dam and when we poured catsup on blacks "sitting in" at lunch counters at Woolworth's we were going through the death throes of the South as it had been socially structured since the Civil War and Reconstruction. This Jim Crow South died like John Q. the "nigger knocker" died. For while I was pastoring the Tylertown Baptist Church I conducted John Q.'s funeral.

Old John Q.'s life ended in tragedy. Courthouse politics in Walthall County is like tabasco sauce—it's red hot. Emotions run deep. John Q. and a man whom I'll call Charlie Ray, another member of my congregation, ended up on opposite sides of the political fence. Feelings between John Q. and Charlie Ray, operator of a local restaurant, became raw. Both men were running for political office. One morning Mr. Ray was driving his truck down Beulah Avenue in Tylertown and saw John Q. standing on the street corner by the Tylertown Drug Store. Mr. Ray (so it was reported) stopped his pickup truck in the middle of the street, got out and walked over to where John Q. was standing, and with his fist let John Q. have an uppercut to the jaw. He turned loose with a real haymaker. John Q. dropped to the sidewalk, blood gushing from his mouth. They carried John Q. to Dr. Pittman's clinic where they discovered his jaw was broken. So they put John Q. in an ambulance and carried him to a hospital in New Orleans where surgeons wired his jaws together. They wired them in such a way that John Q. couldn't talk. Nor could he chew. He had to blend his food in a mixer and sip it through a straw.

People in Tylertown felt sorry for John Q. They stood on the street corner by the bank and said, "Charlie Ray shouldn't have hit John Q. like he did. He should have known John Q.'s bones were old and brittle."

Several months later John Q. died of a heart attack and I conducted his funeral. More people came to John Q.'s funeral than to any other I witnessed while living in Tylertown. Every seat in the sanctuary of the Tylertown Baptist Church was occupied and people were standing outside because they were unable to get inside the sanctuary. Scores of red-faced farmers and farmer's wives from all over Walthall County were present—all having come to pay their final respects to the man who over the years helped them fill in their tax returns and gain their veteran's and Social Security benefits. John Q., the man one went to see if one had a problem with the government, now lay dead and stretched out in a casket with his broken jaw, leaving a widow but no children. No heirs. *None to come after him.*

John Q.'s death was symbolic of what was happening in the Deep South. For just as John Q. died with no one to carry on his name, similarly the blatantly racist South was dying with none to carry on the blatantly racist tradition.

From where we now are it is tempting to look back on those Deep South events of two decades ago and to be moralistic. "The rednecks and the Ku Kluxers were wrong!" we may say. "All of them were big-ots—constituting a moral stain on the fabric of society. The black civil rights workers and the priests from Pennsylvania and the nuns from New Jersey who marched from Selma to Montgomery were right."

Yet I wonder. For in my mind the rural South's race issue has al-ways been a *moral puzzle*, an ethical dilemma immersed in ambigui-ties. The rural South's race question is an elliptical tragedy—a tragedy with two foci. One of those foci is *the rural and small-town Negro*. The rural Negro is a forgotten person in contemporary American society. Subsisting in rural and small-town slums in Mississippi and Alabama and South Carolina, he is a twentieth-century relic from eighteenth- and nineteenth-century slavery.

I experienced cultural shock when I, with my expanded hori-zons, moved back to Mississippi after having lived eight years out of state in Louisville. I'd forgotten about the blacks I'd known in my youth. I'd forgotten about blacks like Aunt Mandy (to whom I once carried "peanut-cracker" sandwiches) and Booker T. (with whom I played at Gulde) and Hip Pocket (who worked for Mr. Tom). Yet when I moved to Tylertown I discovered the Aunt Mandys and the Booker T.'s and the Hip Pockets are still around. When I walked down Tylertown's Beulah Avenue on Saturdays or walked through the black waiting room of Crawford's or Pittman's Clinic I felt, in my racial naiveté, that I was in the interior of Africa. In my youth I had looked at rural Negroes but I had not "seen" them. On returning to Mississippi I for the first time "saw" them and perceived who they were.

Moreover, while walking down Tylertown's back streets and driving over Walthall county's dirt roads, I found myself again and again mulling over what I had been taught concerning the race ques-tion as a seminarian in Louisville. My professors at Southern Semi-nary had viewed the race issue not as a tragedy but as an ethical matter. Knowing the answers, they propounded moral absolutes and theoretical solutions. They said, "Segregation is wrong! Integration is right!" But I, now a working pastor in a two-traffic-light town, perceived that the South's racial puzzle is not exclusively an ethical issue. Rather the puzzle is multidimensional, and one of those dimensions is an *economic dimension*.

The blacks I saw in Tylertown were not the kind of blacks I had seen in pages of *Ebony* or walking across the campus of Harvard or dining in restaurants in Washington. The blacks I encountered in Walthall County were the flotsam and jetsam left over from slavery and the sharecropper system. Living in tarpaper shacks, they have been displaced by mechanized agriculture and made obsolete by scientific farming. For cotton and corn can no longer be profitably raised in the hill country. Thus the land has been fenced for beef cattle and for dairy herds and for tree farms and for soybean fields. Consequently the rural Negro has *no real place* in Southern society. He has *no viable role to fulfill*. In Tylertown all the jobs on Beulah Avenue have already been taken by whites. Whites own the Beulah Avenue businesses and rural blacks are closed out of the business community. To own a business you must have capital and understand leases and have "contacts" and be able to grapple with tax laws and inventory control. And for blacks there is no land, for the land is owned already by white people—by the Stogners and the Conerlys and the Harveys and the McDonalds. Their land holdings are described in legal detail on warranty deeds recorded in the chancery clerk's office at the courthouse, and because they are warranty deeds the title is guaranteed—secure and unassailable—and protected by the power of the state so that white land owners can post on their property intimidating signs that proclaim "Keep Out" and "Posted" and "Private Property."

All this is too bad for rural blacks, imprisoned in ignorance, who sit on the front porches of shantytown hovels and rock and whittle and get by on food stamps and welfare and take care of the children. When they do find a chance to work, it is as if they were still enslaved. Many aggressive, strong-bodied blacks have moved away to Detroit, Chicago, and New York where there are jobs in factories and jobs driving trucks and jobs working on construction crews— jobs where one receives a pay check every Friday. But living up North costs money and the weather is cold and the streets are perceived to be hostile. Often the children are sent back to Mississippi to be reared by grandmas (while their mamas and papas are far away).

We white Southerners refuse to confront or even to acknowledge the economic plight of rural blacks. This refusal is cruel because people not only have civil rights; they also have economic rights—a right to a fair slice of the pie. Should not any society be judged by the way it treats its most unfortunate members? Karl Marx was wrong about many issues, but he was right when he argued that the economic dimension of life is basic. A tragedy of tragedies is that our society has not found a way to offer Southern rural blacks economic opportunity. Perhaps the reason we refuse to confront this issue is because the issue of unemployed and unemployable rural blacks cannot be "solved" within the narrow framework of a doctrinaire capitalistic system, a system that naively posits that for every problem there is a "private enterprise" solution.

Not only did I perceive an economic dimension to the South's racial puzzle, but I also perceived a *social dimension* having to do with conduct, values, mores. Treated across the years with condescension, exploited economically, rural blacks are a damaged people. A question haunting guilt-laden white Southerners is, what has racism and segregation done to the black man's soul? To his psyche? For the black man's psyche is an interior world unknown to whites. We gain fleeting glimpses of that world in the writings of the Richard Wrights and the James Baldwins. These glimpses reveal an interior landscape littered with feelings of anger, rejection, futility. This miasma of hopelessness has produced a black life-style with characteristics puzzling to middle-class whites. One feature is shirking of family roles, a shirking that is disastrous because the family is society's basic unit. Many black men marry, father children, and then disappear, leaving behind single-parent families to be supported on welfare. A saying about black fathers is, "They won't stay hitched." Within the black community giving birth out of wedlock seems not to be viewed with disapproval (between fifty and sixty percent of black babies born in Mississippi are born to unmarried mothers). Is this promiscuity? Is it a "nonwestern" practice embedded in an Afro-American subculture? Or is it, as some observers have suggested, a longing of young black women for the sense of identity, the love, and the rewards of motherhood, and a similar desire of young males for a sense of "manhood" without a corresponding sense of responsibility? Shut out of the dominant culture by economic and social barriers, these young people turn to one another. Tragically, their need for one another is not matched by their ability to provide for one another.

Again many blacks seem oriented completely to the present. Having no sense of a viable future, they quest for momentary pleasure. Insensitive white Southerners, mistaking this behavior as a form of frivolity rather than despair, say, "You've never lived until you've been a *nigger* on Saturday night, drinkin' moonshine and enjoyin' black bottom pie!"

Whatever the explanation, I—living inside the cream pitcher—thought I perceived a lifestyle difference, a behavior gap, separating rural blacks from whites. "Nice people" do not talk about this gap. To do so would be evidence of "prejudice." But the gap—a matter of class and deprivation rather than race—is there, and I came to see that segregation (now "gone with the wind" and never to return) was in part a societal arrangement by which whites attempted to isolate themselves from black behavior patterns that they regarded as distasteful. I wrote an article for the *Saturday Evening Post* in which I attempted to express this sociological insight. I entitled the article "Why Rural Mississippi Fears Integration." This article I should not have written. The editors of the *Saturday Evening Post* gave it another title, "Integration Could Destroy Rural Mississippi." On the magazine's cover they emblazoned the words, "A Mississippi Minister Defends Segregation." Thus I came across not as an observer trying to explain *why* segregation existed but as a racist *defending* segregation.

For weeks following the article's publication the telephone rang around the clock. I received calls from people in Vermont and from people in California. By phone I heard from seminary classmates. The pastor of an all-white Baptist congregation in Louisville (our country's whiskey, tobacco, and horse-betting capital) gave me a tongue lashing, informing me I had no moral sensitivity. Pastors of small-town congregations in Alabama and Georgia phoned and told me they understood. Through the mail I received about three thousand letters. Tylertown's postmaster said, "Damn, preacher, I've had to hire an extra man just to handle your mail." Some letters were empathetic; others assured me I was a bigot.

From this episode I learned a lesson: never trust an editor. The episode also confirmed the Mississippi proverb, "You can't handle manure without getting some of it on you."

But if impoverished blacks compose one focal point of the South's racial morass, then Southern rednecks compose the other. For just as there are blacks with no secure role in society there are also whites without secure roles either. Their grandfathers were conned on the race issue by James K. Vardaman. Their fathers were conned by Theodore G. Bilbo. And they were conned by the Jim Eastlands and Ross Barnetts and by members of the state legislature who carved out political careers by yelling *nigger, nigger, nigger* and who told the rednecks that segregation could be maintained "yesterday, today, tomorrow, and until the end of time."

The rednecks listened to the politicians. They laughed when the politicians said NAACP stood for "niggers, apes, alligators, coons, and possums." The rednecks took Governor Ross Barnett seriously when he talked about "interposition." *Interposition:* that's a fancy word. We white Mississippians, not knowing that interposition had died with John C. Calhoun, didn't exactly know what interposition meant, but it sounded good. Old Ross said he was going to interpose the power of the sovereign state of Mississippi into the integration-segregation issue, thereby making it possible for Mississippi to run its internal affairs without interference from the "liberals" in Washington. Old Ross even promised he'd go to jail before he'd let Mississippi's walls of segregation come down.

During the 1960s we white Mississippians had a leader in Ross Barnett! A real leader! Not one of those bleeding-heart, pussy-cat liberals like Hubert Humphrey or George McGovern. But old Ross! The most successful damage suit lawyer in Mississippi! The plowboy from Standing Pine in Leake County who was the youngest of ten children. We white Mississippians could identify with Old Ross. Everyone knew Ross Barnett had pulled himself up by his own bootstraps. While a youngster he'd carried his lunch—consisting of a sweet potato and fried bacon—to school every day in a lard bucket. He'd paid his way through Mississippi College, the same college I attended, by milking cows and by cutting hair in the basement of the science hall. He'd worked his way through the Ole Miss law school selling insurance. And he'd gone to Jackson and become Mississippi's richest damage suit attorney.

Behind his back Old Ross was called "an ambulance chaser." Folks said that in a courtroom he was "slicker than a greased pig." If you or a relative were hurt in an automobile accident, what did you do? You went to see Ross Barnett and he'd sue the insurance companies and make them pay through the nose. When Eulon, my first cousin, was killed in a head-on collision near Yazoo City, my daddy and Uncle Chester and Aunt Minnie went to see Ross Barnett. A little fellow at the time, I tagged along. To this day I remember sitting with Daddy and Aunt Minnie and Uncle Chester in Mr. Barnett's office, located in downtown Jackson over a shoe store on Capital Street. I was fascinated by Ross Barnett, who was sitting behind a desk the size of a ping-pong table, drinking buttermilk out of a milk bottle. I listened as Aunt Minnie told Mr. Barnett about Eulon's accident— about how Eulon was topping a hill near Yazoo City and right when he got to the top of the hill a truck was coming in the opposite direction on the wrong side of the road and Eulon never had a chance. Ross Barnett sued on behalf of Aunt Minnie and Uncle Chester and got money for them that they used to buy land near Greenville— land that they sold years later to be the site of a shopping center. Over the years Ross Barnett built a reputation across Mississippi of being the friend of "little people" like Aunt Minnie and Uncle Chester.

So when Ross Barnett ran for governor he had contacts all the way from the Tennessee line to the Gulf Coast. He ran for governor on the slogan, "Roll with Ross! He's his own boss!" And we white Mississippians rolled with Ross. We elected him our governor (several of his colonels were members of the Tylertown Baptist Church; Dr. Jewell Pittman, chairman of the Board of Deacons, was one of Governor Barnett's appointees to the Mississippi Agricultural and Industrial Board). On Saturday night, 29 September 1962, we Mississippians rolled forty thousand strong into the Mississippi Memorial Football Stadium in Jackson to watch Johnny Vaught's Ole Miss football team play the University of Kentucky. *Right when the Ole Miss desegregation controversy was white hot.* Everyone in the stadium that night knew Old Ross was at that very moment locked in combat with President Kennedy, the "nigger lover" in Washington who was insisting a black man from Kosciusko named James Meredith be admitted to Ole Miss, our all-white, silk-stocking state university. At half-time Governor Barnett, in the white glare of spotlights, spoke over the public address system to those forty thousand Mississippians. He shouted over the public address system, "I love MisZIPpi! I love her people! Her customs! And I love and respect her heritage!" And the crowd went wild! Screaming, crying, shouting, whooping rebel yells and waving Confederate flags while the Ole Miss band played "Dixie"! This stadium episode lives in my memory as an eruption of primordial tribal emotion with the ghost of Jefferson Davis dancing with glee on the fifty-yard line!

While all this was happening folk in other parts of the country sneered. They looked at Ross Barnett and said, "He's a buffoon." They looked at Mississippians yelling and rioting and burning Ku Klux Klan crosses, and they said of them, "They're bigots! They're prejudiced ignoramuses!" In their moral outrage they failed to perceive that rednecks (and other Mississippians with redneck mentalities) are—like rural blacks—walking tragedies also.

Mississippi rednecks are citizens of the poorest state in the union. Like rural negroes, they have no viable place in American society. They squeeze a living out of the soil and hang on by the skin of their teeth at jobs in needle factories and in chicken-processing plants. As Sam Hill, the historian of Southern religion, has written, "The essence of being a Southerner is to experience a poverty of options."

With less than high school educations, Mississippi rednecks had been pumped for generations on neo-Confederate rhetoric by politicians who exploited the race issue for political gain. Mississippi rednecks had lived all their lives cheek-by-jowl with "cornfield niggers" and they had sense enough to know that they were the ones who would "bear the brunt" of integration if and when it came. For integration would never touch the families of delta planters living on plantations out from Greenwood and Greenville. Nor would integration touch privileged families living in North Jackson. Delta planters and Jackson's aristocracy would send their children to private schools. Nor would integration with "cornfield niggers" come upon the families of Chicago clergymen and Boston rabbis who came South to participate in civil rights demonstrations and to return home as moral "heroes." Mississippi rednecks knew that they were the ones who would *pay the freight for other people's idealism.* To them that some-how didn't seem fair, but nobody else gave a damn about how the rednecks felt or what they thought.

21

Southern Serendipity

ALMOST TWENTY YEARS have gone by; we Mississippians look around us and everywhere there is change. Jim Crow is dead. Mississippi is now this country's most integrated state. Out of civic duty, or necessity, white Southerners finally integrated most public institutions—except the churches—deliberately choosing to obey "the law of the land." Today blacks attend integrated schools, ride at the front of the bus, and patronize the local Holiday Inn. Students from Jackson State, Mississippi's "predominantly black" university come to Hattiesburg and in concert with the University of Southern Mississippi symphony sing the "Ode to Joy" from the last movement of Beethoven's Ninth Symphony and no one thinks a thing about it. A quarter of a century ago blacks on campus would have provoked a riot.

The mad dogs have been muzzled. No longer do politicians yell *nigger, nigger, nigger* and no longer do decent white people cringe before the magnolia Gestapo—the Citizens' Councils. Thus one encounters a Southern serendipity: the Negro's liberation from raw racism has delivered Southern whites from raw racism also. Mississippi's race problem hasn't been "solved," but it has been fundamentally modified—and that's one hell of an accomplishment.

I couldn't foresee this Southern serendipity back in the 1960s when "the woods were on fire" in Walthall County. Then the mad dogs were loose, Ku Klux Klan crosses were burning, and politicians were yelling *nigger, nigger, nigger*. The segregationists in my congregation, with anger in their eyes, time and again backed me into a corner and asked, "Preacher, what do you think about what the niggers are doing?" The high profile in the civil rights movement of Northern clergymen, those twenty-four hour prophets from New Jersey and New York who flew down south on Delta Airlines with martinis in their hands and roundtrip tickets in their pockets, kept those of us who were Southern clergymen on the hot seat. They made our lives impossible. Despondency over the race issue was one of the factors that drove Bob Odenwald, my college and seminary classmate and pastor of the Baptist congregation in Mendenhall, another Mississippi county seat, to suicide. Mississippi clergymen during the 1960s lived exposed every day to the blowtorch anger of steely-eyed segregationists. They lived every day with the grotesque insight that Mississippi, the buckle on the Bible belt and bastion of the "Old Time Religion," was the locus of a monstrous evil, the dehumanizing-through-racism of the Negro. And they lived cheek-by-jowl with parishioners who repeatedly asked, "Preacher, what are we going to do if blacks try to join our church?" For church members, socialized all their lives into a segregated society, this was an excruciatingly painful question. The Christian religion claims to be for everyone. In view of this claim, how could church participation be denied to anyone because of skin color? During the 1960s this was no longer an academic question. For week after week newspapers in Alabama and Mississippi carried front-page accounts of blacks attempting to join or to attend worship services of white congregations. Some congregations stationed deacons outside church buildings to turn blacks away. Thus a volatile issue had emerged that I could not evade: What will be the policy of the Tylertown Baptist Church if blacks attempt to join?

I will carry to my grave a memory of the Sunday night in 1965 when the Tylertown Baptist Church held a churchwide business meeting to deal with this issue. The meeting was announced two weeks in advance. On the night of the business meeting the sanctuary was packed. Visitors came to witness the debate. As I stood in the pulpit and surveyed the crowded auditorium, a bizarre insight hit me. *Everyone was in attendance except the congregation's "liberals,"* members who in private had expressed to me disapproval of segregation. *When the showdown came on the race issue at the Tylertown Baptist Church, the "liberals" tucked their tails between their legs and ran for cover!* I opened the meeting with a brief statement of my views. I told the church that I could not in good conscience deny any person, regardless of skin color, the right to attend the Tylertown Baptist Church. I then opened the floor for discussion, and a torrent of views poured forth. Some expressed *this* view. Some expressed *that* view. A visitor joined the fray by standing up and asserting, "If you folks vote tonight to let niggers come to this church, I want you to know I'll never join!"

Finally, after an hour's debate, the vote was taken. A majority of the good folks of the Tylertown Baptist Church, located in the middle of Ku Klux Klan country, voted to adopt an open-door policy toward Negroes. This open-door decision brought down upon my head a firestorm of criticism, particularly from people who were not members of my congregation. The morning after the business meeting I encountered on Beulah Avenue a member of Tylertown's Methodist church. He stopped me and told me he had heard about our open-door decision. He then said, "You know, Dr. Sullivan, that proves what I've suspected all along. You're a pea-brained, nigger-lovin' Baptist preacher."

Take the race issue as I encountered it in the cream pitcher, combine it with the suffering, the halo, and the pissing-on-a-turtle problems, then add financial insecurity, exposure to carping complaints of some people—"My grandmother was in the hospital for a week, and Dr. Sullivan didn't visit her but three times"—and an absence of any sense of belonging. All these issues collectively ground me down, giving me a feeling of fatigue. Together they constituted my coherence problem, the dilemma of making sense out of being a Baptist preacher in a two-traffic-light town and the puzzle of trying to function as a Southern clergyman with a sense of inner peace, wholeness, and integrity. I had not foreseen any of these issues when, as a naive high school student, I bowed my head one morning in the Heidelberg kitchen and offered myself to God to be a preacher. I made the commitment to be a preacher with an unquestioning, romantic trust in the Southern church; I did not then perceive the entanglement of Southern religion with Southern culture and politics. Encounters with evil and tragedy were not a part of my decision. I became a preacher expecting to be "successful," but instead of success I found bafflement. While in my mid-thirties, I lost in the muck a sense of the grandeur of preaching. Having burned out on the inside, I cringed at the thought of spending the next forty years with windy words and a sense of futility. When the opportunity came along to become a member of the faculty of a state university, I grabbed it. It was a ladder on which to climb out of the cream pitcher, and it was a way of trying to retrieve my sanity.

Other members of the Southern clergy have also encountered coherence problems in the pastorate and, after years of grappling with those problems, have experienced clerical burnouts. Before burning out we repeatedly attempted as preachers "to solve" our coherence puzzles. Yet these attempts were undermined by the pygmy understanding of the church that dominates the rural South. Baptists and other "conservative" denominations across Dixie think of the church primarily as a "local" institution. Churches are like tubs; each one sits on its own bottom. From my youth in Mississippi I have vivid memories of hearing Baptist ministers explain how a church is a "democratically-controlled, autonomous" organism. They eisegetically supported this view by appealing to the New Testament. They reasoned, "Paul in his letters always wrote to 'the church in Rome' or to 'the church in Corinth' or to 'the church in Thessalonica.'" My point is that across the years Southern clergymen have unreflectively advocated an ecclesiastical polity that they like to believe "goes back to the New Testament" and that they label "the autonomy of the local church." This theoretical position has the practical result of every Baptist congregation owning its own property, controlling its own finances, calling its own pastor, and regulating its own affairs. This "local" understanding explains why people say, "No one under the shining sun can tell a Baptist church what to do."

Candor compels the admission, however, that this tendency toward localism in Southern Protestantism does not go back to "the banks of the Jordan River." I do not believe that localism was a part of original Christian practice and belief. Indeed, to posit the existence two thousand years ago of a devotion in the Roman-Mediterranean world to "local" direct democracy would be an ideological anachronism. Instead, Baptists and other conservative denominations have unknowingly borrowed their "local church" conception from New England congregationalism. Even a casual reading of colonial documents like the Cambridge Platform of 1648 makes this obvious. This "local" understanding of the church, coming as it does out of the hills and valleys of prerevolutionary New England, reflects the frontierization of the church in American religious experience, an apotheosis of individualism.

This "local" understanding of the church differs significantly from the view of the church encountered in Roman Catholicism, in Greek Orthodoxy, and in mainstream Protestantism. These churches are connectional. They adhere to the Apostles' Creed with its assertion of a universal church. With wisdom gained from centuries of struggling with a flawed world, connectional churches perceive the value of organization. Acting collectively, they have refined their beliefs and procedures. Possessing a system of church officials, they believe in infrastructures that provide guidance and fellowship for clergymen. In other words, ministers within a connectional church have access to a support system. A clergyman can always go and "tell your troubles" to the bishop or to some other ecclesiastical superior.

By contrast, Baptist clergymen in the Deep South live and move and have their being within a nonconnectional system. Baptist churches, from an organizational standpoint, resemble a massive pile of golf balls—each one self-contained and independent. This each-tub-sits-on-its-own-bottom system transforms Baptist preachers into ordained Lone Rangers. They are caught up in a system wherein it is every minister for himself! They must either sink or swim, for there are no lifeboats!

This system works felicitously for young, charismatic clergymen with John Wayne profiles. Becoming the pastor of an autonomous church, located preferably in one of the expanding suburbias of the sunbelt, provides a wholesome outlet for a minister's aggressiveness and ambition. The sky is the limit! Some charismatic Baptist preachers pastor the same congregations for years, at times transforming those congregations into de facto personality cults. Under their leadership magnificent church buildings are erected, and impressive church programs of instruction and ministry are carried out.

But this every-minister-for-himself system does not work felicitously for "noncharismatic," "average," "ordinary" ministers. Within them it frequently produces feelings of vocational isolation and loneliness. Show me an "ordinary" pastor of a Baptist church in a two-traffic-light town in Dixie, and I will show you a person who is, nine times out of ten, professionally *lonely*.

Indeed, one of my strongest recollections from years spent in Tylertown as the preacher is a memory of vocational isolation. No reason or occasion existed for a close relationship with other Baptist preachers. I was in my Tylertown and cream pitcher orbit; they were in their orbits. Like ships passing at sea, we from time to time acknowledged each other's presence, but no sharing of hearts and souls took place. Once a year, along with thousands of other preachers, I attended the Southern Baptist Convention. These vast gatherings, with their pomp and pageantry, were held in cities like Miami and Detroit. To these massive conventions I went with an aching heart, increasingly concerned about the coherence puzzle with which I grappled day by day as a small town preacher in Southwest Mississippi. Sitting in convention crowds on the forty-second row of Miami's Orange Bowl or sitting toward the rear of Detroit's Cobo Hall while listening to "let's-go-get-'em" sermons delivered by denominational celebrities did not meet my inner needs. At Southern Baptist Conventions I always felt like a lost grain of sand on an endless shore.

This ministerial loneliness is ignored by the denomination's image polishers, who merrily portray the Baptist clergy as Billy Grahams and W. A. Criswells. What they fail to perceive is that for every Billy Graham and W. A. Criswell there are scores of "average" or "insignificant" preachers who fall through the cracks of a system wherein they are ordained and forgotten.

Ironically, Baptist preachers themselves are primarily responsible for implanting across Dixie this "local" view of the church that has resulted in their ministerial isolation. By energetically propagating a theory of autonomous churches Baptist ministers reveal that they have never read Plato's *Republic* with its blistering analysis of a direct democracy. By energetically propagating a theory of autonomous churches they display their devotion to the Haman Fallacy—the fallacy of erecting a gallows for one's own execution. And this is precisely what Baptist preachers across the South have done: they have sawed the wood, driven the nails, and erected the platform for the gallows on which they from time to time are unceremoniously hung. For the Baptist clergy is not always peaches and cream. The clergy has its "perilous" moments. Every year scores of Baptist preachers are "fired" or "dismissed" from their pulpits. Others "wear out their welcome" with a congregation or have misunderstandings or become disheartened. Or they find themselves entrapped in what I have described as a "coherence problem." In these trying and unhappy experiences ministers need professional guidance. They need assistance in moving from one pastorate to another. Yet this needed assistance cannot be provided by a helter-skelter system of rigidly autonomous churches in which there are no authoritative and supportive ecclesiastical officials. Such assistance would offend that sacred cow named "the autonomy of the local church." Thus in "perilous" situations some Baptist ministers hang on by the skin of their teeth (for they can think of nothing else to do) or stew in frustration. This stewing process can last for years. Others, unwilling to stew or unable to maneuver successfully through "perilous" moments, leave the ministry, fade away into the night, or become insurance salesmen.

This exaggerated "autonomy of the local church" polity is also the gallows on which a prophetic Southern clergy has been executed. Such is the case because many "local" churches over the Southland are acculturated churches. They embody the prejudices and values of the society that surrounds them. They are controlled lock, stock, and barrel by their members. As one Baptist layman remarked to me about the church, "We own it, so we run it." Understandably, pastors of such "autonomous" churches pander to the opinions and views of church members upon whom they are dependent for their livelihoods and professional well-being. This dependency explains why few "ordinary" Southern clergymen are spokesmen for social justice. This dependency also confirms the observation of Socrates, "Any person who would fight for justice must do so as a private citizen."

Baptist clergymen, strangely enough, fail to perceive that in advocating an autonomous-local-church system they have shot themselves in the foot. Indeed, they resent any questioning of this system although it has transfigured many of them into cultural toadies and has made authentic ministerial collegiality an impossibility. This curious devotion to furnishing one's own gallows illustrates the truth in Dryden's satirical remark,

> Look round the habitable world: how few
> Know their own good, or knowing it, pursue.

To this day I remember Tylertown and Walthall County with love and respect. My fate was to live there when times were twisted, and in retrospect I perceive that we all suffered together.

PART IV

A Buck Private at Fort McCain

22

USM

THE STATE OF MISSISSIPPI supports three major universities. The oldest and most prestigious is the University of Mississippi in Oxford, known as "Ole Miss" and referred to by its alumni as "*the* University." It is the university with the state's medical school and law school out of which traditionally come Mississippi's governors, congressmen, and legislators. There is an air of refinement about Ole Miss. To walk across its campus in Oxford is to walk across a campus where every building exudes tradition.

The second major university is Mississippi State in Starkville, the university known for its schools of agriculture and engineering. With the bulldog as a mascot and the cow bell as its symbol, it is affectionately known as "the cow college."

The third is the University of Southern Mississippi, the only major institution of higher learning located in the Southern part of the state. This school is the Johnny-come-lately on Mississippi's educational scene. For years it was known as "teachers' college" and for a time it was called Mississippi Southern. In recent years it has been the University of Southern Mississippi, known by the acronym USM.

The University of Southern Mississippi is located in Hattiesburg, a town of about fifty thousand people situated in the middle of the Piney Woods, that Southeast quarter of Mississippi that until less than a century ago was a frontier covered with an awesome forest. In all directions—as far as the eye could see—was an uninterrupted stand of virgin hardwood and softwood untouched by an axe or a crosscut saw. This forest had been centuries in the making. To walk through this primeval forest, early settlers observed, was like walking through a cathedral.

Around the turn of the century a constellation of factors led to the cutting of this forest: the metropolitan centers up north (Chicago, New York, Boston) needed lumber; white pine, for generations the premier wood of Northern states, had become scarce and expensive; railroads (like the Illinois Central and the Gulf, Mobile, and Ohio) had been constructed, providing a means for shipping lumber out of the South. Southern landowners did not perceive the value of timber; to them trees were a nuisance, an obstacle to agriculture. So the timber was sold at a fraction of its value to lumber barons who constructed sawmills, erected dummy lines, and made fortunes overnight. By 1910 more than seventeen hundred sawmills were in operation in Mississippi. In less than three decades the virgin forest, where Indians once hunted and fished, was cut, and its lumber shipped to Northern cities and to Western Europe.

For a time people tried to cultivate the thin soil of the Piney Woods, but the sandy loam was not suitable for cultivation. Thus vast stretches of the Piney Woods became hilly wastelands of broom sage, rattlesnakes, scrub trees, and stumps. Indeed, when members of USM's class of 1932 had their fiftieth reunion and were asked about their strongest memory from their student days in Hattiesburg, they invariably answered: "The stumps—they were everywhere."

In the 1930s tree nurseries were established by the federal government, and a reforestation program was begun by the Civilian Conservation Corps. Gradually, a second-growth forest came to cover the Piney Woods, and industrial plants that used wood as a raw product were constructed—plants like the Masonite factory at Laurel and the paper mills at Moss Point and Monticello. In cultivated areas cotton fields disappeared, and the land was transformed into pastures for beef cattle and dairy herds.

Hattiesburg, where the University of Southern Mississippi is located, began a century ago as a railroad town. Across the years it grew into the largest city in the Piney Woods, serving as its medical and commercial center. To this town, site of the Hercules plant that extracts chemicals from tree stumps, I moved in 1966 as a newly hired professor on the faculty of USM.

The first decision I made on coming to Hattiesburg was to buy a home. The five years I had lived in an open-to-the-public-come-one-and-all parsonage had instilled within me an exaggerated craving for privacy. I wanted a place of my own, and through the J. W. McArthur Real Estate Company I bought a home in West Hattiesburg. During the first months I owned this home I sat for hours in the backyard, soaking up a feeling of privacy. I massaged in my mind the idea that this house and this plot of land on which it stands belong *to me*. No one can come on this property without my permission, and no one can run me off. I found myself enveloped with feelings of safety and security that I had not experienced for years.

While sitting in my backyard I tried to assimilate my Tylertown experiences—a task that was not possible for me to do at the time because I was too close to the trees to see the forest. At the time I felt drained—as though there was a plug at the bottom of my foot, and someone had pulled the plug out and allowed all my energies to drain away.

The University of Southern Mississippi hired me to be a member of its philosophy and religion department. Joining a state university faculty, I discovered, is like jumping into a pool of ice water. It is a jarring, awakening experience. State universities have a unique atmosphere, an atmosphere different from that of denominational colleges to which I had previously been exposed. In some church-related colleges you "play it safe" and you are cautious about what you say. By contrast, a state university is a marketplace for an unfettered exchange of ideas. "Anything goes, and everything sells!" Academicians in secular universities worship at the altar of intellectual honesty and—at times insensitive to the feelings of colleagues—say precisely what they think.

The chairman of the philosophy and religion department when I joined USM's faculty was Dr. John Nau, a man of wit with a keen mind who—as a youngster—came to this country from Germany by way of India, where his father was a Lutheran minister. Dr. Nau assigned me to teach courses in philosophy and in non-Christian religions. As a neophyte professor I plunged into preparing and teaching these courses. But I made a disconcerting discovery about myself: I perceived my ignorance of philosophy and religion. I sensed my intellectual provincialism. Across the years I had filled up a mental bucket with facts and ideas. In my arrogance I thought I knew a lot about religion. After all, I had a doctorate from Southern Baptist Theological Seminary—one of the premier theological institutions in the South. But the tidbits in my mental bucket were from a Protestant-Christian tradition exclusively. There I was in my mid-thirties, and all my life, I had lived inside a Southern Baptist cocoon. From a Southern Baptist family I had gone to a Southern Baptist college to a Southern Baptist seminary and to a Southern Baptist pastorate. All my days I had worn Southern Baptist blinders. *Southern Baptist*—that was all I knew.

I knew nothing about religions like Buddhism or Islam. Indeed, I had never taken non-Christian religions seriously. To my mind they were not worth taking seriously. Buddhists and Muslims were not persons to whom one listened with respect; rather, they were objects for conversion, people to be "delivered" out of "paganism."

Moreover, I knew nothing about philosophy. In the first departmental meeting I attended, I heard Dr. Nau and other members of the department talking about the "pre-Socratics" and the "British empiricists." The first time I heard these terms I did not have the foggiest notion what they meant. In the training I had received to be a preacher no emphasis had been placed on philosophy. Why be concerned with philosophy when the Bible contains all one needs to know on any subject?

Thus on the campus of the University of Southern Mississippi I experienced an intellectual awakening similar to the one I had experienced previously at Southern Seminary in Louisville. Whereas Southern Seminary aroused me from my Mississippi slumber, the University of Southern Mississippi aroused me from my Southern Baptist slumber, making me aware of fields of knowledge and areas of experience which previously I had not explored.

With the renewed enthusiasm and energy of my mid-thirties I gave myself to philosophy. I stayed up all hours of the night reading Plato, Pascal, Locke, and Hume. As a neophyte professor I gave myself to a study of religious experience other than religion as understood by Southern Baptists. For the first time in my life I began exploring non-Christian religions. I discovered the thought of scholars like Huston Smith, Gerardus van der Leeuw, Ninian Smart,

Winston King, Mircea Eliade, Harvey Cox, Peter Berger, Wilfred Cantwell Smith, Walpola Rahula, David J. Kalupahana, and D. T. Suzuki—none of whom I had encountered at Southern Seminary. I spent hours discussing religious beliefs and practices with foreign students who were members of USM's student body.

As the semesters went by I was forced to rearrange the furniture in my mind. The more I read, talked, and listened, the more I found it impossible to ignore reservoirs of sincerity and piety in non-Christian religions. Increasingly I found it difficult to deny alternative religious experiences. To this day I recall the impact made upon me when for the first time I studied in detail the life of Edgar Cayce, the famous psychic. Cayce's life was the springboard that caused me to consider seriously reincarnation, a belief held by thinkers as diverse as Plato, Emerson, and Goethe. Subsequently I have looked at reincarnation through the spectacles of writers like Ian Stevenson and Geddes MacGregor, and against my will, resisting every step of the way, I have come to see reincarnation's plausibility.

A watershed event in my personal pilgrimage was a sabbatical I spent at Temple University in Philadelphia, Pennsylvania. Temple, located on Broad Street in the middle of Philadelphia's black ghetto, has a religion department that concentrates on non-Christian religions. For a year I lived across the Delaware River in Moorestown, New Jersey, and commuted daily into Philadelphia, where on the campus of Temple I immersed myself in Judaism, Islam, and Buddhism. In seminars and in classes I had exposure to Sikhs from India, to Muslims from Indonesia, to Buddhists from Sri Lanka, and to Jews from the Philadelphia area who were studying for the rabbinate. In them was an obvious moral earnestness and depth of religious commitment. The Muslims, Sikhs, Jews, and Buddhists I encountered took their religion as seriously as Christians take their religion. As I came to know these "non-Christian" religionists I had no desire—nor did I see any need—to "convert" them to the Christian faith. To have broached such a possibility would have been insulting or embarrassing. Rather I wanted to listen and to learn from them for I intuited in them God's presence. In other words, on the campus of both Temple and USM I had a head-on collision with *religious pluralism,* perceiving that I live in a world in which numerous religions—with millions of devotees—exist side by side. Southern Baptists are not the only ones. Christians are not the only ones. There are numerous religious alternatives open to mankind.

Who knows, maybe we have reached one of those bends in the road as far as the human religious quest is concerned. For centuries the Christian faith, the religion of the West, has behaved like Little Jack Horner, staying off in a corner by itself. It has claimed to be the "only true" religion while endlessly polishing and repolishing its dogmatic gems. Yet the world is becoming a "global village," and in this global village the Christian religion can neither deny nor ignore religious pluralism. So maybe Peter Berger, rephrasing Tertullian, is right in suggesting that the pivotal religious question of our time is, " What is Jerusalem to Benaras?"

I think I would have been a better preacher in Tylertown if I had been aware of Eastern faiths and of alternative religious experiences. Maybe I would not have gotten so upset over the "fallen sparrow" problem. For the Christian faith provides no rationale for the savage injustices we see around us and for the differences in talents, opportunities, and circumstances that exist among people. But if religions like Buddhism are right in contending we live not one life but many lives, experiencing human existence from different angles, then life's injustices and vagaries might be endowed with meaning or purpose that otherwise is impossible.

23

The General

IF THERE IS TRUTH in Ralph Waldo Emerson's remark that "an institution is the lengthened shadow of one man," then USM during the late 1950s to the early 1970s was surely the shadow of its president, Dr. William D. McCain. Dr. McCain was born in 1907 in Bellfontaine, a hamlet in Webster County in North Central Mississippi. Like Ross Barnett, Mississippi's controversial governor, he was a person who had pulled himself up by his own bootstraps. But whereas Ross Barnett went into law and politics, William D. McCain went into education. Eventually he earned his Ph.D. in history from Duke University in Durham, North Carolina. This was no small accomplishment, for he earned this doctorate in 1935—right in the middle of the Great Depression. Dr. McCain, a man with blue-chip academic qualifications, quipped about his student days, "I figured if I was going to starve to death I might as well starve while working on a Ph.D."

Pussycats do not become university presidents, and Dr. McCain was no pussycat. He was a man of ability and drive and in 1955, while in his late forties, he was appointed by the state's college board to be president of "teachers' college." In Dr. McCain the college board got more than it bargained for. He hit the campus in Hattiesburg as a hammer hits a nail. He had a dream—a vision—for "teachers' college." That dream was to transform it into a major state university. He knew "teachers' college" was the only tax-supported college located in South Mississippi—the most populous area of the state where industries, like the shipyards and refineries at Pascagoula, were booming. Dr. McCain saw a potential and decided to realize it.

During his twenty-year presidency, millions of tax dollars went into new building construction on the Hattiesburg campus, and the student body grew from three thousand students to more than ten thousand.

When I landed a job on USM's faculty my father and father-in-law were delighted. Both knew Dr. McCain from his earlier days in Jackson where for more than a decade he had been director of Mississippi's Department of Archives and History. I recall my father saying, "Son, I'm glad you're going to Hattiesburg where McCain is. He's a first-class man." I too was glad I was going to Hattiesburg, and I moved there with the idea of giving everything I had to the university that had hired me.

Lee Iacocca, former president of the Ford Motor Company, now president of Chrysler, once remarked, "When joining a large organization, stay quiet for the first three years." Those are wise words. For large organizations have personalities of their own, and things are not always what they seem. There are power cliques and recognized "ways of operating." In a large organization time is required to master the territory and to learn where the buttons and trapdoors are.

When I joined USM's faculty I followed Iacocca's advice. I maintained a low profile, kept my mouth closed and my eyes opened. I lost myself in a study of non-Christian religions and philosophy, and I gave myself to lecture preparation. To me USM was a charming, beautiful place with its lily pond crossed by a kissing bridge, with azalea bushes and rose gardens, with magnificent water oaks, golf courses, and ivied buildings. USM was a school, some said, that would soon surpass in reputation the "cow college" in Starkville and "the University" in Oxford.

Yet as the months passed I discovered unanticipated insights into USM. The salient insight that emerged was that many students and many faculty members did not care for Dr. McCain, the university's president. Behind his back they referred to him as "the old man." They called him "Generalissimo McCain" and "Dictator McCain."

For Dr. McCain, a bald-headed gentleman who usually wore a hat and always drove Chryslers, was a curious, complex man—a walking enigma. He had, for example, an exaggerated pride in his Scottish background. Dr. McCain went out of his way to make certain everyone knew about his Scottish ancestry, a matter that interested no one but him. He spent years compiling a multivolumed genealogical study tracing his family's Scottish ancestry. This genealogical study, shelved in USM's library, he aristocratically entitled "The McCain Chronicles."

One of USM's more impressive structures, housing the major auditorium on campus, is the Fine Arts Building. During its construction there was embedded in the building's brick-walled lobby a black rock from the area of Scotland where Dr. McCain's family originated. This prominently displayed rock has above it a rose-colored marble inscription that reads: STONE FROM MIGARY CASTLE KILCHOAN, ARNAMURCHAN, SCOTLAND SITE OF THE ORIGIN OF THE MACIAINS. This rock, like the black stone of Mecca, protrudes out of the lobby wall—curiously out of place.

USM has an excellent school of music, and the university's main marching band, consisting of more than a hundred members, is called "The Pride." In 1963 this marching band, which performs at half-time during football games, added a special unit called the "Scottish Highlanders." This organization was initially a thirty-piece bagpipe and drum corps. During their performances the bagpipers and drummers were "attired in authentic Scottish costumes featuring the plaid of the McCain clan."[1] On occasion at University functions Dr. McCain made "grand entrances" during which he was preceded by the "Scottish Highlanders" playing enthusiastically on bagpipes and drums.

Dr. McCain cultivated a reputation as an orator. An active member of the Sons of the Confederacy, he frequently spoke to service organizations and to ladies' clubs concerning Confederate heroes. In these speeches he used embroidered, extravagant rhetoric. To the Hattiesburg chapter of the United Daughters of the Confederacy, he said of Robert E. Lee,

> He was a foe without hate, a friend without treachery, a soldier without vices, and a victim without murmuring. He was a public officer without greed, a private citizen without wrong, a neighbor

---

[1]Gilbert T. Saetre, *The Pride 1920-1979* (Hattiesburg: University of Southern Mississippi Press, 1969) 74.

without reproach, a Christian without hypocrisy, and a man without guilt. He was Caesar without his ambition, Napoleon without his selfishness and Washington without his reward. He was as obedient to authority as a servant and royal in authority as a king. He was as gentle as a woman in life, pure as a virgin in thought, watchful as a Roman vestal, submissive to law as Socrates, and grand in battle as Achilles. [2]

Dr. McCain had a proclivity for dark suits that he wore year round, even in June, July, and August. Moreover, Dr. McCain prided himself on being physically fit. His first day as president of USM was 18 August 1955. In celebration of that event he always wore on each 18 August the same suit he had worn on his first day as university president. An article, accompanied by a photograph of Dr. McCain, by Roger Brinegar of USM's public relations office in the 27 August 1982 edition of the *Hattiesburg American* reported:

> On August 18 of every year since 1955, Dr. William D. McCain has worn the same suit to work.
> This past August 18 was the 27th straight year that Dr. McCain has done so and he intends to continue the tradition for some time to come.
> McCain currently is serving as President Emeritus of the University of Southern Mississippi, having retired in 1975 after 20 years of service as president of the institution.
> The suit was worn on McCain's first day as president and it is kept in a special place throughout the year for its annual unveiling.
> "People do not believe me," he said, as he produced a faded newspaper clipping. "They simply do not believe that this could be the same suit."
> Dr. McCain has published eight voluminous works on his family's history and is working on six more. This hard work, even in retirement, reflects his Scottish heritage as does his frugality in preserving a suit for a special occasion.
> Why does he wear the same, slightly out of style suit on his presidential anniversary?

---

[2]"Dr. McCain Speaks to UDC on Life of Robert E. Lee," *Hattiesburg American*, 18 January 1978, 9.

"I go around the campus and visit with all my friends who have let their waistlines go," he replied.[3]

But Dr. McCain's distinguishing characteristic par excellence was his *pride in his military career.* While a youngster he had enlisted in the army. Across the years he had served off and on in both the regular Army and National Guard. He served until eventually he became a major general. Not only was he *Dr.* McCain, he was also *General* McCain. On occasion he paraded across campus arrayed in his general's uniform. He made speeches and wrote articles about his military experiences during the Second World War. Time and again he related an episode that became known irreverently among faculty members as Dr. McCain's "Damn the Dago" story, a story that finally appeared in print. In an article about himself for the February 1972 issue of the *Journal of Mississippi History,* Dr. McCain related an episode about an accident in Italy.

> I had an interesting trip to the north late in January, 1945, to check on plans for the coming offensive. I left Rome on the morning of January 25 in an open command car. The weather was quite cold. I had a British major with me who sat on the back seat and covered himself completely with a tarpaulin. He was surprised along the way to Florence when we hit a tree. An Italian cart was going south. We were headed north. An Italian on a bicycle darted out from behind the cart. We smashed into him and left his bicycle a crumpled mass. We ended up against a tree. My right leg was injured and my trousers leg was torn. We left the Italian sitting in the road beside his crumpled bicycle. I instructed the driver, "The next time you have a choice between me an an Italian, kill the Italian."[4]

Even then Dr. McCain had developed an extraordinary ability to reprimand subordinates. As he wrote about a day in Italy when he was an army archivist,

---

[3]Roger Brinegar, "Dr. McCain Is Well-Suited to Mark USM Anniversary," *Hattiesburg American,* 27 August 1982, 4.

[4]William D. McCain, "Some Reminiscences of the United States Archivist in Italy—Dr. William D. McCain on Military Leave from Mississippi Department of Archives and History," *Journal of Mississippi History* 34, 1 (February 1972): 8-9.

I recorded privately this morning: "I have a tongue lashing stored up for some Italians if they can be found today. I am after one of these phony counts in particular. I will teach him to do things without consulting me first." I wrote in the afternoon: "I am having trouble getting Italians told off today. They are hard to find when you are after them. I intend to teach one count to meddle with archives business without consulting me. He decided to appoint a superintendent for the Archivi di Stato of Lombardia. His man went to work at nine this morning. I fired him at ten. We should have some fireworks now."[5]

At USM during the McCain era one might have thought World War II was still being waged. For years ROTC was compulsory for male students, and once a year all the ROTC students marched in review before General William D. McCain. A saying on campus was, "The Generalissimo's concept of heaven is standing throughout eternity in a jeep all decked out in his general's uniform, while an endless column of soldiers marches by in review—all of 'em saluting and singing 'Dixie.' " At graduation exercises at USM more attention was given to students receiving commissions in the armed forces than was given to graduate students receiving Ph.D. degrees. On campus members of the administration and faculty were defined not in terms of academic accomplishments but in terms of their prior military careers. Thus Dr. McCain's right-hand assistant was not referred to as "Mr. Johnson" but was called "General Johnson." The head of buildings and grounds was not referred to as "Mr. Aikens" but as "Colonel Aikens." During the 1950s and 1960s scores of retired military officers came to USM where they served as professors, departmental chairmen, and deans.

Dr. McCain's admiration for all things military had an influence upon the University of Southern Mississippi. For universities, like people, have personalities. Every university has a complex of characteristics that distinguish it from other schools of higher learning. These characteristics are largely molded by the person at the top. A university's president sets the tone; his values and personality, like yeast, leaven the whole. Ordinarily university presidents are persons

---

[5]Ibid., 19.

of refinement and graciousness, but this was not always the case with Dr. McCain. To the contrary, he could be *tough*—projecting a military, macho image. In talking with faculty members he on occasion began sentences with the words, "I order you. . . ." On occasion he cursed and gave tongue lashings. The president's office at USM during the McCain era had about it a barracks atmosphere. Dr. McCain always kept his general's flag in a stand beside his desk. Dr. McCain's devotion to military procedures and values explains why USM was nicknamed "Fort McCain." For members of the faculty said, "McCain runs this place like an army base."

Maybe the outcome of the Ole Miss-James Meredith episode would have been different if James Meredith had chosen Fort McCain rather than Ole Miss as the school at which to break down Mississippi's Jim Crow System. In that case Meredith would have come face to face with Dr. McCain, a man who was not a marshmallow. Perhaps the same thing would have happened to James Meredith that happened to Clyde Kennard, another Negro who years before Meredith had tried to breach Mississippi's Jim Crow society by attempting to enroll at USM.[6]

Clyde Kennard was a Negro native of Hattiesburg. At age twelve he had moved from Hattiesburg to Chicago in order to live with a sister. Eventually he entered the armed forces and served as a paratrooper in Germany and in Korea. After military service he returned to the states and for three years was a student at the University of Chicago. With money earned in Korea he purchased a small farm at Eatonville, a rural community five miles northeast of Hattiesburg. In 1955, at the age of twenty-eight, Clyde Kennard moved from Chicago to Eatonville and started raising chickens for a living on his farm.

Having finished three years of college work at the University of Chicago before returning to Mississippi, Kennard wanted to complete his college education. The University of Southern Mississippi, then all white and called "Mississippi Southern," was a fifteen-minute drive from Kennard's chicken farm. Over a three-year period

---

[6]My account of the Clyde Kennard tragedy is based on an article by Ronald A. Hollander, "One Mississippi Negro Who Didn't Go to College," *The Reporter* (18 November 1962): 30-34. See also Monte Piliawsky, *Exit 13: Oppression and Racism in Academia* (Boston: South End Press, 1982) 21-27.

Kennard had a series of exploratory conversations with Dr. McCain about becoming a student at Mississippi Southern. The possibility of a *nigger* becoming a student at Southern became the talk of Hattiesburg. Kennard, aware of the community's hostile attitude, explained his position in a letter that he wrote to the *Hattiesburg American*, the local newspaper.

> I, too, am a solid believer in the ability of the individual states to control their own affairs. I believe that if this state should lead out with only the smallest amount of integration it would never have to worry about Federal intervention.
>
> I have done all that is within my power to follow a reasonable course in this matter. I have tried to make it clear that my love for the State of Mississippi and my hope for its peaceful prosperity is equal to any man's alive. The thought of presenting this request before a Federal Court for consideration, with all the publicity and misrepresentation which that would bring about, makes my heart heavy.
>
> Mississippi Southern College is the only state supported four-year college in this area and my situation at home makes it very difficult for me to leave home to continue my education. On this account I have been unable to attend school for nearly five years. By attending Mississippi Southern College my problem would be solved, as I could live at home and attend school.

In the fall of 1959 Kennard, now in his early thirties, submitted an application for admission to Mississippi Southern College. On 15 September 1959 he drove his 1956 Mercury station wagon from his chicken farm in Eatonville to the campus. He parked his car and walked into the president's office for an interview with Dr. McCain. Dr. McCain was not by himself. Also in the president's office was Zach J. Van Landingham, chief investigator for the Mississippi Sovereignty Commission, an organization created by the state legislature to maintain total racial segregation in Mississippi. In an interview lasting about fifteen minutes Kennard was told by Dr. McCain that he would not be admitted to Mississippi Southern because of "irregularities" in his medical records and because Mississippi Southern claimed it had not received all his academic records from the University of Chicago.

After the interview Kennard returned to his Mercury station wagon where he was met by two waiting constables, Lee Daniels and Charles Ward. The constables placed Kennard under arrest and charged him with reckless driving. Kennard gave the keys to his station wagon to the arresting officers. They had difficulty starting the car and Kennard showed them how to start the motor. He was then taken in the constable's car to the sheriff's office by one of the arresting officers. The other constable drove Kennard's station wagon to the sheriff's office.

Kennard was escorted inside the sheriff's office for questioning and while the interrogation was in progress one of the arresting constables appeared with a brown paper bag containing five half-pints of whiskey. He explained he had "found" the whiskey under the front seat of Kennard's station wagon. Kennard was charged not only with reckless driving but also with possession of liquor. Liquor possession was illegal because in 1959 Mississippi was legally a dry state.

That afternoon Mississippi Southern issued a statement that "Clyde Kennard, a Negro presumably residing in Forrest County, today appeared at Mississippi Southern College in connection with his request to be admitted to the college. He was denied because of deficiencies and irregularities in his application papers."

Several days later Kennard was convicted in a hearing before justice of the peace T. C. Hobby and was fined six hundred dollars for possession of whiskey. Justice of the peace Hobby said he had never known of a case "where the state proved more clearly the guilt of the defendant."[7] When it was pointed out Kennard did not drink, one of the constables said, "Most bootleggers don't."

Kennard ended up in Parchman, the state penitentiary. Several months after the aborted attempt to enter Mississippi Southern he was accused of buying from Johnny Lee Roberts, a nineteen-year-old illiterate Negro, five bags of stolen chicken feed worth approximately twenty-five dollars. This chicken feed case was tried in the court of Judge Stanton A. Hall, circuit judge of Forrest County. Johnny Lee Roberts, the Negro who stole the feed from the Forrest County Co-op, testified for the state. On the witness stand he as-

---

[7] "Negro Kennard Fined $600," *Hattiesburg American*, 29 September 1959, 1.

serted he had stolen the chicken feed from the Co-op and had sold the feed to Kennard (who—according to Roberts—knew the feed was stolen because he had suggested to Roberts that he steal it). Kennard was charged with being an accessory to burglary, for under the Mississippi Code, "Every person who shall be an accessory to any felony before the fact, shall be deemed and considered a principal, and shall be indicted and punished as such."

Johnny Lee Roberts, after testifying for the state, received a five-year probation sentence and continued working at the Co-op from which he had supposedly stolen the feed. Clyde Kennard, known locally as "the darkie who tried to integrate Mississippi Southern," was sentenced by Judge Stanton Hall to seven years in the state penitentiary: one year for each $3.57 of stolen chicken feed. After Kennard was imprisoned he was discovered to have leukemia. By 4 July 1963 Clyde Kennard, United States paratrooper and Eatonville chicken farmer, was dead.

24

Fired!

DR. MᶜCAIN'S MACHO PERSONALITY and his military style of operation had an impact on USM's students. Intimidated by Dr. McCain's behavior, they had little to do with him. Indeed, when passing Dr. McCain on campus students often looked the other way. This student coldness irritated him, as a 1967 article in the *Student Printz*, the campus newspaper, indicated in quoting Dr. McCain.

> As I go about the campus, I have great difficulty in getting students to speak to me. I occasionally stop one who refuses to exchange greetings and ask for his name and station in life. If a man or woman is too important to speak to the president of his or her university, I need to become acquainted with that person. One of these days a student who refuses to speak to me is going to appear in my office for help when in trouble with the office of the Dean of Student Affairs. I will then have the opportunity to remind him of his previous discourtesy. [1]

Dr. McCain's macho personality and his military style of operation also had an impact on the faculty. Another nickname for USM during the McCain presidency was "the land of the children of Israel." Such was the case because from time to time in conversation Dr. McCain compared himself to Moses. He said, "When Moses led the children of Israel out of Egypt the first thing he did was to organize them. He divided them into companies and appointed commanders for each one. And that's the way it is here at the University

---

[1]"President's Address to Campus," *Student Printz*, 20 April 1967, 3.

of Southern Mississippi. Like Moses, I've organized this place into companies, and I've appointed commanders over each one of 'em." That is the way it was. Every professor who had taught at USM for at least a week knew that around Dr. McCain was a cluster of administrators who were his handpicked "commanders."

In the university community the commanders were a privileged coterie. Indeed, they were in a category by themselves. Composing a campus aristocracy, they did not go by the rules; they made the rules. They gathered frequently in the administration building, nicknamed "The Dome" because of its Byzantine architecture, to drink coffee together and to chew the fat with one another. Many of the "commanders" were members of the Hattiesburg Country Club, a membership they could afford because their salaries far exceeded the salaries of everyone else at USM.

Moreover, concerning these handpicked "commanders" Dr. McCain said in effect, "As a general I believe in backing up my commanders. Their decisions are my decisions." *I believe in backing up my commanders!* This McCain policy presented problems, for some of the "commanders" had reputations on campus for brutality and for lack of sensitivity in dealing with others. These men would call a faculty member into their their offices, chew him out, and without batting an eye or shedding a tear, fire him from his job. These firings occurred at times over peccadilloes. A faculty member could be fired for growing a beard too long, for making a remark in lecture critical of this country's military establishment, or for joining the American Civil Liberties Union.

Dr. Catherine Swan[2] was a refined, gracious woman from New Jersey and a member of the USM philosophy department. A graduate of Rosary College and St. Louis University, she held a Ph.D. in philosophy from Tulane University in New Orleans. She was fired because one of the deans arbitrarily decided she was immoral, on the basis of a telephone call he received from Miss Swan's landlady. Miss Swan's landlady was a Hattiesburg spinster who owned off-campus apartments. She spotted "two strange men" going into Miss Swan's apartment at night. The next morning she telephoned the dean and

---

[2]This name is a pseudonym.

said to him, "I hate to say this, but you need to know you've got a woman of loose morals on your hands." She then told the dean about seeing "two strange men" entering Miss Swan's apartment after nightfall. In fact, the "two strange men" were priests from Hatties-burg's Sacred Heart Church. They had been invited by Miss Swan, a devout Roman Catholic, to her apartment for an evening meal. The visit from the priests was as innocent as water from a hillside spring. They ate waffles, listened to classical music, and sipped hot apple cider. Yet the dean believed the worst about everyone. Accepting at face value the landlady's account, he telephoned the chairman of the philosophy department, and demanded, "I want you to get rid of the whore you've got down there!" The chairman's attempts to defend Miss Swan only antagonized the dean. His response was, "I meant what I said! Get rid of the yankee whore!" The dean's wish was re-alized.

These dismissals were disasters because in the academic world getting fired is professional destruction. Being dismissed meant, nine times out of ten, being finished as an academician. Accounts circu-lated in the faculty lounges about the tribulations of fired faculty members. Was it not true that one of the short order cooks at Sam-bo's on Hardy Street was a fired professor with a Ph.D. from Van-derbilt? Was it not true that a Volkswagen mechanic in Baton Rouge was a fired professor who held a Ph.D. from Edinburgh in Scotland? Thus many members of USM's faculty, I quickly discovered, lived under a cloud of dread and with a sense of impending doom. They spoke to each other in whispers. Many were on edge and afraid. The question faculty members discussed among themselves *ad nauseum* was, "How many more years will it be until McCain retires?" The years to his retirement were calculated with the care and precision that pris-oners use in calculating remaining years of prison sentences.

In the midst of all these firings was I, Clayton Sullivan, worried about my professional future? "Goodness, gracious, heavens, no!" I felt safe and secure. After all, I was from Mississippi. The professors being pressured off the faculty were frequently out-of-staters like Christos Doumas, a political science professor from Greece. What was someone named *Doumas* doing teaching in the middle of the Pi-ney Woods? Or someone with a name like Monte Piliawsky, another teacher fired from political science?[3] Others dismissed were professors who had gotten mixed up with "pinko" organizations, or they were people who popped off in faculty meetings or participated in campus demonstrations against the war in Vietnam.

By contrast, I maintained a low profile, minded my business, and concentrated on preparing lectures and teaching students. I felt I was doing an excellent job as a teacher. The waters might be turbulent *for others,* but for me the waters were calm. Before me was smooth sailing under blue skies. As I have said, my father and father-in-law both knew Dr. McCain from years gone by. I belonged to the same church Dr. McCain attended, Hattiesburg's First Baptist Church on Pine Street with its lovely colonial sanctuary and magnificent steeple. I, so I believed, was in the midst of people who accepted me, and in faculty bull sessions I time and again came to Dr. McCain's defense, expressing my view that he was a misunderstood man.

But then, unexpectedly, what had been happening *to others* at Fort McCain happened to Clayton Sullivan. In the early 1970s a bizarre restructuring of departments took place in the College of Liberal Arts. The academic areas of anthropology, philosophy, and religion were collapsed into one department that became known on campus as the CRAP department (CR standing for comparative religion, A for anthropology, and P for philosophy). Appointed as chairman of CRAP was Dr. Roger Pearson, an English anthropologist who for almost twenty years had been a British army officer in Egypt, Burma, and India. The father of four children, Dr. Pearson was always polite and he spoke with a pronounced English accent.

In the fall of 1971 Dr. Pearson, a man around fifty years of age, called me into his office for—as he expressed it—"a confidential chat" about my tenure at USM. Professors, after serving a probationary

---

[3]Monte Piliawsky, now on the faculty of Dillard University in New Orleans, has written about his own firing in his *Exit 13: Oppression and Racism in Academia* (Boston: South End Press, 1982) 111-14. His book takes its title from the number of the exit from Interstate 59 to the road leading to the campus of the University of Southern Mississippi. Piliawsky defines "the Exit 13 syndrome" as "being completely at the mercy of hostile and malicious forces" (21). As he observes, "The Exit 13 syndrome requires a sense of humor—one must laugh because otherwise one will cry" (xv).

period, are granted what in the academic world is called *tenure*. Tenure can be described as a "union card." It protects a teacher from arbitrary, capricious dismissal. When a university grants a professor *tenure* it is a way of saying, "We accept you. We put our stamp of approval on you. You are a permanent member of the team." I had always assumed that at the end of my probationary period I would be granted tenure. That it would not be granted was a possibility that had never crossed my mind.

But in the course of my "confidential chat" with Dr. Pearson I learned my assumption in this regard was ill-founded. Dr. Pearson told me of his recent conversations with Dr. Claude Fike, dean of Liberal Arts, and with Dr. Charles Moorman, the academic dean. Both Dr. Fike and Dr. Moorman had opposed my receiving tenure.

Dr. Fike and Dr. Moorman were heavyweights in the McCain administration. On USM's campus both were feared. Dr. Fike, a member of the history department, struck terror in the hearts of faculty members. By my colleagues in the philosophy department he was nicknamed "Dean Fang." Dr. Moorman, the academic dean of the university, was reported to be, after Dr. McCain, the most powerful man on campus. Some critics said that Dr. McCain—who was to retire in two or three years—had lost interest in his job as university president and "had turned USM over to Dean Moorman." That these two crucial deans opposed my receiving tenure was disastrous.

I asked Dr. Pearson the reason for their opposition. His response was, "I'd rather not tell you." I found this answer puzzling, and as my "confidential chat" with Dr. Pearson continued I felt within myself a rising surge of anxiety. A sick feeling stirred in my stomach, and I felt my face breaking out with sweat. For in the academic world to be turned down for tenure is a slap in the face. It is being told: "We don't want you. You're persona non grata." Being denied tenure is tantamount to being fired. My anxiety level shot through the roof when Dr. Pearson concluded our "confidential chat" in his office by saying, "Tomorrow you and I are to go to Dr. McCain's office for a conference concerning your tenure situation."

To the office of the Generalissimo himself! What in the devil was going on? I did not have the remotest idea, but whatever it was it was not good. The last thing in the world a faculty member at USM wanted to do was to go to Dr. McCain's office. Yet here I was being told I was to go there the next day for a conference concerning tenure.

When, the next day, Dr. Pearson and I went to Dr. McCain's office, Dr. McCain was there, Dr. Claude Fike, dean of Liberal Arts, was there, and Dr. Charles Moorman, the academic dean, was there. Dr. Moorman was a man short in stature with red face and corpulent build. He had come up through the ranks at USM. A graduate of Kenyon College, he had started out years before as a literature professor and soon became chairman of the English department. He was then appointed dean of the graduate school and finally academic dean of the University. Dr. Moorman was a man with unquestioned academic qualifications, a Guggenheim Fellow who had earned his Ph.D. at Tulane University in New Orleans. He was a man whom I had admired. Dr. Moorman was a medieval scholar, an able lecturer, and a published author. At USM people said, "Charlie Moorman knows more about King Arthur, the Knights of the Round Table, and Camelot than anyone else in Mississippi."

All of us took seats around the conference table in Dr. McCain's office, and Dr. Moorman began the conference by saying, "Gentlemen, all of us know why we're here. We're here to discuss whether or not Dr. Sullivan will be granted tenure. The answer to that issue is *no*. Moreover, I assume full responsibility for denying him tenure, and in doing this I know I am screwing him." That is what the medieval scholar—the Camelot specialist—said. *"I know I am screwing him."* Dr. McCain, sitting like a Buddha at the head of the table, said nothing.

I felt blood rushing to my face. I was embarrassed, so embarrassed my flesh wanted to crawl off my bones and slink across the floor and hide in a corner. The conference in Dr. McCain's office continued, but I heard nothing. I was too humiliated to hear.

The conference eventually ended, and we all stood up and one by one left the room. As I was walking out, Dr. Moorman spoke a final word to me. He said, "Dr. Sullivan, before you leave this office I want you to know that if there's any person I despise and hold in contempt, it is an ordained clergyman." These words pierced my brain like red-hot nails, and with these words ringing in my ears I walked out of the administration building alone and headed across campus.

My encounter with McCain, Fike, and Moorman was a decisive moment of illumination. I saw myself as others saw me. I sensed anew the contemptuous attitude existing in the post-World War II South toward the clergy. I sensed my powerlessness, my vulnerability, my insignificance in the secular world.

I had been living in Hattiesburg in a world of self-created illusions. I had assumed the good will of others. I had thought I was among friends, and in my naiveté and provincialism I had supposed that being a Mississippian assured me of acceptance in Mississippi society. My encounter with Dr. Moorman showed me this was not the case, and a sense of isolation and ostracism descended upon me.

Screwed by Dean Charles Moorman in the middle of the Piney Woods! Screwed forty miles south of where my paternal grandparents lie buried in the Sharon cemetery in Sullivan's Hollow. My Sullivan's Hollow forefathers would not have taken a screwing from Dean Moorman. Hell no, they wouldn't! Or at least they would not have taken it lying down. Old Wild Bill Sullivan would have loaded his shotgun and filled Dean Moorman's duster with buckshot. But I am cut out of different cloth from Old Wild Bill, who fought with his fists and bit with his teeth. I wear a suit and tie, carry a briefcase, and sport a fancy doctor's degree.

Screwed by Dean Charles Moorman, Mississippi's premier authority on King Arthur, the Knights of the Round Table, and Camelot! Everybody at USM said Charlie was the nicest guy on campus until he became Dean. Then he changed. Overnight, some said, a Napoleonic complex emerged, and he started throwing his weight around and knocking people over. That is why people called him "Napoleon" and "the little Caesar." "Caesar Charlie."

What had I done to Caesar Charlie? Our paths had seldom crossed. In all the years I had taught at USM I had had, as best I could recall, two conversations with Dean Moorman. At registration in the coliseum I had asked him who wrote "The Emperor's New Clothes," and he had told me that it was Hans Christian Andersen. In the A & P Grocery in the University Mall Shopping Center I had congratulated him after he had been appointed university dean. Outside these two fleeting exchanges I had had no contact with Charlie Moorman, a man I admired and liked from a distance. Yet here he was, out of the blue, telling me he despised me because I was a preacher. I wanted to say, "Charlie, don't hold that against me! Please understand! God drew near to me while I was scrubbing floors in the Heidelberg Hotel kitchen and called me to be a preacher. Being a preacher isn't my idea."

In campus bull sessions I had heard reports of Dean Moorman's anticlericalism, but I had not taken these reports seriously. Dr. Pearson, my departmental chairman, had discussed this issue with me, and he had said, "You've got to understand—Dean Moorman has no use for religion and preachers." I was familiar with the Don Williams episode. Don was director of USM's Wesley Foundation. He went by Dean Moorman's office to seek the Dean's approval for using Methodist students to assist underprivileged youngsters in learning to read. Don explained the proposed program to Dean Moorman, and the Dean's response was: "I don't give a damn what you do. We could have a good university if we could get rid of all the goddamn Christians on campus."[4]

Screwed by Charlie Moorman, the most powerful dean around. After becoming university dean he divorced his wife and mother of his two sons, and married a professor in the foreign languages department. Charlie and his new wife were a curious couple on campus. She, a French teacher, appeared to be much taller than Charlie. This height difference caused some folk to remark, "Napoleon has married the Eiffel Tower."

Screwed and how it hurt! By then I was a father; I had a wife and baby daughter dependent on me for food, clothing, and shelter. When a person is single and is responsible only for himself, he can tell the world to go hang. But when a man has a wife and child he will do anything for them. For them he will crawl. Crawling is what I decided to do. Dean Moorman had also said during the conference in Dr. McCain's office, "When I screw a person one year, I try to make it up to him the next." To my mind that statement was a glimmer of hope. On the one hand, I had not been granted tenure at USM; on the other hand, I had not been out and out fired. I was neither in heaven nor in hell; rather, I was in limbo.

---

[4]Don Williams is now the minister of the United Methodist Church in Purvis, Mississippi. I have in my files his affidavit confirming this episode.

So I hunkered down like a turtle does when it is kicked. I decided to hang in and not give up. I taught my classes and did my best, for my professional future was at stake. I had done, I felt, an excellent job at USM, and I was determined not to be run out of my job at Fort McCain.

Perhaps my "hang-in-there" decision was not the brightest of strategies. For during the next academic year at Fort McCain faculty dismissals were more common than rattlesnakes in the Piney Woods. Scores of professors were fired from their jobs. The CRAP department was decimated. Dr. Gary Atkinson (Ph.D. from Duke University), Dr. Sanford Wood (Ph.D. from Vanderbilt University), and Dr. Cedric Evans (Ph.D. from the University of Edinburgh) were fired. Dr. Forrest Wood (Ph.D. from the Southwestern Baptist Theological Seminary) was tendered a letter of termination, a firing later rescinded. All received letters of dismissal from Dr. Pearson, the English anthropologist, who acquired on campus the nickname of "Roger the Ripper." In his office Dr. Pearson discussed these firings with me, explaining that all were the brainchild of the dean. With his clipped English accent, Dr. Pearson said, "Damn, Sullivan, all these firings! All this adverse publicity! I'm so embarrassed I don't know what to do! But the dean calls me into his office and gives me orders to fire people, and if I don't carry out his orders I'm afraid he'll fire me."

Thus for the CRAP department 1972-1973 was a year of fire. In the midst of the firings Dean Moorman, the Camelot specialist, had quipped, "Thirty thousand Southern Baptists praying in convention won't save the boys in the philosophy and religion department." Miraculously I survived. But then came the next academic year, and this was to be my year of agony. The week before the 1973 fall semester began Dr. Pearson came into my office in McMillan Hall and ominously said to me, "Clayton, I've got bad news. Let's go over to Sambo's where we can talk off campus."

Over to Sambo's Restaurant on Hardy Street Dr. Pearson and I went. We sat down opposite each other in a booth, ordered coffee, and started talking. Dr. Pearson, a pained expression on his face, said, "Sullivan, in England we have a saying 'to be forewarned is to be forearmed,' and that's why I'm talking to you. You need to be forewarned. Dean Moorman and Dean Fike are still hot after philosophy and religion, and they're hot after you. Dean Fike has given me orders. As he put it, 'Get rid of the goddamn preacher.' So what I'm telling you is: as soon as the fall semester begins, I'm going to have to fire you from your job."

"Believe me, Clayton," Dr. Pearson continued, "I don't want to do this. I think you're a good professor, and you and I've gotten along splendidly. I've told Dean Fike you're a good teacher, but he's adamant and he keeps saying, 'Get rid of the goddamn preacher.' He's given me orders, and like a good British soldier, I do what I've been ordered to do. But I'm asking you to understand. I have a wife and four kids to support. The job market in this country is tight, and I can't go back to England because there're no jobs over there. If I refuse to fire you, you know damn good and well what'll happen. Fike will fire me for insubordination."

What more was there to say? Orders are orders! Like a good British soldier, Dr. Pearson, a gentleman who was always courteous, was going to do what he had been ordered to do. It was either he or I! From Dr. Pearson's viewpoint it was better for me to get the axe than for him to get the axe!

And the axe is what I got. Two weeks later Dr. Pearson called me into his office. He asked me to sit down, and he handed a letter which read:

September 10, 1973

Dr. Clayton Sullivan
Post Box 124, Southern Station
Hattiesburg, Miss. 39401

Dear Dr. Sullivan:

It is with regret that I write to inform you that you will not be offered further employment at this University following the conclusion of this academic year in May 1974.

May I express my personal appreciation of your services during the period that I have been Chairman of this Department.

Yours very sincerely,

Roger Pearson Ph.D.
Chairman

That is what the letter said. "You will not be offered further employment at this University." In other words, I was *fired*.

Fired in the middle of the Piney Woods by a good British soldier. Fired forty miles south of Sullivan's Hollow where my grandfather and grandmother are buried in the Old Sharon cemetery!

Fired, so I was told, at the orders of Dean Fike who said, "Get rid of the goddamn preacher." Fired by "Roger the Ripper" who said, "Like a good British soldier, I do what I've been ordered to do." Count the words in that statement. They total thirteen, the number that always suggests disaster to me.

Fired from my job in Mississippi—the place where I wanted to be accepted, wanted to live, and wanted to invest my life.

Having read the letter, I looked at the Englishman and said, "Well, Dr. Pearson, that's it. I'm fired. But out of curiosity—what's the reason? Why have I been fired?"

"Dean Fike said he wanted to tell you," Dr. Pearson replied. "He ordered me to give you this letter, and then for the two of us to come to his office so he could tell you why you were being dismissed. I'll call him right now and find out if he can see us."

Dr. Pearson picked up his telephone and dialed Dean Fike's office. A brief conversation ensued. Then side by side Dr. Pearson and I walked out of McMillan Hall, and we headed across campus toward College Hall where the dean's office was. We walked past the Student Center, past Danforth Chapel, and past the Commons. Within myself I felt a curious sensation. Here I was walking across campus to Dean Fike's office to find out why I had been fired. I was walking to my own execution.

This was not really happening! It was a nightmare! A bad dream! At any moment I would wake up and discover it was not true. But this was not a dream. This was reality. I was passing through an existential hell.

Dr. Pearson and I walked into College Hall and down the corridor to Dr. Fike's office. We entered the office, and neither one of us sat down. Instead, we stood side by side before the dean who was sitting behind his desk. Dr. Fike, holder of a Ph.D. from the University of Illinois, was a historian whose academic specialty was Cold War issues. Of all "commanders" at USM, he was by far the most feared.

The interview with the Cold War historian was brief. Dr. Pearson and I remained standing throughout. Dean Fike, his face red, asked me, "Dr. Sullivan, is it true you're conducting church services on Sunday?"

I confess this was the last question on the face of the earth I expected Dean Fike to ask me. The answer to his question was yes. On Sundays I was serving two minuscule congregations in logging towns south of Hattiesburg. One was at Beaumont in Perry County, and the other was at McLain in Greene County, both on the highway that runs from Hattiesburg to Mobile. On Sunday mornings I drove down to these logging communities to conduct morning worship services. I enjoyed doing this because it kept me in touch with grassroots Mississippians. So Dean Fike was on target when he asked, "Dr. Sullivan, is it true you're conducting church services on Sunday?"

I told him I was.

He answered, "Are you aware this is contrary to the university's administrative policy?"

I told him I was not aware such was the case.

"Well, it is," Dean Fike said, "and because of your violation of this administrative policy, it has been necessary for Dr. Pearson to fire you from your job."

On that somber note Dr. Pearson and I turned and walked out of Dean Fike's office. As we walked out of College Hall into the September sunlight, Dr. Pearson took me by the arm and in his British accent said, "Believe me, Clayton, I'm sorry. But I had no choice. Fike gave me orders. And like I've told you, I've got a wife and four kids to support and. . . ."

But Dr. Pearson's words were no consolation. I too had a wife and a baby to support. Being fired, I discovered, was a savage assault on my ego. I instantly lost my self-respect. I dissolved on the inside. Capitulating momentarily to despair, I wanted to get in my car, drive home and hide. That is why the most vivid memory I have of that September day was being unable to find my automobile. I wanted to go home, but I could not locate my car.

Where had I parked? I could not remember. Had I parked over by McDonald's on Hardy Street? Had I parked by the football stadium? Or maybe by the Coliseum?

In a state of shock, I walked back and forth across campus, looking for my station wagon, and to this day I do not recall where I found it. But eventually I did. I drove home and told my wife I had been fired from my job. That day I remember as the bleakest of my professional life.

25

Reprieve

IN THE AFTERMATH OF BEING DISMISSED I turned my mind to the question, what am I going to do? At earlier stages in life I had wasted time and emotional energy longing for a father, for someone to lean upon and to run interference for me. Yet the central discovery of adulthood is that no father can protect you. I must take care of myself. I must hustle my interest because no one else will. As a Jewish proverb affirms, "If I am not for myself, then who will be?"

For several days I floundered. I turned *this* alternative and *that* alternative over in my mind. It was like being back on the Baltimore Turnpike, driving aimlessly.

Maybe I should have said, "To heck with it! This world is a big place! There're other things to do besides teaching at Fort McCain. Let Roger the Ripper and Dean Fike take my job and go hang it up!" Yet I was impaled on ego. Pride was at stake. I did not want to succumb to being fired. Moreover, I felt threatened like a cat backed into a corner by a pursuing dog. When you are cornered, and you are protecting your family, you will fight as a cornered cat fights! And that is what I wanted to do. I wanted to fight!

Finally I seized on a plan. I decided to ignore the chain of command at USM and to take my case to none other than General William D. McCain, president of the University of Southern Mississippi. In my mind I hammered out a scenario. I would ask for an interview. I would tell Dr. McCain I did not think my dismissal was justified, and I would ask him to rescind my firing. This seemed an audacious thing to do, but I would do this for my wife and daughter, buying time, hoping to hang in, and to keep my act together.

I called Dr. McCain's office and requested an interview. I was given one, and at the appointed hour to the "Dome" I went, dressed in my very best suit with my shoes freshly polished. I marched into the presence of the Generalissimo himself, sat down, and poured my problem out to Dr. McCain. I told him about my dismissal, about how it had been "ordered" by the dean, and about how I felt my firing was unjustified.

Dr. McCain could not have been more decent! Dr. McCain's way of dealing with people in a one-on-one relationship did not always correlate with his public macho-generalissimo image. He heard me out, and at the end of my recital of woe he responded in two ways. First, he told me he was going to reverse the firing decision. Then he told me his "top sergeant" story. When, he said, an officer in the army gets ready to appoint his top sergeant, he looks around the barracks for the meanest man he can find. That, Dr. McCain said, was what he had done in choosing a dean of liberal arts—he had chosen the meanest person on campus.

By this time I was experiencing bureaucracy-induced vertigo. Roger Pearson, chairman of CRAP, had assured me he did not want to fire me, but he had fired me anyway because he had a wife and four kids and—as a good British soldier—he did what Dean Fike commanded him to do. Dr. Fike, dean of Liberal of Arts, told me I had been fired by Dr. Pearson because I was conducting worship services in two logging towns. In turn, the president of the University of Southern Mississippi advised me to forget about having been fired. Tell me: in a bureaucracy, whom do you believe? In an organization, who tells it straight and whom do you trust?

One thing I do know: I *survived* the 1973-74 academic year. By no means was I out of the woods. For Dr. Pearson, who heartily congratulated me on getting my firing reversed, orally delivered to me a "message" from Dean Fike and the message was: "As soon as Dr. McCain retires and is no longer in a position to 'protect' you, I'm going to fire you again."[1] So I still had problems. But I was *hanging in there!* I was not running away!

Toward the year's end, Dr. Pearson, a man of astonishing intellectual energy, suffered a heart attack. Shortly thereafter he resigned and moved to Washington where today he is editor of the *Journal of Indo-European Studies*, a journal he founded while at USM. In the course of our final conversation, which took place in his home on West Lake, he made what lives in my mind as his "British Empire" remark. For twenty years, Dr. Pearson told me, he had been a soldier in the British army, stationed in every corner of the Empire—England, Egypt, India, Burma, and Australia. He had, he said, heard profanity in every language of the Empire, but he could not find in all of that invective the words to describe his superior at USM, the dean of liberal arts.

Then came the 1974-75 academic year, the last year Dr. McCain was university president. Time catches up with everyone, even with presidents and generals. Dr. McCain was "on his way out," and the faculty was delighted to see him depart. For they reasoned that only by McCain retiring would they be able to escape the tyranny of his "commanders." By the last year of the McCain presidency the hostility between faculty and "commanders" was so intense that USM resembled a Byzantine court with Hogarthian overtones.

This hostility was compounded by the faculty's loss of professional respect for Dr. McCain in the wake of his reprimand for pla-

---

[1]Dean Fike was able to carry out this threat. During the 1974-1975 academic year I was fired a second time, this time by Dr. Robert E. Kuttner, a chemist and cultural anthropologist who had been a research assistant to William Shockley at Stanford and was appointed to succeed Dr. Roger Pearson as chairman of CRAP. Curiously, Dr. Kuttner resigned at the end of the 1974-1975 academic year. On his notorious racial prejudice, see Monte Piliawsky, *Exit 13: Oppression and Racism in Academia* (Boston: South End Press, 1982) 73-75.

At USM the 1975-1976 academic year was significant as the first year of Dr. Aubrey Lucas's presidency and the last year that Claude Fike was dean of liberal arts. In the fall of 1975 Dr. Paul Sharkey arrived on campus to become chairman of the philosophy and religion department; he had been appointed to that post by Claude Fike. In our first interview Dr. Sharkey fired me from my job; that dismissal was reversed by Dr. Lucas, who remarked to me, "Clayton, you hold the record here at USM of having been fired more times than any person on campus." Dr. Sharkey is no longer chairman of the philosophy and religion department.

giarism by the American Historical Association and the American Association of University Professors. Plagiarism, from the Latin word for "kidnapper," is the appropriation, without permission or without proper acknowledgment, of another person's literary work. It is the unpardonable sin of the academic world. Plagiarism is to write something and to pretend it is your own creation when in fact it is somebody else's mental sweat, blood, and tears.

The plagiarism charge descended on Dr. McCain as a result of an article entitled "The Administration of David Holmes, Governor of Mississippi Territory, 1809-1820," which he published in the November 1967 issue of the *Journal of Mississippi History*. This nineteen-page article includes a footnote in which Dr. McCain cites twenty-four sources he consulted. One source mentioned was an Emory University master's thesis by Frances Elizabeth Melton Racine entitled, "The Public Career of David Holmes, 1809-1920." In the footnote Dr. McCain observed that he "relied heavily" on this Emory University thesis and on a University of Colorado thesis by William Boyd Horton. In the footnote he also stated he "consulted" twenty-two other works. Where and how these twenty-two works were used is not obvious because the McCain article is almost verbatim an unacknowledged and unfootnoted quotation of the Emory University thesis by Mrs. Racine.

Somehow (in a way unknown to me) McCain's article in the *Journal of Mississippi History* came to Mrs. Racine's attention. Recognizing plagiarism, she wrote an accusing letter on 9 May 1968 to Dr. John E. Gonzales, editor of the *Journal of Mississippi History* and a member of USM's history department, spelling out her complaint against the unauthorized use of her thesis by Dr. McCain.

> In the centennial issue of the *Journal of Mississippi History*, published in November 1967, there appeared an article entitled "The Administration of David Holmes, Governor of Mississippi Territory, 1809-1817." Its author was Dr. William D. McCain, President of the University of Southern Mississippi.
>
> This article was of more than ordinary interest to me, first, because my own master's thesis at Emory University, on which I worked for several months in 1966, was on the subject "The Public Career of David Holmes, 1809-1820"; second, because the records show that Dr. McCain borrowed my thesis in April 1967; and third,

because the printed article bears so many close and continuous sim-
ilarities to my thesis that they cannot be overlooked.

The first paragraph of Mr. McCain's article has one footnote—
the only footnote in which he even mentions sources; and in that
one footnote he says that he "relied heavily" on . . . [my thesis].
Even a cursory comparison of my thesis with Mr. McCain's article
reveals that he has done more than "relied heavily" on it. He has,
in fact, reproduced essential portions of it without the permission
of any authorized person at Emory University.

In organization, interpretation, and narration, Mr. McCain's
article is identical to my thesis. His article contains sixty-five (65)
paragraphs. Sixty (60) of these vary only slightly, if at all, from what
I wrote in my thesis. Often the language of my thesis is used verbatim; and Mr. McCain has made no pretense of using quotation
marks or acknowledgments in footnotes.[2]

In her letter Mrs. Racine placed side by side sentences from her
Emory University thesis and sentences from the McCain article.
When she did not receive what she deemed to be an adequate response from Dr. Gonzales (who occupied the William D. McCain
chair of history at USM), Mrs. Racine took her accusation to the
American Historical Association and to the American Association of
University Professors. An *ad hoc* committee of historians was formed
to investigate Mrs. Racine's plagiarism charge. The committee, after
investigating the charge, asserted that "Dr. McCain's article repre-
sents a violation of approved scholarly usage with respect to another
author's literary property." The committee concluded that it "cannot
agree with the editor and editorial board of the *Journal of Mississippi
History* that the single reference to Mrs. Racine's thesis embedded in
a long footnote was adequate or proper recognition for such exten-
sive use of her material."[3] These conclusions were expressed in a report, "The American Historical Association and the AAUP: A Joint
Inquiry into an Issue of Attribution."

---

[2]"The American Historical Association and the AAUP: A Joint Inquiry into an
Issue of Attribution," *American Association of University Professors Bulletin* 57 (Winter
1971): 530.

[3]Ibid., 529.

About the inquiry Dr. McCain said nothing because one of his rules was that he would never answer criticism. When approached by the New Orleans *Times-Picayune* for a response to the AHA-AAUP committee report, Dr. McCain said, "It's not worth bothering about. I don't have time to follow that."[4]

But the plagiarism reprimand created shock waves of embarrassment on campus. At Harvard or Yale an administrator charged with plagiarism by the America Historical Association would have been banished by sundown. In the wake of the McCain plagiarism charge, however, nothing happened. USM's faculty had long before been cowed into silence, and apparently no one on the state's board of trustees for institutions of higher learning understood the gravity of plagiarism in the academic world. Indeed, a campus quip was, "Nobody on the college board knows what the word 'plagiarism' means." So all the faculty could do was snicker. "The Generalissimo—caught with his pants down for all the academic world to see!"

The faculty's loss of respect for Dr. McCain was intensified by reports bouncing back and forth across campus concerning possible financial hanky-panky on the part of McCain cronies. Rumors abounded about financial mismanagement in the textbook service and in the campus bookstore and gift shop. Rumors bounced around about coaches buying personal automobiles with money from athletic ticket sales and having thousands of dollars in cash from athletic funds tucked away in safety deposit boxes. And everyone knew that representatives of the state auditor's office had examined the campus financial records of Dr. Raymond Mannoni, dean of Fine Arts and one of Dr. McCain's closest associates, and had brought embezzlement charges against him.

Dr. Mannoni, with a head balder than a bowling ball, was an enigmatic McCain appointee. Every summer USM sponsored band and twirling camps for high school students. These summer camps, which brought scores of students to campus were under Dean Mannoni's supervision. In connection with them, thousands of dollars were collected in student fees. The state auditor's office investigated the collecting and dispensing of these summer camp student fees, and

---

[4]New Orleans *Times-Picayune*, 13 February 1972, 1

as a byproduct of this investigation Dean Mannoni, a crown jewel of the McCain administration, was charged with embezzlement.

The case against Dean Mannoni was handled by Forrest County Prosecutor George Phillips. During the trial Prosecutor Phillips focused on a bank check written in August 1973 for $400.00 This check was made out to one Roy Martin, a retired Greenwood, Mississippi, band director. A USM payroll voucher identified this check to Mr. Martin as an honorarium for twirling instructors and counselors. Yet during the trial Mr. Martin testified he had done no work in 1973 at USM's summer band and twirling camp. Moreover, he testified the signature—the endorsement—of Roy Martin on the back of the check was not his and that he had not received the money. Also during the trial a Hattiesburg bank teller identified Dean Mannoni as the person for whom she cashed the check made out to Mr. Martin and which had Dean Mannoni's endorsement under Mr. Martin's forged endorsement.

In the course of the trial Dr. McCain testified on behalf of the dean. During his testimony Dr. McCain became angry at Prosecutor George Phillips and, upon being excused from the witness stand, walked to the rear of the courtroom and proceeded to call Prosecutor Phillips a damn son of a bitch. He also asserted, concerning the prosecutor, "If I see him on the street, I'll beat his damn brains out." For this temper explosion Dr. McCain was fined $500.00 and given a thirty-day suspended jail sentence by Forrest County Circuit Judge Jack Weldy.[5]

Toward the end of Dr. McCain's tenure as president, the center did not hold. Things went to pot and they began to smell. When finally Dr. McCain retired and moved out of the president's office, the faculty uttered a collective sigh of relief. At Fort McCain World

---

[5]On this incident, see Janet Braswell, "Judge declares mistrial after Mannoni stricken in courtroom," *Hattiesburg American*, 24 August 1978, 1, 16; Braswell, "McCain fined $500, given 30-day suspended sentence in contempt case," *Hattiesburg American*, 8 September 1978, 1, 12. Five days later the judge ruled that he lacked the authority to convict Dr. McCain. A subsequent jury trial ended with a hung jury, and the case was ultimately dismissed See Piliawsky, *Exit 13*, 42-43.

War II was finally over, and the faculty and students celebrated V-E Day thirty years after it had been celebrated in other parts of the country.

26

The General in Retrospect

IN THE DECADE since Dr. McCain's retirement the University of Southern Mississippi has become a changed institution. The McCain "commanders" have been removed or demoted. A new administration has taken over. On campus courtesy has replaced arrogance; compassion has replaced curtness; conferring has replaced commanding. I have been granted tenure in the philosophy and religion department, and faculty colleagues who once were in the administration's dog house have been promoted to places of academic responsibility.

As time slips away and as memories fade, it would be easy to dismiss the antics of General McCain and his commanders as petty tragicomedy in the Piney Woods. Yet there is more to this story than tragicomedy at Fort McCain. The conduct of Dr. McCain and the "commanders" is an example, a microcosmic expression, of *bureaucratized brutality* in American life.

From one end of this country to the other scores of people live out their working lives in bureaucracies. Our society has become a society of organization people. Bureaucracies, properly directed, provide contexts within which people grow professionally, find fulfillment, and experience a good life. Improperly directed, they can be human hells in which bureaucratic brutality becomes the order of the day. Whether an organization is a curse or a blessing is determined largely by its power wielders, by those in places of authority.

On the one hand, some power wielders are supportive in relating to people around them. Seeing the good rather than the bad, power wielders of this genre have a personal maturity which enables them to seek the best for others. On the other hand, some power wielders are abrasive and dictatorial. They revel in relating destructively to people, and they thrive on intimidation. The bureaucratic violence they inflict on others tends to be invisible, not visible. Brass knuckles and black jacks are not needed. Rather, bureaucratic violence is verbal and mental. In the academic world it assumes the forms of rudeness, insensitivity, and misrepresentation. Through bureaucratic brutality careers can be dismantled, and people's good names destroyed, leaving them in the poignant posture of Iago in *Othello* when he remarked,

> Good name in man and woman, dear my lord,
> Is the immediate jewel of their souls:
> Who steals my purse steals trash;
>   'tis something, nothing;
> 'Twas mine, 'tis his, and has been slave to thousands;
> But he that filches from me my good name
> Robs me of that which not enriches him,
> And makes me poor indeed.

Possessing power is a dangerous, disorienting activity, particularly in academia. A power wielder in academia has followers who are dependent upon him for promotions and for salary increases. Followers who are in need of what someone has to offer have a tendency to flatter. Indeed, a standard ploy of faculty members at USM was to ask Dr. McCain, "Doctor, is it true you're thinking about running for governor?" Power wielders are charmed by flattery. Flattery reduces their ability to see reality and to make wise decisions. As the years pass power wielders start conceiving of themselves as all-knowing and unable to do wrong. Surrounded by sycophants who are afraid to point out mistakes (for no person relishes telling the emperor he is naked), they fall victim to the hubris about which the Greek tragedians warned. They view criticism as personal dislike or as insubordination. They have academic chairs named in their honor, place their names on buildings, and think more highly of themselves than they ought to think. They can even think of themselves as gods. A story made the rounds on campus concerning an imaginary professor who died and went to heaven around A.D. 2050. On arriving he was given a tour by St. Peter, and in the course of this heavenly tour encountered a strutting gentleman decked out in a bemedaled uniform. The newly arrived professor pointed at the strutting man and asked St. Peter, "Is that God?" St. Peter answered, "No, that's General William D. McCain."

The McCain era not only brought into focus bureaucratic brutality; it also brought into focus the truth found in Edgar Z. Friedenberg's remark: "All weakness tends to corrupt, and impotence corrupts absolutely."[1] Or to use Rollo May's words, *powerlessness corrupts.*[2] USM's faculty was powerless during the McCain era. This powerlessness was a byproduct of the faculty's behavior. Year after year we supinely "took" the McCain administration (headed in part by men who understood the Russian proverb: "Beat a dog once and then all you must do is show him the stick"). When the "commanders" were not around, faculty members cursed the ground they walked on; when the "commanders" were present, faculty members stroked them, smiled, and spoke words of praise. For USM's academicians were primarily interested during the McCain era in covering our own behinds and protecting our own interests. Having allowed ourselves to be emasculated, we evidenced moral depravity in tolerating the bureaucratic brutality that surrounded us. When colleagues were arbitrarily fired, when academic careers were destroyed, we did nothing. We raised no voices to protest; instead, we cowered in faculty lounges and gossiped. Like the priest and Levite in the parable of the Good Samaritan, we—in the presence of man's inhumanity to man—passed by on the other side.[3]

As time slips away and as memories fade, it would be easy for the USM academic community to continue to say, "The Generalissimo's administration is a thing of the past! A good riddance! Let us all rejoice and be glad!" These are tempting words. Yet they ignore an undeniable insight: the University of Southern Mississippi, on its way

---

[1]Edgar Z. Friedenberg, *Coming of Age in America* (New York: Irvington, 1965) 47-48.

[2]Rollo May, *Power and Innocence* (New York: W. W. Norton, 1972) 23.

[3]One notable exception to this sycophantic policy was Dr. William Scarborough of the history department; cf. Monte Piliawsky, *Exit 13: Oppression and Racism in Academia* (Boston: South End Press, 1982) 83-84.

to becoming a major academic institution in the South, would not be what it is today if there had been no General William D. McCain. The General knew how to relate to Mississippians who lived at the forks of the creek and where the graveled roads crossed. More important, he knew how to relate to Mississippi's power structure. When Dr. McCain took over as USM's president he brought with him years of experience in dealing with Mississippi's political leaders. For almost two decades he had been director of the Mississippi Department of Archives and History. Time and again he had struggled to get his department's budget approved by the state legislature in Jackson. Thus Dr. McCain knew the state's legislative leaders on a first name basis. He knew where the buttons and levers were. Breaking the Ole Miss-Mississippi State hammerlock on appropriations, Dr. McCain secured for USM its fair share of tax revenues. Dormitories, apartments, classroom buildings, laboratories, concert halls, theaters, a stadium, a coliseum, and parking lots went up all over the campus—monuments to Dr. McCain's talents as a shaker and doer. To be sure, at times his methods were dictatorial. But if they are going to get anything accomplished, university presidents must be forceful; otherwise a stalemate ensues.

Yet, alongside multiple strengths the General, like all mortals, had weaknesses. One weakness was exaggerated loyalty to appointees who were albatrosses. Another weakness was an inability to change and to move along with the times. He lived in the past. World War II was his golden age, his Periclean Athens. But while Dr. McCain was USM's president our country went through the wrenching experiences of the Vietnam War and the social revolution of the 1960s. The times were out of joint, and a paradigm shift took place. The heroes for our nation's youth were no longer a General Douglas McArthur wearing sunglasses or a General George Patton with an ivory-handled pistol. Rather Elvis Presley, the Beatles, and John Belushi became heroes for our nation's youth, to whom World War II was as remote as the Thirty Years War.

This paradigm shift struck General William D. McCain as silly. Students started wearing long hair. Some dressed in ragged clothes and walked across campus barefooted. They sang songs and hooted slogans ridiculing the country's leaders. Students appeared on campus decked out in T-shirts emblazoned with the words "Down With

the Draft" and (emulating students at Berkeley and supported by lib-
eral-arts professors) they conducted antimilitary, antiwar demonstrations. These developments infuriated Dr. McCain.

Dr. McCain did not understand that the students were not trai-
tors; they were letting off steam. Dr. McCain did not understand
that the students *may* have been *right* in their judgment that a land
war in Asia against a puzzling, elusive enemy made no sense. As one
student remarked to me, "Dr. Sullivan, if I can't pronounce 'em, I don't
want to fight 'em." And so Dr. McCain—with his military, polished-
shoe philosophy—feared that the behavior and dress of rebellious
students would damage "the image of the university." He summa-
rized his feelings in a 1967 report.

> We continue to have trouble with our weak and emaciated
> males. They still have to cling to the females as they walk on the
> campus or tenderly hang to other portions of the female anatomy.
> Animals carry on their affairs in public. Human beings are sup-
> posed to be trained by their parents to conduct themselves prop-
> erly in public. Some of the students seem to have no knowledge
> whatever of decent public conduct. I have made numerous state-
> ments on this subject. . . . Do not try to tell me that I cannot change
> your morals. I knew that before you were born. I am, at least, ask-
> ing that we conduct ourselves in public so as to give the people who
> pass our way a good image of this University.
>
> We seem now to live in a world where men want to wear their
> hair down to their shoulders and women want to wear their skirts
> up to their rumps. I shall not comment on the skirts. Whatever any
> of you think about long hair on men, beards, and general disre-
> putable appearance, we still do not like tramps and beatniks in our
> midst. We think that it is best for the University of Southern Mis-
> sissippi and for the students if we all dress with reasonable propri-
> ety, and shave and bathe regularly, and visit the barber at decent
> intervals. Smelly and trampish students do the image of the Uni-
> versity no good.[4]

By March 1972 Dr. McCain was telling the members of the USM
Student Senate where they could go.

---

[4]Quoted in "President's Address to Campus," *Student Printz*, 20 April 1967, 3.

I wanted to boast this month to people around here. I have worked a long time in this world and this month I reach complete financial independence, to the extent that I can tell everybody to go to hell. And I'm proud to tell everyone about that.[5]

Later that year he addressed a group of high school students.

Two or three years ago when things were more troublesome on college and university campuses, I had several of the hippie-type here to pay me a visit. And one of the things they said to me was, "You don't love us." And I had no answer for that: I didn't. . . . This thing of young people saying that they don't know who they are, they want to find themselves, they can't identify themselves. And they told me those things; they've been telling me those things here, and I can't understand. . . . And when people come to me wanting to find themselves, I don't know what they're talking about.[6]

What Dr. McCain was admitting was, "I, William D. McCain, president of the University of Southern Mississippi, don't understand and empathize with college students." In this regard he was right.

There has never been—nor will there ever be again—another man quite like the Generalissimo! General William D. McCain! The Good Lord created him and then threw the pattern away. The General was complex. On the one hand, he surrounded himself with appointees he described as dirty, mean sons-of-bitches. He taunted students by telling them he was positioned in life to tell everyone to go to hell. While transforming the campus into a landscaped wonderland, he screamed reprimands at students who walked on the grass, comparing them to cows.[7] Yet on the other hand, in one-on-one situations he could be amazingly compassionate. He never, so far as I know, cursed in a woman's presence. A not-always-obvious gentleness in the Generalissimo's personality is reflected in the dedication that he composed for one of his genealogical studies.

---

[5]William D. McCain, "Report before meeting of the Student Senate of the University of Southern Mississippi," 13 March 1972, as cited in Piliawsky, Exit 13, 20.

[6]William D. McCain, "Our Heritage: Paper read before the meeting of the All American Forum III, Hattiesburg, 17 July 1972," as cited in Piliawsky, Exit 13, 18.

[7]See "President's Address to Campus," Student Printz, 20 April 1967, 1.

To the memory of
my Father, Samuel Woodward McCain,
who taught me the alphabet,
and who instilled in me
a love for books and for the making of books,
and to my Mother, Sarah Alda Shaw McCain,
who never said an unkind word to me,
who never did an unkind thing toward me,
and who never was a party to
an unkind act in my presence. [8]

---

[8]William D. McCain, *Seven Generations of the Family of Alexander Hamilton McCain (1786-1838) and His Wife, Naomi Neely McCain (1800-1874), of North Carolina, South Carolina, Georgia, Alabama, and Mississippi* (Hattiesburg: privately published, 1973).

PART V

A Montage of Musings about Going Home

27

On Looking Backward

YEARS AGO WHEN I STARTED OUT as a whippersnapper preacher I preached revivals in country churches, and during these revivals momentous events occurred. Sinners repented and souls were saved from hell as I expounded the Plan of Salvation and sang the hymns of Zion. To this day those hymns that I sang when I knew the answers and my mind was uncluttered grip me. My eyes become cloudy when I hear Christians singing "The Old Rugged Cross."

> On a hill far away stood an old rugged cross,
> The emblem of suffering and shame;
> And I love that old cross where the dearest and best
> For a world of lost sinners was slain.
> So I'll cherish the old rugged cross,
> Till my trophies at last I lay down;
> I will cling to the old rugged cross,
> And exchange it some day for a crown.

I get a lump in my throat when I hear "When They Ring Those Golden Bells."

> There's a land beyond the river
> That we call the sweet forever,
> And we only reach that shore by faith's decree;
> One by one we'll gain the portals,
> There to dwell with the immortals,

When they ring those golden bells
For you and me.

Hymns like these move me to the roots of my being. Yet I no longer sing "When They Ring Those Golden Bells." Nor do I any longer warn about hell fire, preach revival sermons, or expound the Plan of Salvation.

Instead, as a state university professor, I now attend annual meetings of the American Academy of Religion in cities like New York or Chicago or Boston or San Francisco. And at these meetings I listen to wine-and-cheese theologians who wear beards on their chins and beads around their necks. They read to one another dandy little papers on Parmenides and Gnosticism. Between reading and listening to esoteric essays, they patronize gourmet restaurants, nibble on Camembert, and sip glasses of Chablis.

During an annual meeting of the American Academy of Religion I'll take a cable car all the way across San Francisco so I can go to a Hungarian restaurant with a panoramic view of San Francisco Bay. And as I sit there looking out at the Golden Gate Bridge and munching on Hungarian delicacies I know that this isn't what God had in mind when he touched me in the Heidelberg Hotel kitchen and told me to be a Southern Baptist preacher.

Somewhere along the way things didn't work out. Maybe it was all my fault, or maybe I was just in the wrong place at the wrong time. It could be that, like many people who begin their working lives as fireballs of religious enthusiasm, I burned out because I failed to accept myself for who I was and the world for what it is. Maybe I studied myself away from my roots. What happened? Did I cop out? Or did I grow up? Did I surrender myself to God or was I dominated by ego? I'm not sure.

Yet I am sure of one thing: it is astonishing how time and distance enable one to see things differently. When I was a preacher in the cream pitcher, preaching to the Baptists of Tylertown, I thought I had a coherence problem. I now perceive that what I thought was a coherence problem was in part the burden of growing up. I was forced to come to terms with the world as it is, a world that is imperfect. The people of Walthall County were also struggling to live in a flawed world; every year, my respect for them deepens.

It is astonishing how time and distance have enabled me to see gaps or missing links in my life. I can see now in my life a gratitude gap. If I had to live my life over again, I would go out of my way to say "thank you" to all the people I have taken for granted. I should have expressed gratitude to my father-in-law, Zach Taylor, a reticent man who worked every day of his life until he died at seventy-eight. His generosity was expressed to me in many ways, but I never really thanked him. I should have expressed gratitude to my Southern Seminary professors, Morris Ashcraft and Wayne Ward, who combined scholarship with concern for seminarians as persons. I should have expressed gratitude to Ansel Estess, a paradigm Baptist layman, and to Lois Gulledge, a widow in the Tylertown congregation whose concern for others revealed to me the role of compassion in the Christian religion—a role I had not understood before. I should have expressed gratitude to my wife, a woman of insight and tenderness who has shared her life with mine.

28

Preaching

WHEN I DECIDED TO BECOME A PREACHER they said, "The call to preach is a call to prepare." And preparing to be a preacher, I was told, meant going to seminary and getting a professional education so I'd know something and make sense and not be a dumb pulpit thumper. Uncle Wib, my preacher uncle in Natchez, told me, "The best seminary Baptists have is the Southern Baptist Theological Seminary in Louisville, Kentucky." "It's scholarly," he said. "It's better"—so he said—"than the Baptist seminary in New Orleans or the one out in Fort Worth."

Becoming a Louisville graduate, I thought, was a denominational union card, giving you respectability. So off to the Louisville seminary I went, and I stayed there eight years and studied my heart out. But my fate was to attend Southern Seminary when the times were out of joint. The "mother" seminary was passing through an anomalous period, exposing unsuspecting seminarians from Mississippi and Alabama to disorienting thoughts—parading before them Bultmann and Strauss and Weiss and Wellhausen. It was feeding them on a historical-critical diet, giving them ideological vertigo.

I should have known better. I should have had sense enough to see: "Miss Fannie down in Pistol Ridge won't go in for this J-E-D-P business, and Uncle John and Aunt Henrietta won't swallow this demythologizing line." But no! I ate it all up. Whatever Southern Seminary taught I believed. For eight years I consumed the historical-critical method as a rooster eats corn. All the way through I thought I was on my way to illumination, to certainty, and to acceptability.

Some of us who were Louisville seminarians in the 1950s were unconsciously in rebellion against our rural, small-town upbringings. For the "Old Time Religion" on which we'd been raised was void of aesthetic appeal and intellectual content. We believed that through study we'd make religion "respectable" and "convincing." But we were young and we didn't understand that study gives you *data* but it can't give you *insight*. Insight comes only through experience and suffering. That's why preachers are like Kentucky bourbon: they need to go through an aging and mellowing process.

When those eight years in Louisville were over and the time came for me to leave, some said, "He's a liberal." And some of my acquaintances in Mississippi from years gone by said, "He's changed. Sullivan doesn't preach like he used to. He doesn't shell down on hell like he once did. And we can't understand him any more. He uses words like *ad hoc.*"

"He's changed!" A perilous charge! A charge suggestive of unwise behavior! For on the morning I had left Mississippi for seminary, while I was backing my car out of my father's driveway with that shoebox full of fried chicken on the seat beside me, had not Daddy warned me, "Son, whatever happens, don't let 'em change you!"

Those were wise words, words I should have heeded. But I changed and because I changed they threw stones and said, "He's become a liberal!" The stone throwers didn't know how those verbal stones hurt! They didn't know I was aching on the inside and had rectal itch and had to soak in hot water because I hurt all the time. They didn't know I was insecure, was head over heels in debt, and needed someone (a Barnabas) to show me my mistakes. The stone throwers didn't understand it takes time for you to get over going to seminary and to return to sanity and to normality. Indeed, it took me until I was well into middle age to recover from the distortions and afflictions of a theological education.

From where I am now in life, sensing the sun has passed high noon and is headed toward sunset, I muse, "I couldn't care less about all that's happened. I've gone on to other things." Those are boastful words, arrogant words that massage my ego! Yet within myself I know those words—"I couldn't care less about all that's happened"—are hollow. For God spoke to me in the Heidelberg Hotel kitchen while I was scrubbing pans and slicing oranges and told me to be a Southern Baptist preacher. That was my life's dream and I can't take lightly the collapse of my life's dream.

And if it be true that "I couldn't care less about all that's happened" then why is it that *every day for the past twenty-five years* the words of Dr. Ray Summers, the Texas theologian, have floated back and forth through my mind: "You do not have a moral right to be a Southern Baptist preacher"?

Count the words in that statement. They total *thirteen*—that unlucky number. Thirteen words stuck in my memory—oscillating in my mind like a perpetual pendulum of pain. Damn it! Why can't I forget them? Why do I remember so vividly unkind words and forget kind ones? At some point shouldn't the statute of limitations take effect? Let bygones be bygones?

In maturity I should concede that Dr. Summers, the Texas theologian who played God with my life, may have been *right*. Every religious organization has an obligation and a right to determine its identity. The Roman Catholic Church, for example, has determined its belief structure, and if someone comes along who doesn't believe in clerical celibacy or in papal infallibility the Roman church doesn't change its views on celibacy or infallibility to please the person who disagrees.

In a similar way the Southern Baptist Convention has a right to determine its identity, as it is now attempting to do. Churches of the Southern Baptist Convention are today passing through an identity crisis. Baptists and other Southern denominations are again caught up in the Fundamentalist-Modernist Controversy that rocked American Protestantism in the early decades of this century. Many Southern Baptists managed to ignore the controversy then, even though fundamentalists like the Texan J. Frank Norris did what they could to divert the church's energies into a war on "modernism."[1] Sixty years ago the fundamentalist crusade was a Northern phenomenon, although William Jennings Bryan did bring his campaign against evolution to Dayton, Tennessee, to prosecute the famous Scopes Trial. But then the principal advocates for both sides were found in the

---

[1]See the discussion of Southern Baptists and the Fundamentalist-Modernist Controversy in James J. Thompson, Jr., *Tried as by Fire: Southern Baptists and the Religious Controversies of the 1920s* (Macon GA: Mercer University Press, 1982) 61-82.

North, people like Bryan and J. Gresham Machen on the one side
and Harry Emerson Fosdick and H. L. Mencken on the other.

Recently the conflict has erupted again with renewed fury, this
time in the South. To many observers in other parts of the country,
the return of this controversy must seem curious. Is not fundamentalism, like the Ptolemaic astronomy, a relic of the past? What must
be understood is that we Southerners sometimes lag behind the rest
of the country in our intellectual pilgrimage. Southern Baptists and
other Southern churches are experiencing the full impact of this
controversy belatedly. We Southerners have a nostalgia that causes
us to long for simpler times, for dirt roads and tin-roofed tabernac-
les. We pine for these simpler times even though they, too, have
"gone with the wind." Protestant fundamentalism appeals to this
nostalgia and embodies a refusal to come to terms with the Enlightenment and with modernity. "Bring back the good old days of Billy
Sunday when the answers were obvious!" "Away with higher criticism and the Wellhausens!" "Keep it all simple and certain!"

Fundamentalists, capitulating to this nostalgia and convinced of
the rightness of their position, have a compulsion to impose their
views on others. They are brass-knuckled believers in an infallible
Bible and in a Jesus unsullied by historical relativism. They are de-
fenders of the "Old Time Religion," and militant opponents of "liberalism" and the historical-critical method.

What the outcome of the present fundamentalist controversy will
be, no one yet knows. For the Southern Baptist Convention, unlike
the Roman Catholic Church, does not possess a hierarchical structure of authority. Theoretically no Baptist can impose his creed or
views on another Baptist. Yet, ironically, this is precisely what the
fundamentalists of the Southern Baptist denomination are now trying
to do. I, for one, hope that fundamentalists do not gain a hammerlock on Southern churches. Under their direction the Christian faith
would become an anachronistic curio, a Dixie correlative of Shiite
Islam. But if—God forbid!—fundamentalists do take control of the
Southern Baptist Convention and other Southern churches, they have
an obligation to spell out plainly just what the implications of their
"victory" will be. They should, I suggest, explain to young people
who are contemplating careers in the ministry just what the facts of
life are. To uninitiated and unsuspecting seminary students from

Mississippi and Alabama and Georgia they should say, "You tell us that God has 'called' you into the ministry! That's well and good! But please understand: although God may have 'called' you to be a preacher, he has entrusted to us *control of that 'call'*. To that end, we're warning you, you must live intellectually South of the Mason-Dixon line. Stay away from scientific biblical studies! Have nothing to do with European scholarship or with the kind of research that is carried on at Harvard, or the University of Chicago, or Union Theological Seminary in New York! Rather, you must stay within the borders of the 'Old Time Religion' and believe as Wally Criswell believes. And remember, young preacher, if you don't follow these guidelines, we'll destroy you."

If fundamentalist leaders would tell the truth in this way, then young people from Mississippi and Alabama would know what they are getting into when they become preachers. They would know how to run the race. They could ask themselves: Is this what I want to get into? Do I want to become an organization man, and run the risk of sacrificing personal integrity for institutional acceptance?

29

Majestic Awe

IN LOOKING BACK ON MY LIFE what vexes me most is that I've never found a place where I really belonged. That's the common lot of Southern blacks and landless rednecks; we live in a society where a place of permanence and a sense of belonging are elusive. It's not that, like Thomas Wolfe, we "can't go home again." Rather, we have no home to go to.

When I was a boy and my father and mother were country school teachers, we lived in houses belonging to others—like the fertilizer shack at Lemon—and my parents taught on year-to-year contracts controlled by local boards of trustees made up of farmers who wore overalls. There was no permanence there. Nor was there permanence in Mrs. Craft's boarding house owned by the wealthy Buie family next door. For a time I thought I'd found permanence, a place to sink roots, when Mother and Daddy scraped together enough money to make a down payment on the house they purchased in Jackson on Claiborne Avenue. This was the first and only home my parents owned. It was a modest house with one bathroom, an asbestos-shingle exterior, two pecan trees in the front yard, and room for a garden in the back. It was a home we pampered. We kept the grass mowed and the woodwork painted. We put out camellia and rose bushes. And we struggled over the years to keep the foundation secure, which wasn't easy to do because Jackson is located over a stratum of Yazoo clay that crawls around like a caged opossum.

For a quarter of a century Mother and Daddy struggled to pay the mortgage on this house, every month sending a check to the First Federal Savings and Loan. It was *our house*, the place where Daddy broiled steaks, raised tomatoes, and carried on conversations with Ralph Wadlington, his favorite neighbor. And it was the house where Daddy died.

To learn that your father has died is a brutal experience. Early on a Monday morning in December 1969 the telephone rang in my home in Hattiesburg, where I was struggling with a bout of influenza. I rolled out of bed and stumbled to the phone and picked up the receiver.

The call was from Dr. James Holloway, a physician in Jackson. I'll never forget his words. He said, "Dr. Sullivan, I'm calling you from your father's home. I regret doing this, but I must tell you your father has expired." I tried to absorb those words. "Your father has expired."

Stunned, I said to Dr. Holloway, "Are you telling me Daddy is dead?"

"Yes, Dr. Sullivan", he answered, "he's dead. About an hour ago he had a heart attack, and it was fatal."

With halting words I thanked Dr. Holloway for calling and I asked him to tell Mother I'd get to Jackson as quickly as I could. I hung up the receiver and stood there beside the phone, tears in my eyes, a granite lump in my throat. Five days earlier my wife, baby daughter, and I had been with Mother and Daddy, observing Christmas. Our Christmas celebration together had been an unspeakable joy. My daughter was one year old and Daddy was ecstatic about her, his only grandchild. And now—five days later—he was dead.

I knew that Mother needed me, and I was overwhelmed with a desire to get to her as quickly as I could. Forgetting about my fever and influenza, I dressed and headed for Jackson.

The ninety miles from Hattiesburg to Jackson, on U.S. 49 through Collins and Mt. Olive and Magee and Mendenhall, never seemed longer than they did that cold December morning while I drove as swiftly as I could to my mother's side. As I drove up the highway emotional volcanoes erupted inside me. A recurring theme in literature is the conflict between fathers and sons, and Daddy and I had our share of arguments. Yet between us was a bond of father-son love, and the thought crashed around in my head: "I'll never see my daddy alive again. Never again will I talk to him. It's all over and

I've lost the best friend I ever had." I thought of things I should have said to my Father before he died. I wished I'd thanked him for the things he'd done for me, and I wished I'd told him more frequently how I loved him. My daddy relished broiled steaks; indeed, broiling steaks was his hobby. I'd been planning for months to give him as a gift a box of prime steaks. His death meant I'd never give them to him, and the mental image of a box of steaks floated hauntingly back and forth across my mind as I drove up the highway on that December morning.

When at last I arrived at my parents' house on Claiborne Avenue it was filled with relatives and neighbors. Parking the car, I got out and walked inside the house to where Mother was. Ignoring others in the room, Mother and I put our arms around each other and we wept. Having for several moments given vent to raw emotions, she and I sat down beside each other and started talking. I was curious about the circumstances surrounding Daddy's death, and I, regaining my composure, said to Mother, "I want you to tell me what happened. How did Daddy die?"

"Son," she replied, "this morning your daddy and I got up early like we always do. Clay hadn't slept well. He'd tossed and tumbled all night. We ate breakfast and when breakfast was over I started cleaning up the kitchen and Clay went back to the bedroom and sat down in his chair. The last thing he said was, 'Mildred, leave the coffee pot on.' A few moments later I heard him call out my name and make this strange sound. I ran to the bedroom where he was and I could tell something was wrong. I called the doctor and I got a wet cloth and started bathing Clay's face. But he was dead. I knew he was dead before the doctor got here."

While listening to Mother's account I experienced an odd sensation. Over the years I have collected the last words spoken by people immediately prior to death. My father's last words were, "Mildred, leave the coffee pot on." Odd final words! Yet, for my father, appropriate words! Every day of his life he had drunk from ten to twelve cups of coffee.

Mother and I made arrangements for Daddy's funeral with the Wright and Ferguson Funeral Home. I went through the last rites for my father because there was no choice. The day of the funeral and burial (at the Lakewood Memorial Cemetery) was cold and bleak, and the happenings of that day remain in my mind a mental blur— a montage of events experienced yet difficult to remember with clarity.

In the weeks immediately following Daddy's death I could not bring myself to discuss his dying. My inner feelings were too raw. I wanted to close the episode out of my mind and to pretend it had never happened. Yet time passed, the inner ache subsided, and I found myself eventually *wanting* to talk about my father's death. One day, months after the funeral, I broached the issue with Mother. "Mother, I want you to tell me—in as much detail as you can—what happened the morning Daddy died."

She began by recounting how my father hadn't been feeling well and how he had experienced a restless night. She told about how they had eaten breakfast together, and about how Daddy had gone to the bedroom after breakfast and stretched out in his leather chair. She recalled how he had told her to leave the coffee pot on and then a moment later had called out her name in a bizarre way. She told how she had run to where he was.

At this point Mother paused. She remarked, "Son, something happened that morning which I've never told anyone, but I think I ought to tell you. When Clay called out my name I ran to the bedroom where he was, and when I got there a Power was in the room. There was a Power . . . a Presence. You could feel it. It was so real I couldn't move, and I stood there and looked at Clay and he looked at me and all the time I knew he was dying."

These words startled me. Mother is, I believe, the most honest person I know. She never cheated on her income tax but insisted on reporting every penny she earned. She once paid for ten azalea bushes at Gibson's Discount Store and on discovering when she got home that she had picked up eleven azaleas instead of ten, she promptly drove all the way back across town to return the extra azalea bush to the discount store. My mother is honest, but is not a mystical person, and I had not expected her to say what she was saying. Perplexed, I asked, "Did you *see* anything in the room?"

"Oh, yes!" she answered. "The room was filled from the floor to the ceiling with a billowing cloud. The cloud was like steam or smoke. You could almost feel it."

Nonplussed, I probed, "You say there was a Power in the room while Daddy was dying . . . a Power you could see and almost feel . . . how would you describe it?"

For several moments Mother was silent, searching for words. Finally she answered, "The best way I can describe it is to describe it as *Majestic Awe*. That's it . . . *Majestic Awe*. While Clay was dying he was surrounded by *Majestic Awe*." And then Mother said, "Son, I believe that Power was God. I believe it was the angels coming down and taking Clay away to heaven. And I believe the first thing Clay did when he got to heaven was to sit down and drink a cup of coffee."

Oh, what magnificent theology, more impressive to me than anything in Barth or Brunner! To contend that when we die the angels come and carry us away on a cloud to heaven for coffee.

As a philosophy and religion professor I've read scores of discussions on the question of life beyond death. In this regard, I've read dialogues of Plato, tomes of medieval theologians, and essays by modern thinkers like Pierre Teilhard de Chardin. But none of these discourses on life after death move me as forcefully as my mother's account of Daddy's first cup of coffee in heaven.

30

Beyond Words

IN THE AFTERMATH OF DADDY'S DEATH Mother continued living on Claiborne Avenue. This was the one place on earth that was *ours*. This was the one place giving a sense of permanence and a modest feeling of roots. But then rumors began to circulate. Rumors confirmed by driving through the neighborhood and by talking with real estate agents. The Negroes were coming!

West Jackson—until the 1970s an all-white, middle-class fortress—started going black. Blacks began buying up property like hamburgers. They began near downtown Jackson and started coming out Robinson Road, house by house, block by block. It seemed to be a black tidal wave, irresistible and unstoppable. Some white people said, "We'll never sell our homes to niggers. We've lived here all our lives and this is home. Let the niggers stay down town where they belong." And white people looked each other in the eye and said, "I won't sell to a nigger if you won't sell to a nigger." They shook hands to affirm the agreement.

But inevitably some white property owners did sell to blacks, then others sold, and still others. In a matter of months another area of West Jackson had turned black. The white people packed up and moved out. White people said, "The blacks will never come out as far as Buena Vista and Pecan Boulevard. They can't afford property that expensive."

But the impossible took place. Homes on Buena Vista and Pecan Boulevard, two of West Jackson's most prestigious streets, were sold to blacks. And then it happened: homes on Claiborne Avenue, where Mother lived, were also sold to blacks. Negroes moved into the house where Mr. and Mrs. Bailey had lived, and into the house where Mr. and Mrs. Puckett had lived, and into the house where Ralph and Lida Wadlington had lived.

Blacks bought the house on the south side of Mother's home where Mr. and Mrs. Koch had once lived. Another black family bought the one behind Mother's house. Finally the house on the other side of Mother's was sold to blacks, so that our Claiborne Avenue home was surrounded by Negro families. While all this was happening I said time and again to Mother, "Mother, you've got to move. This part of Jackson is changing." But Mother said, "I'll never move. This is the only house Clay and I ever owned. We worked all our lives to pay for it. This is home." And she added, "The blacks are nice people. They don't bother me."

Months went by, and eventually I received a long distance phone call in Hattiesburg from my Mother in Jackson. Her voice was one of distress. She said, "Son, you've got to come up here. I need to show you something." The "something" she wouldn't discuss with me over the telephone. Up to Jackson I went and Mother showed me the "something" that was bothering her. On the side of the house next door the black occupants had painted in bold letters with red paint the words: SCREW YOU WHITE FOLKS.

SCREW YOU WHITE FOLKS: painted in full view of the house my parents treasured, where in the back yard Daddy and I grew vegetables and where we planted an oak that grew from a few inches tall to a tree spreading branches over the garage.

SCREW YOU WHITE FOLKS: painted in full view of the house my parents paid on for more than a quarter century with checks sent monthly to the First Federal Savings and Loan.

SCREW YOU WHITE FOLKS: painted in full view of the house where on a December morning angels came down and carried Daddy away to heaven for a cup of coffee.

SCREW YOU WHITE FOLKS: words that led my Mother, her voice quivering, to say, "Son, I think I'd better move." We sold our Claiborne Avenue house to a black family and Mother moved down to Hattiesburg where I can take care of her. From time to time I go back to Jackson I drive by the home we once owned, where I practiced my clarinet and studied algebra and stretched out on my bed while listening to the Boston Symphony on the radio. I know now that there was *no permanence there either.* Like the WPA "teacher's home" at Gulde and like Mrs. Craft's boarding house, our home belongs to others.

Since I'm from the landless redneck layer of Mississippi society, where do I find permanence? Where do I go for acceptance? Where do I find a niche to fit into? At the Louisville seminary I was told I didn't belong because I'd become a "liberal." Then when I came back to Mississippi I thought: "I'm coming home. Mississippi—this is where I'm supposed to be, and it's where I'll live the rest of my life." But there was no permanence in Tylertown, because I was a "come and go" preacher and my grandfather wasn't buried in Walthall County. For a family to be regarded as "local people" in small town Mississippi requires three generations of living in the same place. From Tylertown I came to Hattiesburg and to the University of Southern Mississippi where deans who lecture on Camelot tell you they're screwing you and despise you.

Then one day it dawned on me: *maybe in this world there is no place for me.* As the old song says, "This world is not my home; I'm just a-passin' through." I've found anew my identity with Mississippi's *rednecks* and *niggers.* I share their fate of living in a society where you're not wanted or needed. You can't go home because there's no home to go to.

But—with God's help—I have *survived!* I have done whatever I had to do, and I have outrun the hounds. I have outlasted Louisville liberalism, Texas fundamentalism, cream pitcherism, and bureaucratic brutality. I have survived, and *practicing the art of survival* is the essence of a Mississippi redneck. Leo Paxton, my maternal grandfather who lost his thumb in a logging accident, summed up the redneck philosophy time and again. "Don't ever give up," he would say, "because you never know what might turn up."

Sometimes I think it would be money in the bank and I'd be ahead of the game if God had not called me to be a Southern Baptist preacher. But I did become a preacher, I am a preacher, and I will continue to be a preacher until I die. And when I die I know what I hope will happen. I hope that angels will come and carry me to heaven in a billowing cloud, just as they carried my father. When I get to heaven, and I'm at last—I trust—in a place where I belong, a place no one can take away, I hope I'll see Daddy again and we'll sit down and drink coffee together. We'll laugh and reminisce about mashing risins at Gulde, about squirrel hunting in the Pelahatchie swamp, and about going to the Mississippi State Fair in Jackson. And we'll talk about how we used to stand on the brow of the hill behind the Old Capitol Building, and how I would sit on Daddy's shoulders with my legs wrapped around his neck, while looking down on the Mississippi State Fair in all its grandeur, with its red, yellow, and blue lights stretching into the distance as far as I could see. Like a starry Milky Way, beautiful beyond words. . . .

MUP *Called to Preach, Condemned to Survive.*

Designed by Margaret Jordan Brown.
Composition by MUP Composition Department.

Production specifications:
     text paper—60-pound Warren's Olde Style.
     endpapers—Multicolor Antique Jet.
     covers (on .088 boards)—Holliston Roxite
          B 51575 Vellum Finish.
     dust jacket—Printed two colors PMS 185 (red) and
          Black. Varnished.

Printing (offset lithography) and binding
     by Penfield/Rowland Printing Company, Inc., Macon, Georgia.